SUPER HANDYMAN'S DO-IT-QUICK-BUT-DO-IT-RIGHT HOME REPAIR HINTS

Books by Al Carrell

Super Handyman's Encyclopedia of Home Repair Hints
Super Handyman's Big Bike Book
Super Handyman's Fix and Finish Furniture Guide
Super Handyman's Do-It-Quick But Do-It-Right
   Home Repair Hints

AL CARRELL

SUPER HANDYMAN'S DO-IT-QUICK-BUT-DO-IT-RIGHT HOME REPAIR HINTS

PRENTICE-HALL, INC. Englewood Cliffs, N.J.

*Super Handyman's Do-It-Quick but Do-It-Right
Home Repair Hints by* Al Carrell
Copyright © 1981, 1980, 1979, 1978, 1977, 1976,
1975, 1974 and 1973 by King Features Syndicate, Inc.
Address inquiries to Prentice-Hall, Inc., Englewood
Cliffs, N.J. 07632
Printed in the United States of America
Prentice-Hall International, Inc., London
Prentice-Hall of Australia, Pty. Ltd., Sydney
Prentice-Hall of Canada, Ltd., Toronto
Prentice-Hall of India Private Ltd., New Delhi
Prentice-Hall of Japan, Inc., Tokyo
Prentice-Hall of Southeast Asia Pte. Ltd., Singapore
Whitehall Books Limited, Wellington, New Zealand

10 9 8 7 6 5 4 3 2 1

Library of Congress Cataloging in Publication Data

Carrell, Al.
    Super handyman's do-it-quick but do-it-right home
repair hints.

    Includes index.
    1. Dwellings—Maintenance and repair—Amateurs'
manuals.   I. Title.
TH4817.3.C37   643'.7   80-24659
ISBN 0-13-875906-5

To Jean, my wife, best friend, and little pardner

CONTENTS

1.

HOW TO USE THIS BOOK

As we've put this book together, Jean and I have nicknamed it *Do-It,* short for the title we came up with. The files and memos and false starts all have "Do-It" printed on them, so my office looks as if it belongs to some real man of action. Actually, the whole purpose of the book is to sell you on that one thing—doing it. Do-it—the "it" being your own problems of repairs and maintenance around the house.

This is a book for everybody. (Pass the word along.) The competent home handyperson will like the step-by-step directions on accomplishing all these tasks . . . plus he'll love the tips and shortcuts laced into the basics. Most of these ingenious tricks are from the readers of my syndicated newspaper column.

But the book is really written for the person who has never tackled any fix-it project. The first question many people in this group ask is "Why?"

One of the reasons is money. Spiraling repair costs make it worth your while to at least consider doing some things yourself. Materials have gone up, so some projects are still going to cost, but labor prices are really out of sight. So if you can provide the labor, you will come out way ahead.

Another reason lies in the caliber of the people who do the work. There are still many great craftsmen around, but the chances of your getting one of the good ones are about 1 in 482. A good one is hard to find, but even if friends tip you off to one, you know he's booked up. You could spend several days just trying to get beyond his telephone answering device. Even assuming you make an appointment, I'd hate to guess how many people stayed home today specifically for a repairman who didn't show up.

Now, some of the guys who do show up are either incompetent or they just don't care. Their object is to slap it together, get the loot, and get out. The fact that what they did won't last through the month is your problem, as you'll find out when you try to get someone out to make good on what you've already paid for. Usually, you end up calling for someone else. This cycle is good for the economy, but bad on your pocketbook...because even though you got something less than professional work, the guy certainly knew how to charge like a pro.

However, the biggest reason that you should learn to do-it is not money or the trouble in getting skilled craftsmen, it's in just being able to cope. Even if you never install a suspended ceiling or lay down a new floor or roof your house, being able to cope with the everyday home disasters can save you from even greater loss. You should at least know what to do in a home emergency—like when the toilet overflows or a pipe bursts. You may still have to call for help, but just learning how to cut off the water supply in the case of a burst pipe could save your furniture, drapes, and floors from the seventy thousand gallons of water that would gush out before the plumber ever returned your call.

You haven't actually solved the problem, but you've stalled it. And who knows, after the water is cut off and no longer rising up above your boot tops, you may calm down, survey the situation, and decide you *can* do it yourself.

If the book does nothing more than teach you to cope, it'll be well worth the price.

Another reason for you to do-it is one I'll never be able to sell you on until after you've jumped in. It's the sense of pride from being able to say, "I did it myself." I've experienced it. Thousands of my readers, listeners, and viewers have written to tell how proud they are of some fix-it project.

I think the key to having success is to start with an easy task. When it turns out right, you'll gain confidence, and this helps you to go on to bigger and better things. Once you have a few notches in your sawhorse, you'll find the bug has bitten you, and you'll go out of your way to find more projects to get into. Here are a few other keys:

1. Find out as much as you can about the project before you start. What tools are needed? Are parts available? Try to diagnose the problem before you start.

2. Make sure you observe the safety precautions. Protect yourself, and protect the things around the work area.

3. Have the right tools.

4. Have enough time to finish the job.

5. Have confidence that it'll turn out right. (It won't always, but most of the time it will.) Don't panic when things go wrong or differently from what you expected. There'll usually be another way out—and many of these other ways are right in this book.

6. If it's a two-person job, get a helper. Even if it's not, the company is usually welcome.

7. Don't be afraid to ask questions. The hardware or paint dealer can often answer them.

8. If there's any doubt about getting the proper replacement, take old parts along.

9. Keep your sense of humor.

While the book is designed to carry you through the basic steps of a project, it can also serve to convince you that you *don't* want to do that particular project yourself. It may be beyond your abilities; you may not have the proper tools. Or the steps involved may not be your bag. At least when you call a pro, you'll know what he'll be going through.

Unless it's an emergency, use care in selecting a pro. Get more than one estimate, if possible. Ask for recent references, and then check them out. Contact the Better Business Bureau. If it's a very big job, have a contract drawn up so you know what's to be done and for how much.

Since it's going to cost you to have it done, why not get as much for your dollar as possible? Learn while he earns. Watch what he does. If you can ask questions without interfering with his work, do so. Maybe you'll learn enough to tackle the job the next time it arises.

I've mentioned the importance of having the right tools. The saying is, "A poor workman blames his tools." Conversely, a novice with the right tools can turn out surprisingly professional results. In buying tools, avoid the bargain bin and go for quality. I've bought some "bargain" tools that didn't even last through the first job. Many good tools will last a lifetime.

For a list of basic tools, see Workshops, Chapter 16.

2.
BATHROOMS

You probably think that all the do-it chores in the bathroom would be in the plumbing section, right? Wrong, bubble-bath breath. What about mildew, loose tiles, and tub spots?

MILDEW

This is a problem that can happen in the best of homes. It's an airborne fungus among us which is present and floating around most of the time. Given a nice warm, moist surface and a little food, the growth starts. The bathroom is an ideal place because bathing and showers create moisture that may hang around if there's no exhaust fan. The porous grout between tiles can hold that moisture. Furthermore, soap scum that collects on the walls is a very tasty food for mildew to grow on.

In most cases, getting rid of mildew in the bath is a snap. Fill an empty plastic squeeze bottle with liquid laundry bleach. Be sure the bottle is clean. The idea is to squirt the bleach on the mildew. Be sure to observe the caution notices when using bleach, but as you work your way along the wall, you'll be amazed at the speed with which the mildew disappears. If there are stubborn spots, pour a little bleach in a saucer and use a toothbrush to scrub them. (Use an old toothbrush you won't be using on your teeth.) When all the spots are gone, wash the walls with water; and when they are *dry*, wipe them with household ammonia. This helps kill the spores so the stuff won't grow back. *Be sure you never mix bleach and ammonia* as it creates a dangerous gas. (There is another mildew formula in the Painting section for use outdoors.)

If you can't correct the moisture condition, of course, you'll start a new crop of mildew before long. Exhaust fans help. Airing out after a shower works too. In the wintertime, however, this can run up your heating bills. There are chemical dehumidifiers you can buy that absorb moisture from the air.

● In warmer weather, we'd like to open the bathroom window to let air in and moisture out, but this takes away our privacy. The bashful type, I solved the problem by cutting a piece of Peg-Board to fit the lower half of

4

the screen. I attached the Peg-Board to the screen frame with screws. Now we can raise the window. The holes in the Peg-Board let air in, but we still have privacy.

Many folks who have a constant moisture problem in the bath wipe the walls dry after each use. Also, keep the surfaces clean so there's no scum for the fungus to feed on.

TILE AND GROUT PROBLEMS

Ceramic tiles are often used for both walls and floor in a bath. They are easy to clean, and when kept that way, offer a beautiful shiny effect. Tiles also make for a very sturdy surface, an ideal bathroom material— until something goes wrong.

Grout is the stuff between the tiles. It's usually white, but can be colored. Since it's porous, it absorbs dirt as well as moisture. Many household cleaners are made for fighting this problem, but maybe some of these tricks will work better for you:

● One of those round typewriter erasers is simply great for cleaning tiny white grout lines between the tiles in a kitchen or bath. It has a strong abrasive quality, but doesn't dig out the grout.

● One of the best ways to clean the white grout between tiles is with an old toothbrush and toothpaste. It will clean and whiten, but doesn't leave a strong odor like so many other concoctions. Even my wife thought I was smart to come up with this one.

● I saw the old-time grout-cleaning method you ran. My formula is better—and may be older. Mix up two tablespoons of liquid detergent and three tablespoons of vinegar, and scrub the grout with a brush dipped in the solution. Rinse it off, and you'll have gleaming lines.

● Working on the bathroom plumbing left black marks on the grout between the tiles. I tried to remove them, but they still showed up. Then my wife came through with a nail-whitener pencil. She wet it, ran it along the grout lines, and they are white again.

● Your idea of using white liquid shoe polish to whiten the grout between tiles is good, but my way is more permanent. I bought a small can of mat-finish latex paint and used a small brush to paint over the grout. Places where the paint gets on the tile can be wiped clean with a damp cloth. Paint outlasts shoe polish; also, using a brush is less messy and wasteful than the shoe-polish dauber. For more economy, you can even thin down the paint with a little water.

Sometimes the grout comes out from between the tiles. It's easy to replace, and should be done as soon as possible because it lets water get into the crack. This makes more grout come out and can help tiles fall out. The water can also work into wood behind the tiles and rot it.

Now that you're convinced that grout should be replaced, get all the loose grout out of the cracks, using a putty knife to dig with. Then flush out the cracks with water. Clean the surfaces to get rid of soap scum. If there's any mildew, get rid of this *before* you regrout, since the mildew won't go away just because you cover over it.

The grout comes in powder form, or premixed. I think the powdered grout is best and will probably match the old grout more closely. Follow all the directions for mixing, and be sure you get out the lumps. Some folks use a damp, clean sponge, but the best tool for getting the grout in place is your finger. The grout isn't all that good for skin, however, so wear a rubber or plastic glove.

● Rubber gloves will go on and come off easier if you sprinkle a good quantity of talcum powder into the gloves before putting them on. Then dust your hands, too.

Don't stop applying the grout until the lines look like you want them to. Don't worry about getting grout on the tiles. After it dries, a damp terry cloth rag will remove it. "Dries" means when it *first* dries, not when it fully cures, because then you'll have to chip it away.

● I have found that the rounded end of a toothbrush handle does a great job of getting the grout smoothed and curved like it should be.

● A wedge-shaped piece of foam rubber cushioning used in upholstering does a fine job of pushing grout into cracks and then smoothing.

● Regular tile grout that you mix is better looking, I think, than the tub and tile caulk that's really best used between the tub and the tiles. However, the squeeze tube makes the caulk very easy to apply. I make my grout easy to apply, too. After I mix it, I use a funnel to pour it into an old plastic glue bottle. Then I put the cap back on and have a spout that lets me squeeze and squirt the grout between the tiles.

Be sure to allow the full curing time for the grout before getting it wet again. There are also spray silicone sealers that will keep the grout clean, and I'd use these every six months or so.

Tile—When a tile comes out, it can easily be replaced. Most tiles are originally set into a cement mix. If you have many to replace, you might want to chip out the old cement and reset them in a white cement.

● By now everybody knows that you need to soak bricks before they're laid so the porous brick won't drink all the moisture from the mortar. However, many people don't know that the same principle must be used with ceramic tile to be set in cement. The backs and edges are porous and will take a drink just as quickly as bricks do.

However, for the few that usually come out, a tile mastic available at the hardware store will do. Clean out any loose material and carefully chip away the cement on the back of the tile. If it won't come off, don't worry. Better leave it in place than break the tile. If one tile has fallen out, you might check other tiles around it before replacing. Test by tapping with a wooden tool handle.

After you "butter" the back of the tile per the directions on the mastic, ease it into place; and be sure to leave an even space all the way around for the grout.

So that the mastic doesn't slip before it's dry, either tape the tile in place with masking tape or insert broken pieces of wooden tooth-picks to fight the pull of gravity. After the mastic has fully cured, you can add the grout.

Broken or missing tiles are often difficult to match. If the color isn't available from a tile place, try wrecking yards. If you can't locate an exact match, get a close one, and if it offends, maybe a tile decal will make it look like a special decorator touch.

If the broken tile is still in place, you may break several others trying to chisel out the one broken piece. One way to remove without additional damage is to drill a hole in the center of the square. You'll need to use a carbide drill bit; and if you have a variable-speed drill, use a slow speed. Then take a glass cutter and score a pair of lines diagonally across the piece to form an X. Now you can use a hammer and cold chisel to break up only that one tile and get it out of there (Figure 1). (When using a hammer and chisel, safety goggles are always in vogue.) Here are some other tile tips:

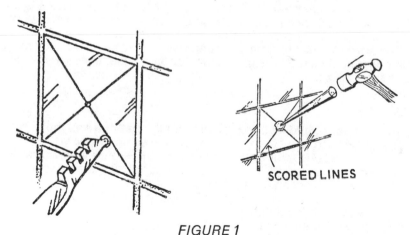

SCORED LINES

FIGURE 1

● Odd-shaped ceramic tiles needed to fit around pipes and fixtures can easily be cut with a jigsaw. You'll get better results if you cover the face of the tile with masking tape before you begin the surgery. It gives you a much better surface to mark on, and you'll get smoother edges—without the risk of scratching the surface.

● Those glazed ceramic tiles used in the bath are treated just like a pane of glass when it comes to cutting. All you need is a straightedge, a glass cutter, and a pair of finishing nails. Score the line to be cut on the glazed side. Place the finishing nails under the tile at a point under the scribed line. Then exercise hand pressure on each side of the line, and the tile will snap right down the line. Any time you use a glass cutter, you should lubricate the cutter wheel. If oil or kerosene aren't handy, just spit on the wheel. This will be all the lubrication you'll need.

SOAP DISHES, TOWEL BARS

These and other ceramic pieces that were set in the tile wall with cement also have a habit of coming out. Junior likes to use them to chin himself on. If you can break him of the habit and insure that not too much weight will again be applied to the fallen piece, you can use a tile mastic to replace them. Then add the grout, and everything will look fine. However, it's best to again reset these parts in cement or plaster. Use plenty of tape to hold the piece in place while it's setting up. It's even a good idea to lean a chair or something against the piece to hold it tightly against the bed of cement or adhesive.

● When I chipped out a place in our bathroom wall for a recessed soap dish, I was discouraged to find there was nothing of substance for the receptacle to rest upon. My neighbor came to the rescue with a wad of excelsior packing material. He mixed up a batch of plaster of paris and dipped the excelsior into this. He then stuffed this all around in the hole. The excelsior was springy enough so it stayed in place against both inside walls. We then pushed the receptacle in place and caulked around the edges. With the excelsior and plaster as a base, the soap dish is a solid installation.

TUB CAULK

Caulk is what should fill the gap between the bathtub and the tile wall above. Don't use grout here. Grout has no give, and when you fill a tub with water and add your own body weight, the tub pulls downward. A rigid filler in this gap will come loose. Be sure you get a tub caulk for this, not the regular caulk that you'll use around the house.

Remove *all* of the old caulk. Use your putty knife, but don't scrape with such force that you chip the tiles above or the tub below. Then use a solvent to clean away all the soap scum in the seam. Rinse away the solvent, then wrap a rag around the putty knife and dry the surfaces inside.

Now you're ready to apply the new caulk; but first fill up the bathtub, then do all the work while standing in the tub. This way, you'll have as much weight as you'll ever have, so the tub will be pushed down to its lowest point. Snip the nozzle on the tube of caulk at a point that will give you a bead of caulk slightly larger than the crack. Snip it at about a forty-five–degree angle. The idea is to start at one corner and go all around the entire tub in one continuous bead (Figure 2). It will seem awkward, but it works best if the tube is slanted so the nozzle points in the direction you're going. Once you've traveled the entire route, a wet

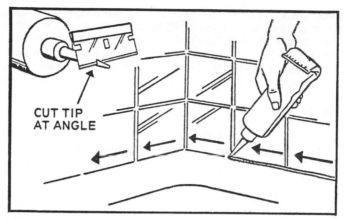

FIGURE 2

finger will let you smooth the bead and make it look like it should. Be sure to remove the excess caulk before it sets up. When you get out of the tub and pull the plug, the seam will be compressed and can expand to take care of maybe even the entire family during bath time.

OTHER STAINS AND SPOTS

Grout isn't the only place in the bath that can become ugly looking. Here are some tips to solve these other problems.

● Those adding a bathroom can save considerable money by looking for used fixtures at a wrecking yard. If there are stains on the fixtures, I have a magic formula that will remove most of them. Sprinkle cream of tartar over the spot, then pour a few drops of hydrogen peroxide on the cream of tartar and mix until it's about the consistency of sour cream. Leave this on until it dries, and when you wash away the residue, the stains go right down the drain.

● For removing rust stains in a china or porcelain enamel sink or tub, make a thick paste from blackboard chalk dust and household ammonia. Spread this on the spot. By the time it dries out completely, the spot will be gone. I make the chalk dust by running it back and forth over a cheese grater. You'll probably say this is just an idea I made up, but if you'll try it, you'll find out it is not a put-on.

● My wife was complaining that she couldn't get some stains out of the lavatory sink. I had been using some oxalic acid for bleaching stains out of wooden furniture. I decided what the heck, mixed a paste of oxalic acid, and smeared this over the stains. When the paste dried, the stains washed away, and I became a hero.

● Hydrogen peroxide is often used to remove spots from marble.

The kind you get at the drugstore may be strong enough, but if not, a store that carries marble-care supplies has a stronger solution. The process will go better if you heat the surface with a strong light bulb before peroxiding. Rig a lamp to hang just a few inches above the marble, and leave it there for about a half hour. A heat lamp will do, but don't use a sun lamp. Now pour on the peroxide and let it set for a while. Stubborn stains may take several treatments.

● Some stains in a sink or tub that won't respond to regular cleansers will come up with a pencil eraser. Just rub the spots to see if this will do the job. If not, you haven't lost anything but a little time. Don't use a typewriter eraser, however, because they seem to be too abrasive on some fixture finishes.

LEAKING SHOWER STALL

One very sobering bathroom problem is a tile shower stall that leaks. If it's in the upper floor, the water soon ruins the ceiling and maybe other things below. On the ground floor, it may only rot out wood, ruin carpets, and heave the foundation from the excess water.

If you call the plumber or a tile man or whoever, he'll tell you it's a leaky shower pan. You may not even have known you had a shower pan, and now he tells you it leaks. To replace it, he'll have to tear up your tile floor and remove anywhere from five hundred to fifteen hundred dollars from your bank account.

If it *is* the shower pan and not some other source of leaking water, there is the nonguaranteed-but-usually-successful Super Handyman way to fix it. It only works about ninety-nine out of one hundred times, and will only cost you about twenty dollars plus some time to find out if you're the unlucky one.

Before you do anything else, though, find out if the leak is through the pan or somewhere else. Seal up the drain completely, using waterproof tape. Then run water into the shower and let it stand. If it disappears and then reappears on your carpets or wherever, you know your shower pan's the problem. Other places for leaks could be around a shower door, around the holes where the knobs come out of the wall, or in the plumbing drain. But if you're sure it's the pan, you're ready for the twenty-dollar cure.

This involves coating the shower floor and at least the first row of tiles up with an epoxy paint. I'm talking about the two-component type that is brushed on, *not* the spray-on variety. This paint can be found in colors or clear. If you want the clear, you may have to call around to find it or even have the paint dealer order it. Here are the steps:

1. Repair all loose grout seams and recaulk any areas that will be painted.

2. When the grout has set up, clean the floor and the portion of walls to be painted with a muriatic acid solution (three parts water to

one part muriatic acid). Be sure to use a plastic bucket, wear your rubber gloves, and be careful. Most hardware and paint dealers carry muriatic acid, but if it's hard to find, talk to swimming pool maintenance suppliers.

3. Rinse the acid away.

4. Let the surfaces dry totally by not using the shower for about a week. (Hopefully, you have access to another shower or tub, or you'll get a little gamy.)

5. Apply two coats of the epoxy paint to the floor and at least one row of tiles up on all four walls. Use a natural bristle brush. Since epoxy is a little difficult to work with, be sure to follow all the directions on the label. Be sure to allow adequate drying time between coats.

That's all there is to it, and hopefully you'll have saved yourself hundreds of dollars. It takes a little time and patience, but is usually worth it. The epoxy can last for years and years before you'll have to repaint ... *if* you have followed all the directions.

Here's a "potty-pourri" of other bathroom hints:

● When I broke the lid to the toilet tank, I found that a replacement was going to be hard to find and more expensive than I'd like. I had some scraps of the wallpaper used for the bath, and after gluing the lid together with an epoxy, I covered up the still-very-visible crack by papering the lid. The glue didn't hold the wallpaper in place. I tried again, but this time painted the porcelain with wall sizing (a sort of glue used on walls before wallpaper is applied).

The sizing didn't hold to the slick surface, so neither did the paper. Being bullheaded, I next tried using the same epoxy I had mended the lid with. It held the paper, and now I have a great-looking bathroom. Maybe if others have the same problem, they'll go to school on my mistakes.

● I couldn't find a replacement toilet-tank lid for the one I broke, so I made one from wood. The lid was cut to size, and has a wooden lip all around so it can't be knocked off. The neatest part is that the lid is also a planter: There are holes in which small clay pots fit. The pots don't stick down far enough to interfere with the tank parts. Short pieces of rope reach from the hole in each pot (Figure 3) to the water in the tank to act as wicks to keep the plants watered.

Plants in the bath look great and often benefit from all the humidity in the air. According to some people, they even help control excess moisture.

● I have a tip that I learned the hard way. Please tell those with chipped places in a porcelain sink or tub that they had better patch them up right away. I didn't, and water got under the finish and caused much more of it to pop up. Then it was too big to patch, and I had to have it refinished. Even if you only paint over it with clear fingernail polish until

FIGURE 3

you can get a porcelain-patching kit, you'll have prevented the problem from getting bigger.

● The two bathrooms in our apartment are back to back, and we discovered that the medicine chests—also back to back—let noises come through from one room to the other. I removed one chest from the wall and stuffed insulation batts all around inside the opening. Then I glued acoustical tiles to the back of the chest in the other wall. Next I glued acoustical tiles to the back side of each medicine chest door. There's still room to close the door without hitting the shelves, and now there's practically no noise coming through the chests. Maybe this will help others who have the same annoyance.

● As an added protection for bathroom mirrors, I have sprayed the back with clear shellac. This eliminates the possibility of their being damaged from moisture, and also gives them a stronger shield against scratches.

● One of the more dangerous bathroom hazards is the shower-curtain rod that isn't securely attached to the wall. If a person starts to slip, he'll grab at the rod; and if it's just screwed into the Sheetrock, it's not going to hold. Why not check to see how yours is attached before someone breaks a leg . . . and takes out a chunk of your wall?

● I installed one of those fiberglass shower kits that snap into place. It was an easy do-it-yourself project, but I soon learned that regular scouring cleanser was taking the sheen off, and I guess would have ruined the finish. After a little experimentation, I came up with the perfect cleanser—baking soda. It is mildly abrasive enough to clean, but won't scar the surface. Why don't the makers of fiberglass tub enclosures warn you about using a cleanser and tell about soda?

● Soap dishes and glass holders are often held to the wall by a suction cup. It can get frayed around the edges and will no longer hold. If this happens, you may be able to operate and save the patient. Take very sharp scissors and carefully trim off the frayed parts. This will probably solve your problem temporarily. Usually when the edges start to go, it's a sign that the rubber has gone bad, and it won't be long before more will fray.

● You once ran a hint about how to keep suction cups stuck to glass longer by moistening them with glycerin instead of water. I have an even better way: Rub the suction cup over a moist bar of soap. It'll stay put for months.

● Warm water to which a few drops of olive oil has been added will keep a shower curtain from becoming stiff and cracking.

● Kerosene is an excellent cleaner for all bathroom surfaces because it dissolves soap scum and leaves the tile and porcelain sparkling.

● Those appliqués to make a tub slip-proof leave a tough adhesive when they finally wear out. If you'll take a single-edge razor blade and carefully remove as much of the backing and adhesive as possible, you can usually dissolve the rest with a solvent. I used fingernail-polish remover and 0000 (superfine) steel wool. It came clean.

● Old bathroom fixtures, including even the inside of bathtubs, lavatories, and toilets, can be colored with fabric or wallpaper with dramatic results. The key is to use epoxy glue. Then you put several coats of exterior varnish over the surface to seal out water. Done right, it lasts for years and looks socko.

3.
CEILINGS

When things—and guests—are looking up, you hope their vision isn't good enough to reach the ceiling. Ceilings are mainly forgotten, but there are a few things you can do to enhance yours.

Maintenance may be all you need to do, and this is easy. You mainly just have to dust. A rag held around a straw broom, with maybe a little dust collector sprayed on, will do the job. In the kitchen, you may have grease from cooking. Most people ignore this until it's time to paint. If it gets noticeable, clean it as discussed in Chapter 12 on painting.

Patching holes is the same as described in Chapter 14 on walls.

Maybe you want to change the look of the ceiling. Painting is the most common way. But there are other ways:

PAPERING A CEILING

I discourage this. It's not all that difficult, but becomes a real pain in the neck. I've always tried to sell the nice contrast between papered walls and a painted ceiling.

Preparation of the surface is the same as for walls. Now you'll want to run your strips crosswise so you'll be dealing with shorter lengths. It's best to have some sort of scaffold instead of having to go up and down a ladder.

● The ideal height for papering a ceiling would put you about six inches from the ceiling. I use a couple of those sturdy milk cases turned upside down as a base for a two-by-twelve. It's an ideal scaffold.

Start by snapping a chalk line out from a wall. Measure so it's one inch less than the width of the roll. Apply paste to your first strip and fold it, paste to paste (Figure 84, page 209). If you're right-handed, start in the right-hand corner. Be sure the strip lines up with your chalk line. Now comes the fun: Unfold only about two or three feet at a time as you

14

hold the rest of the accordion mess against the ceiling with your left hand. An extra roll of paper or a wide smoothing brush in your left hand can help keep the folds from drooping down on you. I just use my right hand to do the initial smoothing (which isn't easy to do since I keep my fingers crossed that the paste will hold as I work all the way across). After the strip is up, I come back and do the serious smoothing.

● After applying ceiling paper, if I spot places that need additional smoothing, I use a short-napped paint roller. The extension handle means I can do the job without having to move my ladder around.

Other techniques are covered in the section on wallpapering.

CEILING TILES

These are an easy way to have a new ceiling, providing the old ceiling is a sound surface. It's also a way to dampen sound in a room. Even though nearly all these tiles are referred to as acoustical tiles, not all are. Many folks install them to block out noise—they don't. However, they do absorb noise if they are acoustical. This means that the noises within the room won't bug you as much and won't travel to other rooms with as many decibels.

There are two popular ways to install tiles: with an adhesive and with staples. Both are easy. If the old ceiling isn't a sound surface, you can nail furring strips at right angles to the joists in the ceiling, and then staple tiles to these. Ceiling molding will cover any rough edges as well as exposed fasteners.

Most ceiling tiles aren't washable if they get stained. Here are a couple of tricks that may work:

● The water spots on the ceiling tiles didn't respond to household cleansers, so I tried a cover-up. My wife's powder puff and talcum powder covered over the stains, and you can't tell the difference.

● To clean an acoustical tile that had a bad stain, I finally tried using laundry bleach. I dipped a rag into the bleach and wrung it out well, then lightly wiped over the stain. It's gone.

SUSPENDED CEILINGS

Another easy-to-install ceiling, a great way to lower a too-high ceiling; and an even greater way to hide the plumbing pipes, heating and cooling ducts, steel beams, or electrical wiring in basements and garages that are being converted to living space—the suspended ceiling hides all these uglies, but still allows easy access.

There are also special lighting fixtures that fit into these suspended systems.

FAKE BEAMS

Hand-hewn beams are impressive in many rooms. The lightweight plastic jobs are very authentic looking and most are easy to apply. Hollow them out, and you can hide pipes and wiring.

HANGING THINGS FROM THE CEILING

With the use of hanging baskets of greenery comes the frustration of loud crashes in the middle of the night. This doesn't have to happen if you'll use the right fasteners. Toggle-type hangers as we discuss for walls will hold fairly heavy items (Figure 4). Screw hooks driven into the

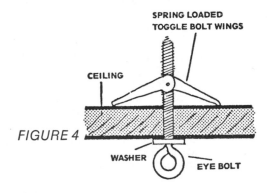

FIGURE 4

joists above will hold even more. You can locate the joists in the same ways you find studs in the wall.

● A hanging divider called for drilling dozens of holes in the plaster ceiling. As I started turning my twist drill for the first hole, the plaster specks began to fall like snow into my face and my eyes. By the time I got through, I'd be blind. I solved the problem by poking the drill bit through the bottom of a small aluminum pie plate. The dust fell into the plate instead of my face. After each hole, I dumped the dust into a paper bag, and when the job was done, there was practically no clean-up.

When you no longer want the basket in that place, you have a hole to patch. Try this:

● Let me tell you about my system for repairing a hole in a plaster ceiling. First I trim a scrap of screen to use as a backing piece. To keep the screen in place while I apply the patching compound, I let gravity hold it for me. I run a length of string through the screen and tie a weight to the end. The weight needs to be heavy enough to pull the screen down firmly.

After the patching is done and dry, the string can be clipped off flush with the surface and will never show.

SPRAY-ON CEILINGS

Lots of homes and apartments have a spray-on acoustical material on the ceiling. I call it popcorn ceiling—it looks great, but if you touch it, it crumbles. There are now companies that make repair compounds. It comes in new (very white) and old (sort of dirty white). For cleaning:

● We had a water spot on our sprayed-on textured acoustical ceiling. From past experience, we knew touching was a no-no. I filled up a child's water pistol with a solution of half water and half laundry bleach. I shot the spot and held a rag under it to catch the drips. After a few rounds of this ammo, the spot disappeared.

Also, the same trick of using talcum powder and a gentle dab with the powder puff works to hide spots on this ceiling.

● That blown-on acoustical texturing they put on some apartment ceilings looks fine, but did you ever try to put hangers into it? It crumbles when you touch it. Rather than take the whole ceiling down, we came up with another way to hang our plants. We put screw eyes in opposite walls from each other and used a strong wire between them. With the wire painted white, it can't be seen. The plants hang from the wire. Even people who have a different type of ceiling might like this idea.

Here are a couple of other room-top tips:

● Many remodeling features require cutting holes in ceilings to accommodate new light fixtures or skylights or decorative panels. You'll make less of a mess if you can cut from above and have a helper hold a great big corrugated box below. The box will catch every bit of the sawdust or Sheetrock. Also, you don't run the risk of cutting into a wire or something else that shouldn't be cut as you do when cutting blind from below. Of course, there is always the danger that you'll step through the ceiling if you don't watch out.

● You know how difficult it is to put up Sheetrock or other large material on a ceiling, even if you can get your wife to help hold it in place while nailing. The solution is to make T-shaped supports from scrap lumber. Make the long piece about an inch or so longer than your ceiling height. Nail a three-foot crosspiece at one end. For strength, nail braces from the ends of the crosspiece back to the upright. This can be wedged in place against the Sheetrock and will hold it while you nail. Actually, a pair of them will let you do the whole job with no help from your wife.

4.
CLOSETS, SHELVES, AND STORAGE SPACE

We all seem to collect more and more things we can't bring ourselves to throw away. Whether yours is a three-room apartment or a thirty-room mansion, if you've just discovered lots of things in piles on the floor instead of in closets and cabinets as they used to be, you probably need more storage space. Rather than spend thousands on an addition to your home, why not steal some storage space from what's already there?

CLOSETS

For storage space, the clothes closet is about the first place everyone thinks of. Although you never seem to have anything to wear, there's never enough room. Here are some suggestions for stretching closet space.

●Slip lengths of chain over the hook of a wire coat hanger. Now hangers with blouses can be hooked into the links of chain. Space them out so you can see at least the collar of each one. Hang as many as you can until no more will go on without the last one brushing the floor.

● We desperately needed more closet space in the bedroom. Since the room was twelve by eighteen feet, I decided we could take two feet off the end of the room and never miss the space. We put closets the full width of the room, which left the room twelve by sixteen feet—plenty big enough for a bedroom.

● The standard home closet has hanger bars and above them, a shelf about twenty-six inches from the ceiling. I suddenly realized that over half the space above the shelf was wasted because most of the stuff we piled on it wasn't very high. I added a shelf halfway above the original. Now that we use the upper shelves for things we don't need too often, we have more storage space than we need.

● I converted the inside of the closet door into a giant shoe rack (Figure 5). I bought some inexpensive screw-in–type doorstops and spaced them in rows of four on the door so that each row holds two pairs of shoes.

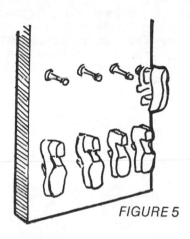

FIGURE 5

Most closet doors are hollow-core, so for each row, you might do well to put a strip of wood on the door to give the threaded doorstops something to bite into.

● Most apartments won't let you hammer nails anywhere, but here's a way to double your closet shelf space without using nails. I make stack shelves to rest atop each regular shelf. The new shelf is cut to fit, and legs—of two-inch-thick stock, the same width as the shelf—are added at each end. There's usually room for one, sometimes two extra shelves above the built-ins.

● In a storage closet, the rods for hanging clothes don't have to be at a convenient height. They can go right up next to the ceiling. My husband made a high-hanger retriever from an old broomstick and a metal clothes hook. The clothes hook has a threaded screw tip inserted in the end of the broom handle, and this hook allows me to lift a hanger right off the rod from ground level.

● I added shoe racks inside the bedroom closet door by attaching a number of curtain rods all up and down the door. The shoes hang by hooking the heels over the rods. My 'shoe door' holds over twenty pairs of shoes and uses only space that was being wasted.

● To double the hanger space in a child's closet, I cut a dowel about an inch shorter than the regular hanger bar. Then I drilled a hole in each end so I could install an eye bolt. To the eye bolts, I used an S-hook and chains connected to another pair of S-hooks over the regular hanger bar. It looks like a trapeze.

● A walk-in closet will often have shelves along each side and maybe a cross shelf along the back. Add a cross shelf in the wasted space over the door. Cut the shelf piece to size so it will span the area. Then attach two straight metal mending plates to each end of this new shelf. The plates go on the top of the shelf and are positioned so that half of each plate extends beyond the end of the shelf (Figure 6). Four-inch plates will do, and this leaves two screw holes on the new shelf. With all four plates in place, the shelf can be installed so the ends of the plates rest on the two side shelves. They don't even have to be attached.

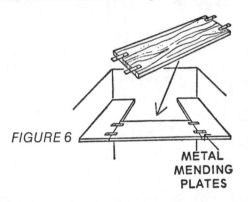

FIGURE 6

METAL
MENDING
PLATES

● Most people are content to put one coat hook on the inside of a closet door. Since I needed more closet space, I put a number of large cup hooks into the door, spaced far enough from the edge that a wire hanger on the hook won't stick out beyond the edge. I use the lower hooks for slacks and skirts, the higher ones for dresses.

● Over half of the clothes in my closets are short blouses, jackets, and skirts. After putting all the long dresses, coats, and robes together at one end of the closet rack, I bought a cheap pine chest at a garage sale and put it in the space underneath the short items. Now I have extra storage space that isn't attached to the wall.

● Here's how I gained additional closet space, and at the same time ended up with a better-organized closet. I took a wooden hanger, installed cup hooks on both sides, and use it to hang all my belts.

● With six children, you have to have hangers for everything or drown in a sea of unhung clothes. We needed a number of coat hooks in the back entryway. Rather than buy them, my husband cut lengths of dowel about four inches long and drilled holes in the center of the end of each one. The holes, about two inches deep, accommodated headless (finishing) nails. He drove the nails into place in the wall, leaving about two inches sticking out. He coated this part with glue and inserted it into the holes in the doweling. When the glue dried and the pegs were painted, we ended up with lots of nice cost-free hooks.

● Ever try to get a twelve-year-old boy to hang up his clothes? I found a way: The basketball net we had taken down when we moved into our apartment wasn't going to be used, so I repainted the metal hoop and attached it to the wall. It looks very much in place in a boy's room, and gives me a place to hang lots of his clothes. As this is something he could relate to and is always in sight, he now hangs a few things up himself.

CLOTHES STORAGE

Now that the clothes worn every day are taken care of, where do you store the out-of-season threads? Here are some ideas for stolen storage space—and other ideas.

● I came up with a good idea when it comes time to store out-of-season clothes. About the only time we use our luggage is for our two weeks vacation each summer. The luggage holds a lot and makes good use of some valuable space.

● Most of us use corrugated boxes for storage. A full one is hard to move because it has no handle. Give bulky boxes a handle ahead of time. Each handle consists of a scrap of board with two holes drilled in it. Punch corresponding holes in the box. With the board inside, run a rope through the holes to form a loop on the outside, and knot both ends inside to prevent their slipping through. The board takes much of the weight off the corrugated box.

● If you live in a humid climate, you know that sometimes moisture in the air works its way through the corrugated boxes used to pack winter clothes. Before you pack the boxes, a light coat of thinned shellac inside and out will make them moistureproof and a lot stronger. Naturally you want to wait for the shellac to dry before packing.

● Although I didn't have enough space for a cedar closet, I did have extra drawer space. I lined the drawers in one chest with thin cedar slats, and we have a cedar drawer.

● We needed a cedar closet to protect winter woolens, but there just wasn't one to spare. I built a cedar chest to the exact size of a window seat for our living room picture windows. It's painted the same as the woodwork and butts up to the window. We added an upholstered pad, and it looks just like a built-in. We needed the extra seating, and also we can move our closet when we move to our dream house.

GUEST CLOSETS

There often isn't room left over for a guest or coat closet, so here are some helpful hints for this storage problem.

● Our small apartment has no guest closet. When we have a party, I always rig up a temporary coat rack. In the corner next to the door, I inserted two large screw hooks, one in each wall. At party time, I put between the hooks a length of chain, cut at the hardware store to fit exactly. Wire coat hangers fit into the links, and we have our coat rack.

● We conquered the problem of no guest closet. I bought three tall shutters from the lumberyard and put them together with hinges. When folded into a U shape, this structure will stand alone (Figure 7). Painted, the screen stands next to the entry door. A metal curtain rod that's flat and has curved ends was also painted to match, and rests across the top of the two end shutters. We've got our guest closet.

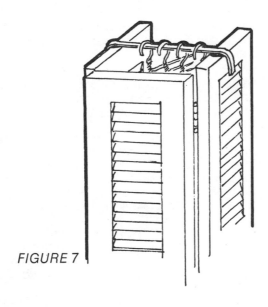

FIGURE 7

SHELVES

Almost every home and apartment has one or more walls that could handle a shelf unit. Places to add shelves are endless. Maybe these hints will help you realize you have lots of unused space for all those books, knickknacks, treasures, and junk you now have piled on the floor.

● We have a fireplace that sticks out about twelve inches into our den. The space on either side was wasted until we added bookshelves flush with the fireplace to the walls. They hold a lot of books and magazines we accumulate, and really look good, too.

● We selected our apartment because it had an entry hall, but soon realized we were paying for a lot of wasted space there. We make better use of the space now that we have added shelves along one wall. This solves the problem of what to do with the books and makes the entry look great. On the opposite wall we installed colorful coat hooks, and can therefore convert our guest closet into a storage closet for other things.

● A hallway or passageway is generally wasted space. If it's wide enough, you'll probably never miss the space if you install shelves or cabinets along one wall.

● A Lally column (the metal support post used in many basements) can be used to handle shelves with this simple installation: Select a metal shelf bracket and attach it to the post using a pair of worm-gear-type hose clamps. Cut a U-shaped section out of the back edge of the shelf so that it will fit around the round column, and secure the shelf to the bracket. It will be steady and secure. You can add several such shelves to each post. Just don't try to make the shelves too wide, since they have only one support.

● If a door or window is seldom if ever used, you can board over the opening on the outside, remove the door or window, and fill the cavity with recessed shelves for all sorts of small items.

● Instead of using bricks to hold up book shelves, I have painted tin cans and stood them on end between planks. I used short cans as a base and tall cans where the books go. Two cans at each end will hold the shelves steady. Anytime I want to change color schemes, I just respray the cans.

KITCHEN STORAGE

Although your kitchen seems crammed to the rafters, there is probably a better way to utilize the space. Following are some hints to help you relieve kitchen clutter.

● When we added a utility room, we moved the fold-out-of-the-wall ironing board from the kitchen into this new room. Rather than cover over the space left in the wall, I converted it into a handy spice cabinet. I made a simple frame for the cabinet, added shelves, and constructed a door to match the rest of the kitchen cabinetwork. The space isn't very deep, but is ideal for spices and other small condiments.

● Our tiny apartment kitchen didn't have enough space for our pots and pans, so my roommate painted a colorful tree on the kitchen wall and installed cup hooks around on the tree. She outlined each pan and put a stick-on flower underneath so that when the pot is being used, the tree doesn't look bare. It not only solves a space problem, but is a unique decoration.

● The one closet in our kitchen has shelves, and between the door and the shelves there's no room to store a broom or mop. By cutting a notch for each handle in each shelf, the mop and broom can stand in the closet, and the door can shut. Pretty slick!

● I like my storage idea for the grocery sacks I save for garbage and other uses. I clip the sacks on a wooden pants hanger, hung from a nail on the back of the pantry door. The sacks are easily accessible, but completely out of the way.

● I have no place in my apartment to store a stepladder, but I'm always needing one. So I painted my ladder to match my kitchen furniture, put it in a corner, and set potted plants on each step. When I need the ladder, I transfer the plants to the drain counter.

● My wife complained about the lack of space in our new apartment's kitchen cabinets, so inside of each door to the cabinet under the sink, I stapled a pair of those expansion files used in offices. These sturdy paper folders hold many flat things such as lids, trivets, and other small items.

● We needed room for pots and pans, so we came up with a hanging utensil rack—a square frame made of scrap wood (Figure 8). A chain is attached to a screw eye in each corner. The four pieces of chain hook onto a screw eye in the ceiling. We painted the chain black and stained the wood. Utensils hang from cup hooks placed around the sides of the frame. It takes care of our excess and looks pretty neat.

FIGURE 8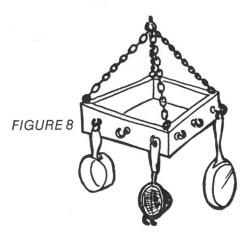

● Although I have no room in my apartment to store all the tools I need, I went out and bought all I needed anyway. Many tools come with bright-colored handles or grips, and some are even painted all over. I bought tools by color. Then I bought several sections of Peg-Board, painted them, and mounted them on a kitchen wall. Finally, I played around with the tools until I had a pleasing arrangement. It's an interesting wall decoration and solved the tool-storage problem.

STAIRWAY STORAGE

If you have a stairway, chances are there's a big wasted space under there—as well as storage space in the stairs.

● Remove one of the steps at the back door. Reattach it with hinges. The space under the hinged step is ideal as a catchall for boots, overshoes, baseball bats, and other sports equipment that would otherwise end up in the house.

● All of the area under a stairway can be used for storage by making a triangular unit on wheels that just fits under there. It can be one unit, or divide the space up into three or four units that fit together.

● I boxed in each step under our basement stairs so each step is now a small storage chest. It was quite simple to nail a back and bottom on each one, and then I hinged the treads to act as lids. A screen-door hook holds each lid in place, and this insures the steps are secure and safe to walk on. Our basement steps are the open kind, so it was easy to get under them to work. But even closed ones will usually have an access. Or you can insert a drawer into each riser, as shown in Figure 9.

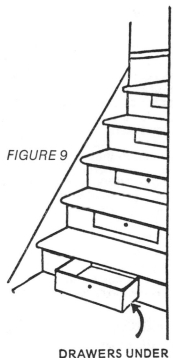

FIGURE 9

DRAWERS UNDER
EACH STEP

ATTIC STORAGE

Speaking of stairs, go up to the attic and see what extra storage area you can make use of.

● For storing things in the attic, I made boxes that fit under the attic eaves, and added rollers to them so they can be rolled out of the way, and yet can be pulled out easily for access.

● Build a storage chest from the floor to the slanted ceiling in the eave area in the attic (Figure 10). I built one and bought drawer units to fit the chest. It's a great place to store lots of things.

NEW ATTIC ROOM

FIGURE 10

STORAGE DRAWERS
GO BACK INTO
UNFINISHED ATTIC

● The access to our attic is through a manhole in the top of an upstairs closet. Each time I needed to get into the attic, I had to carry a stepladder upstairs. Finally I got smart and built a ladder in the closet. It's just a pair of two-by-fours nailed to the wall with crosspieces for steps. Painted the same color as the closet, the ladder doesn't look bad—and sure has saved my having to lug that stepladder up and down.

● Our attic lacked any closet or hanger space. Since it was just a large square room, there was really no place to run a hanger rod without building a closet. Rather than do that, I made an open closet at each corner. Each closet was made from scrap wood and a scrap length of iron pipe. Measuring out from the wall the length of the pipe, I mounted a small scrap of two-by-four. To this, I attached a triangle of wood that stuck out about fourteen inches. It had a V notch about 11 inches out. Back on the wall I had measured from, I mounted another scrap at the same height, with a notch to line up with the first one. The length of pipe rests in the notches, and I have a sturdy hanger pipe.

● To store a roll of carpet in the attic, my husband attached to the rafters long pipe strapping that comes in rolls. These hold the roll of carpet up out of the way against the rafters.

STORING CARD TABLES AND CHAIRS

Card tables and chairs are great to have, but present a storage problem. See if these hints help.

● Card tables stored in the closet have a way of sliding away from the wall and crashing down. But the table bottom edge can't slide past a strip of molding tacked a few inches from the wall. The top of the table just leans against the wall.

● We solved the problem of storing our card table by converting the table into a wall hanging in our entry hall. When we need to use it, we just take it down and set it up. Otherwise, it looks great as a decoration. To the top we glued a print cut from a poster and covered it with varnish. (Before we arrived at our plan, we talked about making a montage of photos, gluing on wallpaper, and even handpainting a design.) The print is square, and a border of the old tabletop runs around it. It really looks wild and solved a problem.

And if you still have a few boxes in the middle of the floor, here are some leftover ideas for your space program.

● Our living room/dining room was one long, narrow room, and we wanted to divide it into two separate areas. By adding a storage wall as a divider, we got not only the desired effect, but a whole wall for storing dishes, glassware, knickknacks, and books as a much-needed bonus.

● We decided we could live without one small guest closet, and have converted it into a neat little bar. I removed the shelf and hanger bar, then found a low chest that fits in the closet to act as a counter top. Above this, I installed new shelves for glassware. It keeps guests out of our tiny kitchen as well as keeping out the glasses, booze, and other bar accessories.

● Stepladders are a pain to store, but I have tucked my five-foot ladder away on the back of a closet door where it's never in the way, yet easy to get to. Near the bottom of the door I made a sort of shelf out of scrap lumber. It's wide enough and long enough for the ladder's feet to fit onto. Then around the shelf I added a lip, so the ladder stays in place. At the top, I nailed to the door an old belt that fastens around the ladder to keep it snug against the door.

● A TV movie showed jewels kept in a wall safe behind a painting. This gave me the idea for storage space. I installed shelves behind two of our bigger pictures. Then I hinged the picture frames so they're really the cabinet doors. It's not like another closet, but we do have some storage space we didn't have before, and nobody knows it's there.

● I get lots of extra storage space underneath many pieces of furniture. The beds can accommodate roll-out bins that aren't seen. Upholstered living room furniture with skirts will also provide extra space.

● Many times installing a room divider can screen out an unwanted view or make two rooms out of one. If your front door leads right into the living room, a divider can create an entry hall. If you have two kids in one bedroom, a divider can make it two rooms, or separate the study area from the sleeping part. A divider will separate the kitchen from the eating area. Dividers can be partial or full walls. They can be actual walls or only a separation that still lets you see through, but creates the feeling of two definite areas.

5.
DOORS

Doors are designed to open, close, latch, and lock. If they refuse to do any of these functions, or won't do them willingly and quietly, they need help. Here's the swinging story of how to help your doors. It's an open-and-shut case; you *can* do-it.

HARD TO OPEN

A stuck door is the most common door problem. If you do get it open, then it won't close. The first thing most people do is get a plane and take a little off the top. This may be the right answer, but about 90 percent of the time it's not. The first step in solving the sticking door is to see exactly where the problem is.

Usually you can see the trouble spot where there's been rubbing on the door, the frame, or the floor:

● Usually a door that's sticking can be easily remedied if you know exactly where the tight spot is. You can pinpoint it by wrapping a sheet of carbon paper around the general area. Put the carbon side against the door. When the door is closed, the tight squeeze will mark itself on the door. Then you can work only where the need is.

● Your trick of using carbon paper to locate exactly where a door is sticking is fine—except our door and frames are stained dark, and carbon paper marks don't show. I take a piece of chalk and rub along the door facing. When the door is pushed shut, it picks up chalk where contact is made and tells me where I need to go to work. A damp rag wipes the chalk away.

● One of the best ways to track down the areas where a door is sticking is to insert a dollar bill between the facing and the door and move it around until it sticks. Mark this place with chalk, then skip over and work the bill back to find where the high place ends. This is the quickest way to find all the sticking places so you can plane them down.

Now close the door, if possible, and look at the edge opposite the sticking place. If there's a big gap there, you may have loose hinges. Even the slightest bit of looseness will let a door sag enough to cause problems. That is, in fact, probably the most common cause and the easiest to fix. First check to see if the screws holding the hinges are still tight. If not, tighten them. If the screws won't stop turning, the holes have become too large. Here are some tricky stopgap ways to tighten up the hole:

● Wrap the screw threads with steel wool. Re-insert. The steel wool will take up the slack and allow the screws to be turned down tight.
● Wrap the threads in cotton. Dip in nail polish, glue, or shellac. The cotton does the same as steel wool would, and the adhesive helps set the screw and cotton in place.
● Insert pieces of wooden matches or toothpicks in the hole to give the screw new bite.
● Use larger, longer screws. However, the heads must be the same size as the old ones to countersink in the hinge plate.
● Rather than remove and reseat the hinges when the screw holes get too big, I've been very successful in just drilling new holes in the hinge leaf. This can be done without even removing the door. Of course, the new holes have to be countersunk. The metal used in most hinges is easy to bore through with an electric drill. Usually you will only need to drill one new hole, but most hinge plates have enough room to drill even three new holes.

If none of these tricks works, rebuild the wood and start with a new hole.

The best way is to drill out the holes so you can glue new pieces of dowel in place. After the glue has set up, use a hacksaw blade without the frame of the saw to cut off the ends of the dowels. Some people use plastic wood to fill the holes, but I don't think this is as effective.

If the screws aren't loose, but the diagnosis is a hinge problem, shim up or recess the hinges to relieve the sticking place. Look at the door. If there seems to be plenty of space around, and if it sticks at just one point near the top of the latch side, it means the bottom hinge side needs to come out some. This calls for a cardboard shim between the hinge plate and the jamb (Figure 11). Shirt board is fine. Cut the shim to match the hinge plate and then cut slots so it can slip over the screws. Loosen the screws on the frame side and slip the shim in place. Retighten the screws and see if the problem is solved. If one thickness isn't enough, add another. If the door sticks at the bottom, then go through the same routine at the top hinge.

● When you have to shim out a striker plate or hinge to correct a door problem, instead of cutting shirt boards to fit under these metal plates, I spread a thin layer of caulk over the area and reinstall the plate. This is quick and easy, and it works because you can adjust the thickness of the bed of caulking to suit your needs.

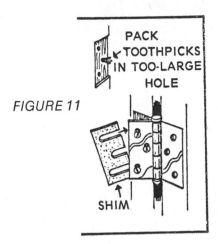

PACK
TOOTHPICKS
IN TOO-LARGE
HOLE

FIGURE 11

SHIM

Sometimes you need to move the door back away from the latch side. This can be done by taking the door down and cutting deeper mortises.

A door that sticks across the top but has plenty of space at the bottom can be corrected by lowering the hinges in the frame.

If, when you close the door, it doesn't qualify as a hinge problem, check to see if there is very little gap all the way around. This could indicate that moisture has caused swelling of the wood. If so, it requires that you remove some of the door. But hold it! Does this door stick just every so often? If so, extra humidity may be doing the damage right now, but if it dries up a little later, the door might shrink back to size. If it's just seasonal, live with it until it dries out. Then seal all the edges so moisture can't get back in.

If the swelling isn't just a passing fancy, you will have to sand or plane. If it binds at the top, try to remove the excess while the door is still hung. Always plane toward the center when planing on the top or bottom so the plane can't catch on the edge of the side rail and rip off a chunk of the door edge. Coarse sandpaper or a rasp will often take off enough and do it easier than a plane. Another tool I like is called a Surform tool. The blade of a Surform-type tool has a series of raised lips around openings in the metal plate. This is an inexpensive tool that cuts smoother than a plane and is much easier for the average person to use with good results.

● If you ever have to plane off part of a hung door, you know when you work above your head you get an eyeful of shavings. When I do this, I rig up a catcher on the plane. Place a plastic sandwich bag over the opening where shavings come out and then tape it to the knob. You catch the shavings in the bag, not in the eye.

● When planing a little off the top of a door, if you don't have someone to hold the door steady, it usually moves to one side just as you're starting a cut with the plane. You either botch up the door or fall off the ladder. The simple solution I use is to put a wedge under the front edge of the door so it can't swing.

● A door that binds at the bottom can often be sanded off without removing the door. Place the sandpaper or a rasp on the floor and move the door back and forth over it. However, the biggest problem is to find the exact spot that's binding. A small purse-size mirror will do the trick. Hold it down at the floor, and it will show you the bottom of the door.

If surface must be removed from the side of the door, avoid planing on the latch side. Whether you know it or not, most doors are beveled on the latch side to allow them to close without hitting the facing. Plane from the hinge side. This may mean deepening the mortise later, but this will be easier for the layman than putting on a new bevel. When planing along the side, cut toward the edges.

● When you remove a door for planing off the excess, it's about as unhandy as any workpiece you'll ever have. However, I have found that there's an easy way to anchor a door. I use two wooden apple crates and attach them with a C clamp to each end of the door on opposite sides (Figure 12). For extra weight, I put a couple of bricks in each crate. Now the door stands on its side, and I can plane away without it falling on my foot.

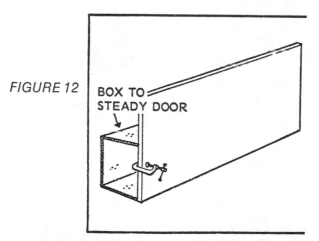

FIGURE 12 | BOX TO STEADY DOOR

When you have finished the planing and have ascertained that your door will once again swing properly, seal the edges where you have exposed new wood to keep moisture out and help prevent future swelling. A coat of paint to match the door is best.

Sometimes the problem is that your house has settled and

forced the frame out of kilter. If so, there is very little you can do. Try placing a padded 2-by-4 against the frame and hitting it with a hammer. Sometimes this will reset the frame just enough to solve the problem. If at first you don't succeed, forget it and go to work on adjusting the hinges or planing off the door to make it fit the frame's new shape.

● Most people never think that an extra coat of paint can sometimes be just enough to prevent a door from working properly. By the time you've repainted several times, the extra paint on the door and the frame can mount up. If you'll examine the tolerance all around the door before you start, you may save yourself some time and effort. If it's getting snug, sand away enough of the old paint so you won't have the problem.

● A warped door can sometimes be fixed without having to take it down and prop weights on it or use heat and moisture to draw it back into shape. Often just adding a third hinge at the middle of the door will force the warp out. If you can push on the door at the hinge side and see the warp go away, this plan will work. This will also let you know where to place the hinge. It won't always correct the warp, but if it does, it'll be easier than doing without the door for a few days.

DOOR WON'T LATCH

A door that won't stay latched may be worse than no door at all. You may be lulled into thinking the closed door means privacy, and all of a sudden it swings open.

Diagnosis is the key to taking care of the illness. Look at the latch bolt while the door is shut. You should quickly spot the problem. If the bolt doesn't come far enough out from the door to engage the hole in the strike plate, either the bolt is hung in the latch or the door or strike plate needs to be shimmed to move the two closer together. Obviously, shimming out the strike plate is easier. However, sometimes you have to shim both strike plate and hinges.

If the latch bolt isn't quite lined up with the opening, you must adjust it in some way (Figure 13). Either file an edge off the latch bolt or remove the plate and enlarge the hole with a file. If the alignment is far off, however, you'll need to move the strike plate up or down. This means extending the mortise up or down. Fill in the old screw holes with plastic wood or a plug, and then replace the plate. Also fill in the gap left by moving the plate.

If everything is lined up, and the bolt comes out far enough but still the door doesn't latch, the opening is too far in. Usually this is only a fraction off, and the easiest way to solve the problem is to remove the plate and file to enlarge the hole toward the front. If it is more than you wish to file, reset the plate farther out on the frame.

DOOR NOISES

Most door noises are squeaks in the hinges. All you have to do to stop the noise is to lubricate the hinge pin. Wedge something under the

FIGURE 13

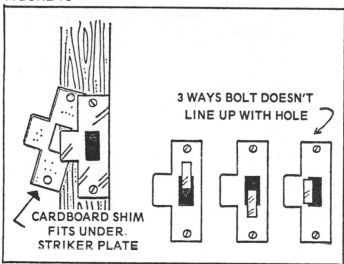

3 WAYS BOLT DOESN'T
LINE UP WITH HOLE

CARDBOARD SHIM
FITS UNDER
STRIKER PLATE

door to prop it up, then remove the hinge pin. Clean it with steel wool. The best lubricant is either powdered graphite or silicone spray. These are both dry and won't drip on the floor. If neither is handy, a light coat of petroleum jelly will do. In a pinch, even machine oil can be put on— lightly, so there will be no chance of a drip.

● The easy way to oil a squeaky hinge is to squirt the oil on the hinge pin and hope it will seep down the pin and into the sleeve. Sometimes it works on down, but often not. So we put more oil on until it goes down and drips on your shoe. The better way is to remove the pin, put oil on a pipe cleaner, and run this around in the opening. This will distribute the oil where it should be.

● Getting oil down along a hinge pin is impossible in many cases without raising the pin each time you lubricate. However, if you'll tap it up slightly you can wrap several turns of string around it. Then tap it back down: The string will be held in place, and you can squirt oil under the head of the pin. The string collar spreads the oil all the way around, then lets it flow down the pin. Of course, it's best to use oil only on outside hinges, since oil could drip on your oriental rugs.

The next most common noise is a door rattle. This indicates that there is too much play between the bolt and the hole in the strike plate. You need something to keep the bolt pushed against the plate. Little felt dots that stick on the bottom of ashtrays can be put on the stop, and this will do the job. They have enough give to allow the door to close and latch, but will bounce back with enough pressure to keep it tight. Small tabs of foam rubber glued to the stop will also stop the rattle. Here are some more noise stoppers:

● A quick way to stop a rattling door is to staple small tabs of cardboard around the doorstop part of the frame. Cut them the width of the stop and staple them at several points. This takes up the gap between the door and the stop, and leaves no room for the door to move and cause noise. If one layer isn't quite enough, use more. These tabs and staples can be painted over to match the door frame and won't be seen. The more conventional solutions all require a trip to the hardware store.

● Don't throw away any leftover self-sticking foam rubber weather stripping. It will come in handy in many ways. A few tabs in a door frame will stop a rattling door. A few tabs can be placed on the bottom of heavy objects to prevent their marring furniture. I'll bet if you have the stuff around, you'll come up with dozens of good uses.

● Most door rattles are caused by too much space between the latch and the plate. The space can easily be taken up if you remove the plate and raise it a little. Instead of cutting a backing piece as most people do, I merely butter the plate with putty. A thin layer is all that's needed. Fill the screw holes with putty too. When the plate is put back in, turn the screws until they are flush, but don't turn them down tight enough to squeeze the putty out. When the putty hardens, the plate is raised and on good and tight, and there are no more rattles.

● If you have kids, live in an apartment, and have crabby neighbors, you get complaints. We have learned many tricks to help keep the noise down. One way to soften slamming doors is with a few wide rubber bands. Slip the bands over one doorknob, then stretch them over the knob on the other side of the door. Be sure the bands are tight enough so they can be positioned above and below the bolt—the rubber band should not touch the bolt. Now when the wild ones come through and slam the door, it makes much less noise.

● With a new baby who needs lots of sleep and a four-year-old monster who doesn't know the meaning of the word *quiet,* we've tried to noiseproof everything in the house. We soon discovered that there are gadgets to stop the sound of screen doors that slam, but nothing to keep the hook from banging against the door. I put an end to this "baby rouser" by slipping a slit fishing cork over the hook (Figure 14). Now the cork hits the door, the baby sleeps, and our four-year-old doesn't get shushed quite as much.

● Almost every home has a door that stays quietly in place until early summer, when the house is open for airing. Then when you are about ready to take a Sunday afternoon nap, *wham!* The wind blows it shut with a slam. We had a couple of these surprise slammers until I installed a screen-door hook and eye. Now, with the doors hooked open, we can enjoy the breeze and fresh air without the boom!

● When the weather is right for opening windows, I found that the wind made one of our doors rattle. I stopped the rattle by cutting off the tips of two pencil erasers and gluing them at the corners of the door frame. This makes the door snug when closed, and it can no longer make noise. The rubber has enough give so the door can easily be closed, and the latch will engage.

● For a rattling, loose doorknob, just remove the knob and drop a

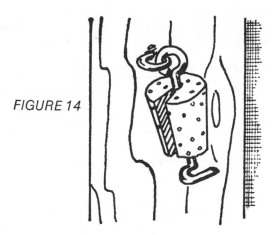

FIGURE 14

ball of putty into the hole where the spindle fits. When the knob is put back on, the putty will form around the spindle and take up the space that caused it to be loose and to rattle.

DOOR STOPS

We mentioned the stops that are in the frame—these are strips against which the door closes. The other stops are those that keep the door-knob from knocking a hole in the wall or keep the door from hitting something. Here are some stopgap tips:

● A door that just won't stay open can be remedied with a door-stop. Around our house, however, the kids are always using the door-stops for some game or project. I staple half of a soft kitchen sponge to the bottom of the door, placed so it sticks down far enough to be compressed some against the floor. The sponge has enough give so the door can be moved across the floor. However, when the door isn't being pushed, the sponge presses against the floor and acts as a friction stop, keeping it in place. Put the sponge on the side of the door next to the wall, and it'll never be seen. When the sponges start to wear down, they are replaced, but are still good for use in the kitchen.

● Here's a hint that might help mobile-home owners or anyone with low ceilings. It's a way to keep doors open without having a wedge or hook that makes it difficult to close them again. Install one of those spring-type doorstops in the ceiling instead of the wall. Position it where you want the door to be when open. The door will push past the spring, which will straighten out after the door goes past. It will keep the door from closing until you add enough force to push past the spring again.

● Here's another way to use that retired garden hose. Cut a piece about two inches long and then split it for a dandy two-way doorstop.

Bend the hose opposite the split, making it fold out sort of flat. Slide this under the door, with the inside of the hose facing the floor. The part that sticks out on each side will curl a little, and the door won't move either way.

● Those rubber wedges that keep doors from blowing shut always seem to stray. I've fixed ours so they stay by the door: I drilled a hole in each wedge so when not in use, it hangs from the doorstop sticking out from the wall. A simple, easy way to keep those little devils around.

● You can quickly have a pair of ready-made doorstops if you happen to have an old wooden coat hanger around (Figure 15). Remove the cross hanger. Then cut the hanger in half, and each shoulder becomes a doorstop. The stops are tapered and can easily be wedged under the door. Since the wood is a good hardwood, it can be stained and finished or painted to suit you.

● The rubber tip came off the end of a doorstop, and the metal was punching a hole in the door. Rather than buy a new stop, I forced a slip-on rubber pencil eraser over the end of the stop. Works fine, looks fine, and cost much less than a new doorstop.

HANGING A DOOR

Sometimes you may decide to add onto your house, or maybe you want to knock a hole in a wall and add a door. Or maybe you've knocked a hole in the old door and want a new one. Some doors come with frame

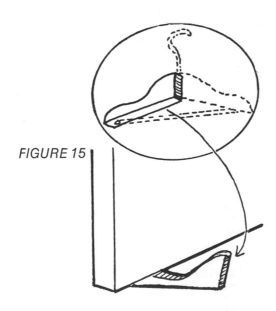

FIGURE 15

and door already together, which makes for an easier installation. If you just go out and buy a door, you'll have to mortise out for the hinges and drill the proper holes for the lock set. In an existing frame, match the hinges and lock set to existing mortises on the frame. In a new situation, remember the seven-eleven principle—not a crapshooter's term. Position the top hinge about seven inches from the top of the door, and the bottom about eleven inches from the floor. Some new doors come with a stile extension—a protrusion on each end that protects the bottom and top edges. This must be sawed off. Mark the door for size and saw off where needed. To check the fit, use wedges to hold the door in place and let you see that there is proper clearance on all sides. Use the plane for slight adjustments in fit. Mortising is generally done with a wood chisel. Use the hinge to mark the mortise.

● If you're going to hang a door, maybe a single-edge razor blade will do a better job of outlining the hinge. In fact, after you've marked around the hinge, the razor blade can be tapped on in to the desired depth of the mortise. It will give a smoother, straighter cut than most of us can get with a chisel. Of course, you'll have to use a chisel to finish the mortise.

Practice with your chisel on scrap lumber before you try a mortise on the door.

● The best template for pilot holes for hinges is, of course, the hinge itself. To hold the hinge in place during all this activity, I use a couple of pieces of cellophane tape. I drill right through the tape, then insert the screws with the tape still in place. Just before the screws are turned down tight, the tape can be peeled off. This sure saves a lot of grief.

DECOR

The door can be part of your decorative scheme. The new door you buy can be painted or stained and can be carved or paneled. Here are some ways to add pizzazz to your doors:

● Many times a plain door bores the homeowner so much he'll buy a new fancy job to replace it. There are other ways to go. There are carved pieces called plant-ons that are glued to surfaces. They are plastic, but look, take stain, and paint like wood. Molding can also be put on a door to jazz it up. One of the newest door decorations is a color photo with paste on the back. It comes in standard door sizes, but can be trimmed if you've cut the door down. The variety of pictures is so wide and the colors so varied that you'll be hard pressed not to find one to fit your decor. Hanging a strip of photo is sure easier than hanging a new door, and costs quite a bit less.

● Jazz up an otherwise plain apartment door by just covering the panels with strippable wallpaper. This can be done either inside or out.

When you move, the strip can be peeled off with no damage to the door. Any adhesive left can be easily removed.

● Paneled doors can be converted to the flush type by adding a layer of plywood veneer or hardboard. Contact cement usually does the job. So that the layer can't sag, you may have to fill in the hollow sections.

● Rather than replace a door that had gotten all beat up, I swapped it with a good door in our basement game room. Then we glued over the old door dozens of magazine ads from the Twenties and my wife decoupaged it. The door is a real conversation piece and a natural for a game room. The "distressed" texture of the door looks as if we worked hard to get it that way.

● I was going to glue some veneer on a door and knew I'd need clamps all up and down the surface. Since I'd never use that many clamps again, I decided that rather than invest in them, I'd make some. I cut strips of one-inch-wide scrap wood a little longer than the width of the door. These boards were positioned on each side of the door. Then I cut rubber bands from an old inner tube. The bands were crisscrossed about the ends to bring the pressure to bear. I got a good glue job, and the "clamps" didn't cost a cent.

● Our mail slot in the front door also let rain blow in until I put a small canopy over it. The canopy was made from one quarter of a large juice can, including a triangle of the top and bottom. In addition to the curved fourth of the can, I left enough on the long side to form a tab through which screws could fit. A similar tab was left on the two triangular parts that form the sides. The canopy is painted to match the door.

Some of the "decor" is done by kids who go through a door as if it were the practice dummy on the football field. How about this?

● We had a few leftover squares of vinyl floor tile from the kitchen. We also had a place on the kitchen door that our youngsters always seem to kick when coming into the house. After cleaning off this area, I placed floor tiles on the door to form a kick plate. It hides the scuff marks and also matches the floor inside.

Another reader used a strip of plastic laminate left over from the kitchen counter top.

SCREEN DOORS

The same techniques used in repairing, replacing, and maintaining the screening in windows would apply to doors. However, the door is subject to more rough treatment. Here's a sag solver:

● Almost every screen door develops a case of the sags after a while. One way to help prevent it is to install the spring at an angle. Place the end connected to the frame higher than the end connected to the door. The upward pull of the spring will keep the door on the up and up.

● Leftover wire screen can best be stored if you will provide a sleeve to keep the roll from coming undone. An easy-to-make sleeve can be fashioned by using a tin can with both ends cut out. Use a coffee can for a large roll or vegetable cans for smaller rolls. Anything that's stored rolled up can be held with this type of sleeve.

And here's the last of the door prizes:

● I used to come in with groceries, and have to put them all down while I opened the several locks on the back door of my apartment. Then I added a small wooden shelf by the door. This holds the packages so I don't have to stoop.

● When we converted our garage to a den, my wife decided on Dutch doors at one entry. It seemed that the job of hanging would be a lot easier if the door could be hung as one unit. I made them one piece by nailing boards along each side. To make sure the space between the halves would still be there, I inserted strips of shirt board before joining them. After the door was hung and the boards removed, filler and paint hid the nail holes.

● Maybe you have a door that sticks out into a room and always seems to be in the way when open. Maybe by simply remounting it to swing back the other way, you can solve the problem. We had such a door, and this simple maneuver meant no more cracked noggins in the dark and more usable room.

● Here's my way to keep an outside door with a key slot in the knob from freezing. I cut a hole in an empty plastic dishwashing-liquid bottle. The hole is just big enough to fit over the knob and is close to the bottom of the bottle. With this shield slipped over the knob, no moisture gets into the lock. By putting the hole near the bottom, the bottle hangs upside down so no water goes in the top. In fact, if snow gets in, the opening lets moisture drip out. This is also a great way to keep toddlers from opening a door you don't want them to.

6.
ELECTRICAL REPAIRS

Lots of people don't understand electricity. It just plain scares them, and so they shy away from anything electrical. I'm not going to try to explain the science of electricity because there are many electrical repairs that you can make *without* understanding how it works. Besides, I find it's much better to just write the whole electrical system off to magic. Otherwise you'll go crazy trying to figure out how an invisible force traveling through tiny wires can make things cold in the refrigerator, hot at the stove, and at the same time pick up thirty-year-old reruns of *I Love Lucy* on TV.

About being scared. I say *respect* electricity, but don't be *afraid*. You won't be in danger if you keep in mind the old Spanish-American War slogan, "Remember the Maine." If you turn off the *main* switch at the entry box, there'll be no current going to the gadget you're working on. Actually, you don't even have to be that drastic. Remove the fuse or trip the circuit-breaker switch for the particular circuit you're working on, and you've also removed the danger. In the case of a lamp or an appliance, just pull the plug, and you're OK. (There are exceptions. Some electronic gadgets—the TV is a prime example—store power that must be discharged before you go inside. But most gadgets are safe with the power source removed.)

CHANGING A LIGHT BULB

If you're one of those folks who laughingly says, "I can't even change a light bulb, much less make repairs," I'll try to prove you wrong. In fact, some electrical repairs are easier than some bulb changes. What if the bulb is broken? Here are some ideas from readers:

- Push a sponge-rubber ball firmly against the jagged remainder of the bulb. The ball will catch, and you can unscrew the bulb without slicing your finger.

● Get a scrap of wood, preferably a two-by-two, and sharpen one end to a shallow point. (Don't make it a long, tapered point.) Jam the point into the bulb base. If it doesn't seem to be secure in the base, tap the other end lightly with a hammer. When it is secure, you can twist the bulb base out by turning the stick counterclockwise. Just be sure not to damage the socket while getting the stick in place.

● I just use my dust mop. Pushed against the broken bulb and turned, the mop grabs hold and will back the bulb out without any risk of cutting your hands.

● A spring-type clothespin will grab hold of the leftover stem in the bulb without any danger of cutting your fingers. Once it's clamped on, you can turn the base right out.

Another old standby is to jam the end of a large rubber-handled screwdriver into the base. But my all-time favorite is to use a large Idaho potato. Doesn't do much for the flavor of the potato, but it will let you back out the bulb. Remember, it turns counterclockwise; and also, be sure the power is off!

ENTRY BOX

So much for the lighter side of electricity. Let's go to the fuse box or circuit-breaker box. It's there to save your house—and maybe your life. If things inside the wiring or an appliance start to go wrong, the fuse blows or the circuit-breaker switch trips, thus preventing continued overheating that could cause a fire. When this happens, it's a signal that either the circuit is overloaded or that there's a short circuit. An *overload* means the wires are being asked to deliver more current than they are capable of. A *short circuit* means that bare wires are touching so your current can't travel its normal route.

In the case of an overload, the blackout usually comes just after you turn on some gadget or when a motor starts. If it's a gadget, check to see what other appliances are on that circuit, and move some of them to another circuit. This is more likely to happen in the kitchen where we keep adding appliances, and where they may all be on at once during a meal preparation.

If the fuse blows when a motor starts, it is probably just a temporary overload. Much more juice is required to get the motor going than to keep it going. This rarely happens with circuit-breaker switches because they are usually able to handle a temporary overload (though they will trip when a central air-conditioning system starts up). However, regular fuses will blow. If you find it's a motor-starting problem, replace that fuse with a time-delay fuse. It will handle the extra load for a few moments, but will blow in the face of a real overload or a short.

If you don't correct whatever caused the blown fuse or tripped switch, you'll just keep on having blackouts, so it's folly to just hope things will continue to run. With fuses, it can get pretty expensive, so do your investigating to find the problem.

● If you've ever had a fuse blow and opened the box to find that wasps had built a nest in the fuse box, you'll appreciate my tip. Keep a few mothballs in the bottom of the box, and these pests will look elsewhere for their home site.

It's a good idea to keep spare fuses. It's also a good idea to keep a flashlight *in working order* at the box. However, be sure your replacement fuse is the same size (number of amps) as the one that blew. A larger fuse will keep the current going longer before blowing, and that might be just long enough to let a fire get started. *Never* use the old penny or foil-under-the-fuse trick. Also, *do not* use larger-rated fuses. Either trick is asking for a fire. The fuses are there for your protection, so let them do their job.

Here are a couple tips for handling the entry box, which is another name given the fuse or circuit-breaker box.

● Whenever I have to throw a switch at the circuit-breaker box to do some electrical work inside the house, I leave a note on the box that says, "DON'T TOUCH! WORK IN PROGRESS!" This prevents any other member of the family from seeing an open box and trying to help by flipping the switch on again.

These boxes are often located in a basement or garage, and since concrete is a heavy drinker, there is always the possibility of a moist floor. So you don't become a conductor, why not provide a two-by-four platform to stand on (Figure 16)? A discarded rubber floor mat from the car is also a good protection. It's best to wear sneakers or rubber-soled shoes. Experienced electricians use only one hand, often gloved, when working on the entry box. To be sure you do that, put the other hand in a pocket.

FIGURE 16

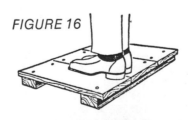

● You can usually tell *why* a fuse has blown by looking at the glass face. It won't always tell you, but often does. If the window is discolored, it is likely that the fuse blew because of a short circuit. A clean window usually means an overload.

If you suspect that there is a short within the circuit, remove or turn off everything on that circuit. Then restore power. If it doesn't blow again, you know that the offender was in one of the lamps or appliances. Plug them in and turn them on one by one. When you reach the guilty party, you'll again trip a switch or blow a fuse. Now you know where to look for the trouble and repair.

If the fuse blows again as soon as you restore power, you know you have a short in the wiring. Check all the fixtures, switches, and wall outlets for loose connections or bare wires touching each other.

● Many times a circuit-breaker switch requires very positive action to get it to reengage. It may look like it's back to the on position, but nothing happens. Pull it back all the way to off, and then give it a firm push to the on position. This'll usually do it. Also, at times a switch will be tripped, but it appears to be still on. Pull it back, then set it again.

If you can't find the problem, it's probably inside the walls, and in most cases, you'll need a licensed electrician. As you progress, however, even complete rewiring jobs are not beyond the do-it-yourselfer. Just be sure what you do complies with the local electrical code.

● Now, while everything is in good working order, is an excellent time to make a diagram of your fuse box or circuit breakers. The trial-and-error method is the best way. Flip the switches or unscrew the plugs one at a time to find out what rooms they control. When the chart is complete, glue it to the box or put it on the wall nearby. Then in an emergency, you'll know what controls what. (And don't forget to reset the electric clock after it's been off.)

REPAIRING A LAMP

Almost everyone has a lamp that lights up only if you stomp on a certain board in the floor while twisting back against the turn-on button. But lamp repair is usually simple.

First, be sure the dead lamp is in a good working outlet. Next check the plug and the cord. A faulty plug is an easy and safe repair—easy because with lamp cord, there are clamp-on plugs that require only that you be able to insert the wire into a hole. It's safe because there is no current involved; the only way you could hurt yourself is if you poked a sliver of wire into your finger.

There are several types of clamp-on plugs. If the lamp has a heavier cord, or if you prefer another type plug, it's still easy because you just zip the two sections of wire apart about two inches and strip back about a half inch of insulation from the end of each. This exposes many-stranded wires, and these are twisted together tightly to form a compact unit in each section. Next, curl the end so it will fit around the screw. Then place it under the screw as shown (Figure 17) so that the

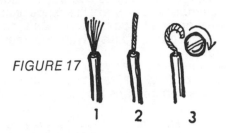

FIGURE 17

1   2   3

curl will be pulled closed as the screw is tightened. A knot is desirable; this means that any pressure on the cord is against the knot, not against the connection.

● Your wife's potato peeler will do an excellent job of stripping the insulation off electrical wiring. It does this without cutting the wire inside.

To check a cord, first give it a close eyeball. Then, with it plugged in, flex the cord at several points to see if it causes any flicker. If so, you either need to replace the cord or cut out the bad part by shortening. Here's a trick from a reader:

● When replacing a lamp cord that has to be pulled through a tube within the lamp base, it may seem impossible to poke the wire through. Before you remove the old wire, attach the new wire to the ends of the old. When you pull the old wire out, it'll pull the new wire through and save some fussing.

If everything else is OK, it's probably the bulb socket. If there isn't just a loose connection at the socket, replacing it is an easy and inexpensive way to make the thing work again. The components of the socket (Figure 18) are the outer metal shell, the cardboard sleeve, and the innards, (the socket, the terminal wires, and the switch). The brass base cap, the last component, is usually attached to the lamp. To replace a socket, unplug the lamp, then press on the side of the outer shell, using your thumb and forefinger. Remove the sleeve and loosen the wires. Reattach the new socket to the wires using the twist-and-curl technique previously discussed. Be sure to include the cardboard sleeve because this is a protective insulator. Snap the whole thing back together.

You replace three-way sockets the same way. The magic that the switch does is built into the switch and the bulb, and not in the way it's wired. In fact, you can convert a regular lamp into a three-way just by replacing the regular socket. Same goes for a dimmer socket—in most cases.

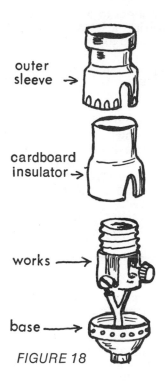

outer
sleeve →

cardboard
insulator →

works ——→

base ——→

FIGURE 18

● Most of us will throw away old lamp cord that has to be replaced. Granted, it's no longer good for electricity, but it's great for use as plants ties. It's flexible and strong; it's soft and won't cut through stems and branches. It can be used as is, or can easily be stripped in half.

WALL SWITCHES

With the success of a lamp repair behind you, you can now try a more difficult replacement—the wall switch. A faulty switch usually isn't repairable, but replacements are very inexpensive. First remove the current from that circuit. Then, to be sure you have the right circuit, use a simple tester.

● Before you use a tester light to make sure there's no electrical current in a wire, test the tester in an outlet tha. you know is good. Then you'll know that the tester is OK. Otherwise, your tester might lie to you about the current, and you might grab a hot wire and get zapped.
● Even though I don't have any kind of electrical test equipment, here's how I test to see if the light switch is faulty or if the problem is in the

wiring. First I cut off the current to that circuit. Then I remove the plate covering the switch, loosen it from its switch box, and pull it out far enough to expose the wires connected to the switch. Next, I connect a piece of wire to the two screws. This completes the circuit. Now with the power restored, the light will come on—if the switch is the problem. If so, again cut the current and replace the switch. If not, you know the problem is either in the wiring or the fixture.

Be sure to note how the switch is wired up before you remove it. You'll want to rewire the new switch the same way. After you remove the unit from the wall, you can use a continuity tester to be sure the switch is faulty. The continuity tester is a simple gadget that's battery-powered, so no house current need be involved. Clip one end to one switch-terminal screw, and touch the probe to the other. With the switch handle on, the test light should glow; with the handle off, it shouldn't. Next clip the tester to the metal mounting strap and touch the probe to each terminal while flicking the handle to both off and on. The tester should not light at all. If the switch flunks either test, replace it.

If it's the only switch that controls that particular fixture or maybe even a circuit, it's called a single-pole switch. If another switch also controls the same fixture, the switch is a three-way switch. A single-pole switch must be replaced with another single-pole switch; the same is true for a three-way. There are also four-way switches that work in conjunction with three-ways when there are three different switches for one fixture.

While you must have the same type of switch, you do have some choices. You might want to get a silent switch so you don't wake up Junior when you flick the light. If there's nothing but lighting involved, you might want to replace the old switch with a dimmer switch. (Talk with your dealer to be sure you get a proper dimmer, and that one can be used.) Or maybe you'd like a lighted-handle switch so you can find it in the dark. Other switches have pilot lights to let you know that the fixture in a remote area is either off or on—great for that switch in the house that controls a light in the garage.

● Out-of-sight lights may stay on all night without you knowing about it. Of course, you can install a special switch with a small pilot light that indicates the light is on. Rather than spend the extra money, I coated the tip of my regular switch handle with bright red fingernail polish. It's easy to tell at a glance if the switch is up or down—and whether the light it controls is on or off. I did this for switches to the light in the garage, a tool shed, the attic, several storage closets, and the water pump. No longer do I pay the power company for my forgetfulness.

If you'd like to be the only person who can operate a particular switch, replace the old one with a locking type that requires a key for operation. This could prevent someone from turning off the power to your freezer when you have a side of beef in it, or could protect your tools from unauthorized use. If you'd like to have the porch light go on after dark even when you're not at home, get a time-clock switch. And if you have a switch in the garage and are tired of tripping over the ladder on your way into the house at night, get a time-delay switch that gives you just about enough time to get in before the light goes off.

Actual replacement means putting the wires back just like they were on the old switch. Once again, curve the loop around the screw clockwise so the wire is pulled tighter as the screw turns. These wires will be solid instead of stranded.

WALL OUTLETS

A wall outlet is about the same. However, you should get the same type of outlet as the one being replaced. Most common household outlets will either have two or three holes. The third hole is for use with three-pronged plugs. You can't ground an outlet by merely replacing a two-hole model with the grounded type. If you have the grounded type, the ground wire goes to the green screw. As with switches, take a close look at the way the old outlet is wired before replacing it. Here again, be sure that the current is off before you touch anything.

CEILING FIXTURES

That plain bare bulb hanging in the living room could easily be exchanged for a Tiffany lamp or crystal chandelier. The electrical changeover is quite simple. Remember the Main. Observe the way the old fixture is wired, and then make the change. The wires are usually twisted together in what is called a pigtail splice. Then you should twist on a solderless connector—these little caps secure the splice and also insulate. The electrical part may be the easiest step, compared to making sure that the new fixture is adequately held up, as it may be heavier than the old one. The hardware store or lighting dealer will have straps and other hardware that will secure your new chandelier.

● Many modern light fixtures have more than one bulb in them. So when one bulb burns out, why not replace all the bulbs in that fixture at once? This means you can do it all with one ladder climb and not have to risk the balancing act again for quite some time. The good bulbs you take out can be used as replacements for lamps and other fixtures that aren't up high.

When wire is lengthened, after the splice is made, it's good to solder the wires before wrapping with tape or—better still—covering the bare wires with shrink tubing. This tubing slides over the bare wires and then shrinks to secure itself with the application of heat on the tubing. Be sure you slip the tubing on *before* you join the wires, or you have to tape the joints.

● Sometimes the working space is too small to let you tape electrical wiring splices properly. A tube of silicone-rubber sealant may come to your rescue. The slender tube may reach down to the splice, and the silicone rubber can be spread around the wires. When dry, this provides an excellent insulated cover for the wires. Be sure to allow full drying time. Also be careful not to get the rubber on anything that shouldn't be coated because it's not easy to remove.

When you splice a cord, tape each splice separately, then tape over the entire area. Here again, the shrink tubing is best; and for the overall wrap, just use a larger size that will go around everything.

FLUORESCENTS

The energy crisis has made people aware that fluorescent fixtures provide more light while using less current than incandescents. In fact, a forty-watt fluorescent gives more light than a hundred-watt incandescent—and at less than half the wattage. And fluorescents throw off less heat, which makes a difference in the summer air-conditioning bills. The fluorescents cost more, of course, but they do last about ten times longer. But while folks have tumbled to the use of these money savers, most haven't the foggiest notion of how to repair them if things go wrong.

The brain center is the black box called the ballast. Some fluorescents have starters, but two types—the rapid start and the instant start—do not.

● For those of you who buy a new starter, be sure you get the right size. The number is on the side. Otherwise, they look alike and are interchangeable—except the wrong size won't work.

Now when your fluorescent light goes on the blink, or if any of the other problems shown occur, you can probably once again light up your life.

● If the fluorescent tube falls out of the workshop fixture, the reason is that the tube fits too loosely in the holder. Vibration from power tools gradually turns the tube so the prongs no longer hold. If you can't adjust the holder to grasp the tube tighter, try this simple trick. Cut a circle from a shirt board and punch holes so it will fit over the prongs and against the tube. This washer will take up the slack and make the tube fit tight. If that doesn't quite do it, add another circle.

ALUMINUM WIRING

If you have warm cover plates, sparks, arcing, or odors at switches or outlets, you have a potential fire hazard—and it could be aluminum wiring. During certain times, copper has been in short supply, and in many homes built during these periods aluminum wiring was used—

FLUORESCENT LIGHT TROUBLESHOOTING CHART

Problem	Possible Cause	What To Do
No light	Tube burned out	Replace
	Faulty starter	Replace
	Tube tips not making contact	Remove and reinstall tube in holder
	Too cold	Warm room. (Below 65° fluorescents start to lose efficiency and much colder won't light)
Only ends light up	Faulty starter	Replace
	Improper ground	Check ground wires
	Too cold	Warm room
Flickering	Tube tips making poor contact	Remove and reinstall tube in holder checking tightness
	New tube	Let "season" for a short while
	Faulty starter	Replace
	Tube going	Replace
	Too cold	Warm room
Ends dark	Tube going	Replace
Hum	Ballast	Check for proper hookup and for proper size ballast. (Wiring diagram and specs usually on ballast)

and it created a potential fire hazard. Aluminum expands and contracts more than copper, and this causes loose connections at switches and wall outlets. Corrosion is another problem. This can happen when dissimilar metals are connected, and bare aluminum can oxidize when exposed to air. Corrosion can cause overheating, which can cause home fires.

So what do you do if you have aluminum wiring? Some electricians will try to sell you on completely rewiring. This solves the problem, but is very costly.

Another solution is to have special switches and outlets made for use with aluminum wire. In the case of regular fifteen-to-twenty amp outlets, these special devices are called CO/ALR. Higher-rated units are called CU-AL. In most areas, these can be installed by you, the homeowner, to replace the old. Check your local code to be sure.

When installing, be sure the current is off. These attach exactly as do the conventional units previously discussed. Be sure to tighten the screws into the wires firmly. I'd also suggest the use of an oxide inhibitor—a salve that coats the bare aluminum wire to stop the corrosion problem. There are several such products on the market, and your hardware store will probably have one if there is much aluminum wiring in the area.

The third solution is a process called "pigtailing," very easy and very inexpensive. It's acceptable to many electrical codes, but check first. The basic idea is to connect a short piece of copper wire to the end of the aluminum wire by a pigtail splice. The copper is then connected to the outlet. This, plus the use of an oxide inhibitor, will solve the problem.

Here are the general steps, but be sure these comply with local code:

1. Remember the Main!
2. Remove the face plate and loosen the terminal screw on an aluminum wire. Release only one at a time. That way, you can't get the thing hooked up wrong.
3. Snip off the exposed end. Strip back about a half inch of the insulation.
4. Apply a thin coat of the oxide inhibitor to the bare wire.
5. The copper pigtail piece should be about four inches long and of number 12 single-strand wire. Strip both ends—one-half inch on one, three-fourths on the other.
6. Use the pigtail splice to join the one-half-inch copper to the aluminum.
7. Use a solderless connector UL rated for aluminum.
8. Now connect the other end of the copper wire back in place. (It is not necessary to pigtail the ground wire, if any.)

Sometimes this pigtailing can't be done properly because there isn't enough room. In the case of an overcrowded junction box, you'll do well to get the CO/ALR replacement.

Electrical repairs can be exhilarating, and we've only touched on the basics. If these turn you on, you may wish to progress—if so, be sure you know what you're doing and that what you plan conforms to the local electrical code. In many communities, the building code will allow the homeowner to do even elaborate wiring jobs if he presents a plan that is correct and proves he knows what he's getting into. Then after the job is done, the inspector will come out to be sure.

Above all . . . Remember the Main!

Now, here are some miscellaneous hints from readers that will electrify you.

● If you live in an apartment with plain accessories, here's a clever way to make an unusual light fixture. Get a number of those double sockets that screw into a single light socket to make room for two bulbs. By putting them together, they'll branch out to become a sort of tree-pattern fixture of any size you wish (Figure 19). You can custom-make your fixture to suit your taste. Use 7½-watt bulbs in the empty sockets. When you move, just unscrew the fixture and take it with you.

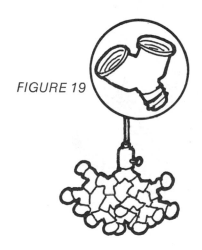

FIGURE 19

● If you need to know the wattage of a particular light bulb, and there's not enough light to read it, you know you can't see it by turning it on—the brightness is too much. Take an ordinary piece of typing paper and hold it against the bulb. In most cases, the wording on the bottom of the bulb will shine right through. It sure beats having to unscrew the bulb to carry it to another light source.

● There is a recessed outlet made so that wall clocks can be hung and plugged in and still hang flush to the wall. By using this outlet behind a chest or dresser, you can plug in a table lamp and still have the piece of furniture flat against the wall. The changeover from a regular wall outlet is a simple do-it-yourself task. Be sure you flip the circuit-breaker switch or remove the fuse so there's no juice while you're making the change.

● The electrical wire that hardware stores carry comes on metal reels about eight inches around. When they sell all the wire off the reels, they just throw them away. But they make excellent storage holders for extension cords in the shop or garage. Ask your hardware dealer to save you a couple. This sure is a lot better than having to untangle the cord each time you need it.

● To make a holder for an extension cord, I cut off the bottom three inches of a large plastic bleach bottle. Then I removed the plate from an electric wall outlet in my garage. I traced around the openings and cut these out of the bottom of the plastic. I also punched a hole where the screw goes through to hold the plate in place. I remounted the plate with the plastic bottle part underneath (Figure 20). The three-inch section that sticks out provides a nice place on which to wrap the extension cord and keep it handy to the outlet. And those cardboard tubes from paper towels or toilet paper will hold extension cords.

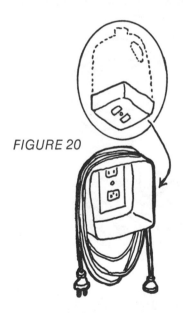

FIGURE 20

● I'm an insomniac. It used to be that when I got up in the night, I either barked my shins on something from groping in the dark, or I woke up my wife by turning on a light. Now I have rigged up a light under the bed that gives me enough light to see by, but isn't going to shine in my wife's face. I just wired a socket under the bed and installed a switch on my side of the bed frame.

● One time you suggested in your column that if you placed your door bell on the heat ducts, they would carry the sound throughout the house. I tried this, and it worked fine. The sound was greatly increased. However, you didn't tell me that after a while, the ringing would cause the bell unit to walk off the duct. When this happened, I went back up in the attic and attached the bell by using self-tapping sheet-metal screws to fasten the bell right to the duct.

7.
ENERGY SAVING

There are some who feel there is no energy crisis, just a plot on the part of oil companies, utility companies, Middle Eastern sheiks, and politicians. Whether you believe there is such a crisis or not, you can certainly agree that your utility bills are going up—and there seems to be no indication that the rates will stop rising. We have all learned that we have been wasting energy dollars. Many houses were built before the shortages, when energy was cheap, and builders didn't bother to put in lots of insulation. There's no longer any cheap energy, and so we have to make our houses as energy-efficient as possible. In fact, if the shortages were solved and if the utility rates dropped, we should have learned a lesson and *still* want to have our homes energy efficient.

INSULATION

In many older homes, this is one of the most important things you can do (or have done) to save energy. Insulation should wrap all of the living spaces of your home to separate them from the outside or from non-living spaces. The illustration (Figure 21) shows what to consider as a likely candidate for insulation.

     Once you know where the stuff goes, then you need to know how much you already have, if any. You don't want to know how many inches or pounds of insulating material you have. What you need to know is the R-value. The *R* stands for resistance, and different materials have different R-values. The higher the R-value, the greater the insulation's effectiveness. The table shows the approximate R-value per inch of thickness for the most popular types of insulation used in homes. If you don't know what type insulation you have, however, take a small sample to a dealer or to the utility company. They'll be able to tell you what type it is and its R-value. They'll also tell you what R-values you should shoot for. I'd be happy to include a map showing the R-values

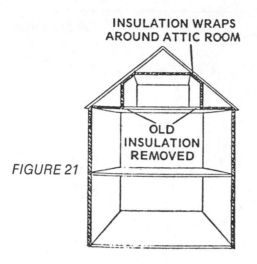

INSULATION WRAPS
AROUND ATTIC ROOM

OLD
INSULATION
REMOVED

FIGURE 21

for the various zones in the country, but these can change. As utility rates go up, it may become economically advisable to add more insulation—and when this happens, the recommended R-values will also go up.

In most homes, it's not all that difficult to get into the attic to check the insulation. This is also a place where the do-it-yourselfer can add his own insulation. If there isn't any flooring in the attic for you to walk on, be careful not to step on anything but the joists or you'll come crashing through to the room below. To check the insulation, just place a ruler against the floor and measure the depth of the insulating material. In the attic, you'll find either a loose type or a batting type. Now if you know what the substance is and its thickness, you can apply the figure in the chart and know just about what R-values you now have.

If you have a floored attic, you may have a small problem. If the boards are just butted together, you can find the end of a board where you come into the attic and pry up enough to inspect. If the boards are tongue-and-groove, drill a hole in the flooring, and then use a flashlight and a wire probe to check. If you have to get a sample out so someone can tell you what type insulation you have, make a hook on the end of the wire.

If you have an unheated basement or a crawl space that is accessible, it will be easy to measure the type of insulation under your floors, if any.

Unless you have X-ray eyes, checking the walls is a real problem. If patching holes in walls as discussed in Chapter 14 sounds like fun, that's one way to find out. A less drastic trick is to probe around electric outlets on the wall. With the power off, remove the face plate

Basic Material	Approximate R-value per inch of thickness
Vermiculite	2.1
Perlite	2.7
Fiberglass	3.3
Rock Wool	3.3
Polystyrene	3.5
Cellulose	3.7
Urea Formaldehyde	4.5
Urethane	5.3

and see if there isn't room between the outlet box and the wall material for a wire probe. If not, take a utility knife and cut away some of the wall. But be sure not to cut so much that the face plate won't cover it. A flashlight and a wire will let you know what's there. Remember, there will be insulation only on outside walls or those next to an unheated space.

Now that you know what you have, if you fall very short of the recommended goals, you should consider adding what you need. The attic can be an easy do-it-yourself project. All types of attic insulation are compatible. So it you have rock wool loose fill and want to add fiberglass batts (Figure 22), it's OK. What you need to do is figure out the least expensive way to reach your desired R-value.

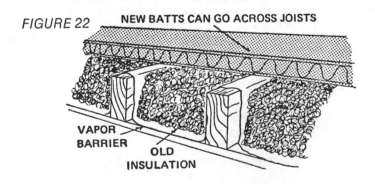

FIGURE 22   NEW BATTS CAN GO ACROSS JOISTS

VAPOR BARRIER

OLD INSULATION

Another consideration is your method of installation. Accessibility might make it easier to install one type over another. Or if you plan to convert the attic into living quarters, the batts you lay down flat on the floor can later be lifted and stapled to the rafters when you make the conversion. Loose fill could not be used as easily.

Loose fill can be poured and raked into place or else blown in. Many insulation dealers will rent or loan blower units made for this purpose. A common garden rake turned upside down can do a pretty fair job of spreading the insulation. One reader suggested:

● Cut a wide rubber band from an old inner tube, stretch this over the tines of your rake (Figure 23) and you have a much better insulation-spreader.

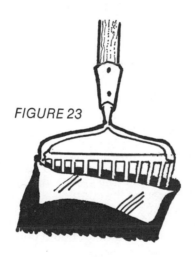

FIGURE 23

When purchasing loose fill, ask the dealer to help figure the amount needed. You must know the square footage of your attic plus the additional depth needed. The bags of insulation should tell what square footage they will yield for various depths.

● The trap door into an attic is usually not insulated, particularly if the attic has blown-in insulation—the stuff just wouldn't stay in place. But it'll pay you to insulate even this small area. The best way is to cut a batt to fit, and staple or glue it to the trap door. Also, it's a good idea to weatherstrip around the opening to further seal it. Any place where the air you've paid to heat can escape, it will.

Although batts and blankets are made in standard widths to fit between most joists, you may find that it's better to lay the pieces at right angles to the joists. When adding this type of insulation, you must not use the kind that's faced with a vapor-barrier material. This could trap moisture between the layers and have an adverse effect on the bottom layer of insulation. If the only type available is faced with foil or some other vapor-barrier material, use your utility knife to slit it every few inches. Often the facing can easily be peeled off. Buying the unfaced type should cost less, so if you don't need the facing, shop around.

In the case of an attic with no insulation, the vapor barrier is needed. If you put loose fill into such an attic, there are plastic sheets that are made for this purpose. Sold in rolls, they can be laid over the entire area before you put in the insulation. If the attic is to be insulated with batts or blankets, get the type with a vapor-barrier facing. The vapor barrier always goes between the insulation and the heated space. So in an attic, the vapor barrier should face down. If you find there is no vapor barrier under existing insulation, you can do a pretty good job with special paints made to be applied to the ceiling from below.

Here are some special safety tips for working in the attic. To avoid the possibility of crashing through the Sheetrock if you make a misstep, put some wide boards up there to use as walkways. Lay them across the joists, and move them as you go along.

With some types of glass-fiber insulating material, you can either cut your skin or get a rash from handling it. Wear protective clothing, including gloves and goggles. If there'll be any floating particles, as when you're blowing insulation in, wear an appropriate mask. If you're like I am, be sure to wear a hard hat. I always stand up to admire my handiwork and conk my head on a rafter. Besides, most attics have nails poking through that could stab you.

Be sure not to place any insulation over vents in the attic (Figure 24). Those vents are there for a purpose. Also, don't cover any recessed light fixtures, as the insulation could cause them to overheat and thus become a fire hazard.

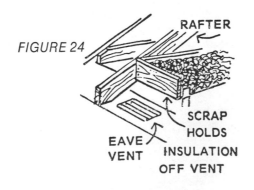

FIGURE 24

RAFTER

SCRAP HOLDS INSULATION OFF VENT

EAVE VENT

In an unheated basement or crawl space, under-the-floor insulation can also be a do-it-yourself project. Here you have to use batts or blankets. Measure the width between floor joists and buy the insulation to fit. There are insulation support wires that will hold the batts and blankets in place. These have points that hold into the wood and are a little longer than the space they fit into, so they "bow" into the insulation. I think a better way is to either staple chicken wire crosswise (Figure 25) or to zigzag wire across the joists using partially driven-in nails to fasten wire to (Figure 26). Then you just slip the batts in place. The dead air space between the insulation and the subfloor is OK because dead air acts as insulation too (Figure 27). Remember the vapor barrier goes toward the heated or living space, so it faces up.

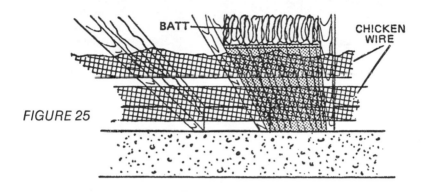

BATT

CHICKEN WIRE

FIGURE 25

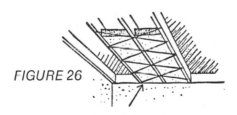

FIGURE 26

ZIG ZAG WIRES HOLD BATTS

Now for the basement that is heated—or may eventually be heated. You don't want to have insulation under the floor between the basement and the upper part of the house. This would mean most of the heat down there would be trapped and couldn't rise to help heat the parts above—which is desirable.

The walls of the basement are your first consideration. If they are concrete, many people think that's all that's needed. But concrete

DEAD AIR GAP

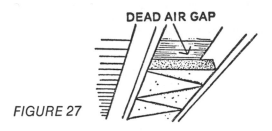

FIGURE 27

isn't all that good an insulator, no matter how thick it is. After you get down below the surface of the earth outside, the dirt starts to act as insulation, but it's still cooler than you want your home to be, so it's best to insulate the walls from top to bottom. If there are exposed studs against the concrete, insulation blankets can be stapled in place. Then the paneling or whatever can be put up to hide the insulation and finish the walls.

If there are no studs, rigid-type insulation can be glued or nailed either to the wall or to furring strips you've added. This is then covered over with an appropriate wall covering. Some building codes specify which materials should cover certain rigid insulation.

One of the big problems with basements is moisture—condensation, leakage, and seepage. Find out the source of any moisture and take care of this before you start to insulate.

The floor in the basement also needs insulation. It's not as critical as with above-ground floors, but the ground below will most likely be cooler than you'll want your floors to be. It's not possible to get underneath most basement floors, so you have to apply insulation atop the floor. Rigid foam is the way to go; then install a flooring over the insulation. However, many people forego this and let carpets take the chill out of walking on the slab.

The home with a slab foundation and with carpets and floors already in can still be insulated. However, you would insulate only the perimeter of the slab. You must dig out around the foundation and attach sheets of rigid insulation to cover. Check with your local utility company to find out how deep this material should extend for maximum efficiency. Then check the local building code to be sure it's properly complied with.

Adding insulation between the walls is usually not a do-it-yourself project. It can be, but it requires more equipment and expertise than most folks have. Walls are usually made with an inside wall attached to studs. Next to the outside of the studs is attached a sheathing. Then there's the exterior wall. To add insulation, you must drill into the wall between every stud (Figure 28) and add either foam- or blow-in insulation. Also, the space under a window cannot be reached from a hole above the window, so where there is any type of obstruction

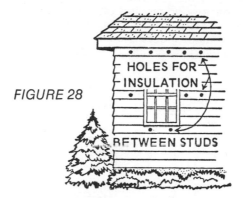

FIGURE 28

HOLES FOR
INSULATION

BETWEEN STUDS

within the wall, an additional hole must be drilled. (Sometimes there are even fire-stops within each cavity.) A two-story house will need holes at the top of both floors. Figure 28 gives you an idea of where all these holes might have to go.

If you decide to have the walls done by a pro, be careful about who does the job. Foam-in insulation is great, but if the contractor doesn't do it just right, you can have all sorts of problems. In fact, check out any insulation contractor, whether it's the foam-in type for the walls or some other type for other parts of the house. There are many good, honest insulation contractors around. There are also many fly-by-night gyp artists and total incompetents.

Before you sign, get three estimates, then check out the one you decide upon with your local utility company, the Better Business Bureau, and with whoever else might be a source of reference. Know what R-values you require and have the contractor specify how much of whatever material he'll use to attain this. Make sure he has insurance to cover his employees, as well as any possible damage to your home. Have a clear understanding about how the finished job will look. It's even a good idea to take a look at what is being installed while it's going on to be sure he has enough of the same material you agreed upon. Done right, insulation is an investment that will pay for itself in heating and air-conditioning costs. And don't forget there are provisions for a tax credit for this and other energy-saving measures you take. Adding insulation is a big-ticket item, but will result in big energy savings.

WEATHER STRIPPING AND CAULKING

While insulation costs quite a bit, caulking and weather stripping cost very little but can really pay off in comfort and savings.

While these are two entirely different applications designed to go on different parts of the house, they accomplish the same thing: They dodge the draft.

Many folks get confused about which goes where. Weather stripping is used to seal around moving parts like doors and windows, while caulking goes into stationary cracks (Figure 29)—usually places where door or window frames meet the side of the house, at corners, or where two different building materials come together.

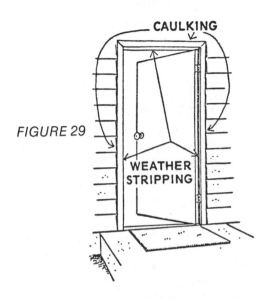

CAULKING

FIGURE 29

WEATHER STRIPPING

What's the big deal about a few cracks? Well, if you have a one-eighth-inch crack all the way around a door, it's the equivalent of a six-inch-square hole. If you have lots of doors and windows and seams with gaps, you're going to have lots of fresh air that you may not need.

Even though these are different steps using different materials, it's good to consider them as companion chores. Not all steps will go together, but if you've climbed the ladder to weather-strip outside a window, why not caulk on the same climb?

First, determine what your weather-stripping needs are. Unless you can see wide gaps, you may think the doors and windows are tightly sealed. Find out for sure, using a hand-held hair dryer outside and an accomplice with a damp back of the hand following your moves inside. Any air getting around the door edge will make the wet hand feel suddenly cool. You may find many openings are drafty, and you may find some have only one edge that isn't airtight.

● A lighted candle will help to determine air leaks. The slightest bit of air will make the flame flicker. Move it slowly around the suspected area, and you'll be able to really pinpoint the trouble spots.

Weather-stripping is available in many forms, with a type for every situation. Rather than try to describe each type, I suggest a trip to your biggest hardware store or home center. Have a list of all the places where you need weather stripping, and let your specialist tell you the different types for each problem. Then pick out the type you can handle best.

● I have found that the self-sticking type of weather stripping doesn't always stick well to enameled wood. However, by using a hand-held hair dryer, you can run warm air across both the wood and the adhesive side of the weather stripping, and the stuff will stick a lot better. I don't know why, but it works.

● When self-sticking weather stripping will stick no longer, use contact cement on both wood and weather strip. It will hold.

● We have aluminum windows, and air comes in around the bottom. I tried stick-on weather stripping, but it didn't hold. For now I have stopped the air with homemade weather stripping. I took aluminum foil and cut strips long enough to go all along the bottom of the window. Next, I folded these over so there are three thicknesses. I then pressed these narrow strips over the edge of the frame where the window goes. When closed against this, there is no longer a gap for air to come into. The strip is mostly covered, but even where it sticks out, the foil matches the metal enough so it isn't noticeable.

● An unusually big source of cold air that many people don't think about is the electrical switch plates and wall outlets. Air comes up through the wall and can enter the house around these. You need only hold your hand over them for a few seconds, and if they are a problem, you'll feel cold air. With the plate removed and the current cut off at the fuse box, you can stop the air with caulk and/or scraps of insulation poked into cracks and crevices. Anything mounted in the wall, even medicine cabinets, can be letting the cold in. These small energy-efficient ideas can save lots if everyone does them.

The gap at the bottom of an outside door is different from those at the sides and top. On the floor, along the bottom of the door, there is usually a hump called the threshold.

A small gap problem can be solved by adding a weather-stripping piece called a door sweep. Most sweeps are made with a rigid spine (usually aluminum) which attaches to the door with nails or screws. Sticking down below the door will be a flexible piece that will rest against the threshold to seal the gap. Sweeps come in standard sizes, but still have to be trimmed to fit. Aluminum is easily cut with a hacksaw. There are several variations of door sweeps, and one will solve your problem.

Sometimes the threshold is shot; it can wear down so there's too big a gap. But it's easily replaced. Metal thresholds are usually held down by several screws that may be hidden under a flexible vinyl insert. Wooden thresholds are often held down on the ends by the doorstops. Gently pry out the stops. Then you can pry up the old threshold. Others are under the door frame. These are best removed by sawing at each end. Use a backsaw and saw straight through, being careful not to scratch the floor—masking tape on the floor will protect it. Pry up the threshold after the two cuts are made. With either type, if prying doesn't work, use a chisel and hammer to split the threshold. The new aluminum replacements are super-easy to install and come in a wide variety to solve all sorts of problems.

Most caulking problems can be spotted if you know where to look. We mentioned the places where door and window frames meet the other parts of the house. Also check where the siding meets the foundation, where pipes go through the walls to enter the house, where steps or porches meet the main body of the house, and around where any two different building materials meet. Don't forget to check around the window air-conditioner units (Figure 30).

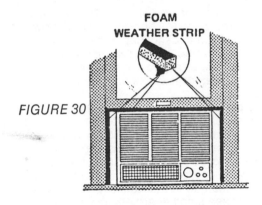

FOAM
WEATHER STRIP

FIGURE 30

There are several types of caulking compounds on the market. The cheapest is oil based, but it's not one of my favorites because it doesn't last too long. Silicone is super. Latex is the easiest to work with because before it hardens, it'll clean up with soap and water. And with a wet finger, you can smooth the bead for a neater-looking result. There are now latex caulks that are supposed to give twenty years of life. However, latex isn't the answer in all cases. High-moisture areas, certain materials, different-sized gaps, and the desired appearance can call for different caulks. Here again, you need your list and a visit to the expert.

● Caulking compound works better in warm temperatures, but the job won't always wait until summer rolls around. Before going outside to work with the caulking gun, I place it on top of a radiator for a few minutes. Then I wrap the tube in foil. This keeps the heat in for a long period of time, and makes the caulking compound much easier to work with.

If you don't have radiators in your house, any heat source will do. To work well, the compound has to get only moderately warm.

● I wrap a heating pad around the caulking cartridge and turn on the heat. After a few minutes, I can put the cartridge in the gun and go outside with very warm and pliable caulking.

● If you have especially large cracks to caulk, use lengths of plumber's oakum to provide backing. Cut the oakum to the proper length and wedge it in the crack. Then instead of the crack devouring the caulk, there is a base to work against.

● I made a simple tool that smoothes the bead of caulking after I apply it. I took half a wooden clothespin and used my grinding wheel to form the end of it into a convex curve. I dipped this tool into shellac, then let it harden. To smooth the caulk, I dip the tool into water; it glides right over the caulk, giving it a smooth, rounded effect, and at the same time poking the caulk firmly into the crack.

● If you don't use all the caulk in a cartridge, there's always the problem of the compound in the nozzle hardening before the next use. My cap for the nozzle seals out the air, and thus prevents hardening. I use a slip-on rubber pencil eraser. It fits snugly over the nozzle and stays in place until it's pulled off for the next caulking job.

● I use a cap from a toothpaste tube to cap the end of the caulking cartridge. The cartridge has a softer tip than the plastic used in the cap, so when the cap is turned down around the tip, it holds tight and seals the end.

I've always used a long nail to plug up the end. After all, you have to use a long nail to puncture the cartridge anyway.

● Some of the caulking guns on the market get all but the last inch or so out of the tube of compound. The plunger just doesn't go down far enough to push it all out. If yours is wasting part of your valuable compound, it's easy to rig it to squeeze out the last drop. Lengthen the plunger by placing a small block of wood between the plunger and the end of the tube. If it's a tight squeeze, put the block in after you have used part of the compound. The size of the block is determined by the amount of compound your gun doesn't push out.

● In some homes, the base molding around the seam where the floor and the walls meet may be hiding a crack that's letting in cold air. Check this possibility, and if you find a problem, carefully remove the molding and seal the crack with caulking compound. If the crack is large, poke scraps of insulation in before caulking. Then when you replace the molding, run a bead of caulk along each inside edge of the molding. This will do away with any possible air entry.

● The next time you finish up a tube of caulking, why not convert it into a funnel? Use a stiff section of coat-hanger wire to poke through the nozzle to back the moveable bottom out of the cartridge. Then clean out as much caulk residue as possible, making sure the opening is clear. When the caulk left inside sets up, you have a funnel that'll be very handy.

● Caulking guns and other squeeze applicators are great for getting compounds into cracks and holes. Sometimes you mix up a small batch of glop and wish you had some way to squirt it into a tight place. One way is to form a cone from waxed paper, leaving an opening at the tip (Figure 31). Poke some of the mixture into the cone, and then you can squeeze it out through the tip. But don't fill the cone too full or the compound also squeezes back into your hand.

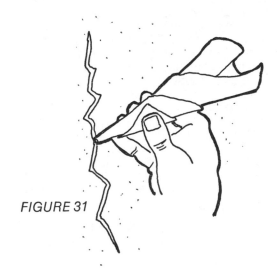

FIGURE 31

Be sure to buy a quality brand of caulk. Most caulking is done from outside. However, feel around pipes and along baseboards inside. You could dodge drafts here with inside caulking.

Even if you don't have high heating bills, caulking and weather stripping do other good things. They help seal out dirt and dust that get in the house. They can help stop bugs who wish to visit. Caulking also seals out moisture that gets into walls and other places to cause all sorts of damage.

In areas where you do have those high bills, these simple, inexpensive steps have been estimated to account for as much as a 30 percent saving. (Of course, lots of other things have to be right too.)

STORM WINDOWS

Even if the windows are weather-stripped and caulked, the glass itself is almost like having an opening in the wall. Glass loses heat two ways—through conduction, and through radiation.

Conduction is the direct transmission of heat through the glass. You see, heat always travels from warmer spots to colder ones. If the temperature on one side of your panes of glass is 68 degrees, and the temperature on the outside is zero, your heat will move toward the zero side. If there is nothing but a single pane of glass in the way, the heat will move very rapidly because glass is a good heat conductor, offering very little resistance. To learn this firsthand, pour steaming coffee into a drinking glass. You won't be able to pick it up because the glass will be too hot. A coffee mug, on the other hand (the unburned hand), is made of clay, which has much more resistance to heat transfer.

Radiation isn't as big a factor in the winter, but it does take some heat away. In the summer, however, it can add appreciably to the burden on your air conditioner.

The loss by conduction (with a little help from radiation) on a single pane the thickness of an average-size window is the equivalent of a seven-inch-square hole in your wall. If you have a house with twenty windows, you have the equivalent of almost a thousand-square-inch hole. That's almost like having a Dutch door and just removing the top half.

As you can see, you are literally throwing heat, and thus energy dollars, right out your window. In many homes, windows are the biggest single heat wasters—and thus offer the best opportunity for big savings.

How can you stop this waste? The addition of another single pane of glass with an air space in between stops the heat transfer by about 50 percent. You can either replace the present single pane of glass with double-paned thermal windows, or add storm windows. Unless the primary windows you now have are really bad, the best path is probably to go with storm windows.

You can find storm windows priced from maybe as low as fifteen dollars on up to well over a hundred bucks. Legitimate differences between these windows cause the difference in price. However, there will be no difference in the effect on heat loss through conduction. In fact, if you wanted to merely staple a clear vinyl or plastic sheet over the windows, you'd end up with the same energy savings, and this would probably cost you less than twenty dollars for the entire house. It won't be as durable or look as good, but it will save you money.

One of our readers couldn't afford real storm windows, so he used this plastic sheeting to begin with and bought the storm windows a few at a time when he could afford them (Figure 32). He figures the temporary jobs saved him enough in utility bills to be able to pay for the permanent units. (Personally, I'd just settle for being able to keep up with the rate increases from the utility companies.)

People ask me if storm windows are a do-it-yourself proposition. They certainly can be. Several companies make systems that allow you to custom-make tracks of aluminum, fit the glass or rigid plastic that you cut to size, and then frame this with a vinyl lip that holds the window in place. Other ready-made windows can be installed easily if your windows are the right size.

If you have the entire job done, however, be sure of the people

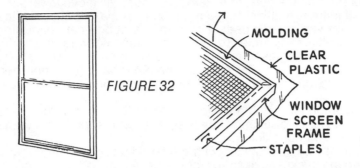

FIGURE 32

MOLDING

CLEAR
PLASTIC

WINDOW
SCREEN
FRAME

STAPLES

you hire to do it. Some people show you a super window, and then install one of inferior quality—so check out the company first.

Storm windows won't pay for themselves quickly. It will take several years; but if they are well made, after they have paid for themselves, you'll continue to get dividends for years to come. In fact, the return on your investment is much better than even blue-chip stocks in most cases.

● If you have air conditioning, your storm windows will save as much energy during the summer as in wintertime. Incidentally, if you want to make your storm windows more effective in summer, look into the thin material designed to reflect the sun's heat. It's now being put out for the do-it-yourselfer and can let your air conditioner work a lot less. For winter and summer, add that sponge-type weather stripping between the storm windows and the house, and you've got another winner.

● We used to remove our storm windows each spring and put up screens. Now that we have air conditioning, I have learned that the storm doors and windows save just as much power in the summer as in the winter. So we ended up with a big bunch of useless window screens. Rather than throw them away, I put on my thinking cap and came up with a super idea. I built a frame and attached the screens around all sides and on the top. This lightweight collapsible frame is now a bugproof outdoor picnic house where we can enjoy the outdoors without the visitors.

Storm windows also make your house more snug. In some cases, they stop window sweating. They also block out a lot of outside noise, so you won't have to hear your neighbors grousing over their high heating and air-conditioning bills.

WRAPPING PIPES AND DUCTS

If you have pipes carrying hot water to taps or fixtures, they can lose a lot of the heat before the water ever gets there. Since you've paid to heat this water, the loss is costing you money. Sure, you still have water hot enough to scald your bod, but if you don't stop the loss on the way to the faucet, you're getting scalded in the pocketbook as well.

The ducts that carry conditioned air, whether hot or cold, can change air temperature on the way to the vents that let this (expensively) conditioned air into the rooms. An uninsulated duct will let that transfer occur right through the ducting. If there also happens to be a seam that isn't sealed, it could allow a lot of conditioned air to pour into your attic, basement, or crawl space.

Both pipes and ducts are easy to control. First, inspect all the pipes and ducts. Trace the route of the hot-water pipes and see if there are uninsulated stretches. Pipe insulation is easy to apply if you can get at the pipes.

There are several types; the newest a flexible foam-type material formed to various pipe diameters. It's slit so it fits right around the pipe, then a sort of zipper arrangement closes the slit. There are also types that spiral-wrap around the pipes. Most are self-adhering and so are easily applied, but before they'll stick well, you must have a clean and dry pipe surface. While you're going after the hot-water pipes, consider all the other pipes. Not only do insulations stop much of the heat loss, but when applied to cold-water pipes, they'll also prevent sweating. If pipes are subject to freezing during the winter, there are insulating wraps to protect them.

All ducts should be inspected for seams or joints that leak air. Usually duct tape will seal these leaks. Sometimes, however, they first need to be joined with some sort of fastener. If the ducts ever have to be taken apart, you'll want to use sheet-metal screws. But most won't ever need to be separated, so you can use blind rivets applied with a pop rivet tool. Then apply tape around the seams. Tape can lose its effectiveness after a few years, so it won't hurt to check it from time to time.

Then wrap the ducts with insulation. These rolls of insulation are available in one- or two-inch thicknesses. If the ducts carry only hot air, there's no need for a vapor-barrier, although most wraps will have this. If the ducts also carry cooled air, you really should have the vapor barrier facing outward when installed.

Round ducts can best be covered by spiral-wrapping the insulation and letting it overlap about half of the previous round. Use duct tape to hold it down at the ends. With rectangular ducts, cut strips that will circle the duct and tape each strip together (Figure 33). Since there's no overlap, get the thicker two-inch type.

Where vents connect to ducts, there may be no neat way to wrap the insulating material. If not, staple it against the framing around the vent, then tape the ends to the wrap.

Sometimes doing ducts and pipes means crawling in an attic or other not-too-spacious or unpleasant space. Think of it in terms of money: In many homes, the loss from uninsulated pipes and ducts can add as much as 10 percent to the heating costs.

In some parts of the country (and in some homes), the money you save on heating and air conditioning through these minor steps

FIGURE 33

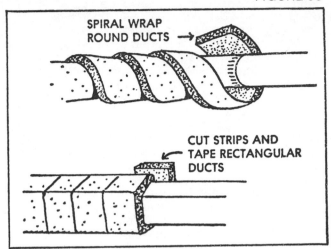

SPIRAL WRAP
ROUND DUCTS →

CUT STRIPS AND
TAPE RECTANGULAR
DUCTS

will allow you to move to a tropical island where you don't even need heat or air conditioning.

WATER HEATER

One other waster to check is the water heater. Touch the side of the unit; if it feels very warm to the touch, ask yourself where the heat comes from. If you guessed from the hot water inside, you're right.

Even if the tank doesn't feel hot, you could be losing heat. A metal jacket as warm as 85 degrees will feel either cool or neutral. Take the temperature of the metal and compare it to the air temperature. There are jackets or overcoats you can buy or make from insulating blankets that will wrap around the heater tank to stop this loss. Be sure to follow the instructions so as to make a safe and efficient installation.

LIGHTING

Even though the average light bulb could burn for days for only pennies, lighting accounts for over 20 percent the total electricity an average family uses. Shows you how those pennies mount up! In many cases, you and your family can cut down on consumption without creating eyestrain or making it so dark as to become dangerous to walk.

The first lighting suggestion most experts make is to replace incandescent fixtures with fluorescents: A forty-watt fluorescent gives more light than a hundred-watt incandescent, while using about half the current. The experts don't point out, however, that in most cases, you'll have to spend a bundle for fluorescent fixtures. I do recommend that you consider a changeover every time you have to replace a fixture, or whenever you add one.

Probably the biggest light saver is remembering to turn off all lights when not needed. This is easy in a room where you see the light. How about a bulb left burning in the closet, attic, or basement?

Maybe you don't need quite so much light. If the light is for fill-in and not for reading or safety, try out lower-wattage bulbs. A dimmer switch can also save if you turn down the light when you don't need so much. Three-way lamps can do the same thing.

Certainly you want to get all the light you pay for. A layer of dust on a bulb or tube will shade part of the light. Darkened bulbs, dirty reflectors, and fixtures can also cut down on the light.

Outside lights can be connected to a photoelectric device so they will cut off automatically when daylight comes.

Speaking of daylight, it's free. Take advantage of as much natural light as possible. Open windows and blinds, clean the glass, and let the sunshine in. Reflective light is also free, so use light colors to help reflect available light.

ENERGY SAVINGS AND THE IRS

You may wonder why someone who can't even spell IRS is going to try to explain the tax laws regarding energy-saving expenditures you make for your home. The reason I'm doing this is because the explanations I've seen have all been from either CPAs or from IRS people and they just don't speak our language.

The idea is that the new tax laws let you, as a homeowner or tenant, use money you'd otherwise pay in taxes to purchase energy-saving improvements. There are two sections loosely termed Insulation Credit and Solar Credit. The insulation credit part allows a tax credit of 15 percent of the first $2,000 you spend, up to a $300 credit. That allows you to get started, but many homes could easily (and wisely) spend more than $2,000. Even without any help from your Uncle beyond the $2,000, if you buy wisely, the expenditures will pay off in savings on your utility bills.

Here's what applies:

1. Insulation for attics, walls, and floors
2. An insulating "overcoat" for your water heater
3. Duct-type insulation for air ducts
4. Wraps that insulate hot-water pipes
5. Storm windows and doors, or replacement windows with thermal glass
6. Reflective film installed to control heat transfer
7. Electrical or mechanical ignition systems that replace a gas pilot light
8. Caulking and weather stripping for exterior doors and windows

9. An automatic clock thermostat or other set-back device
10. Furnace replacement burners designed to reduce consumption by increased efficiency. (This is tricky because I got different opinions from IRS people, and you might wait until there have been clearer guidelines.)
11. Meters that display energy usage.

About things that are *not* included—there is a provision for the IRS to add all sorts of things that they feel are qualified. However, there are some things that do *not* qualify. The highly touted heat pump doesn't make it. Nor does exterior siding, even if it's been given some insulating qualities. (I've heard of a few siding salesmen who have claimed it would qualify.) Everybody knows that fluorescents use less energy than incandescents, but these improvements will have to be all on you. Fireplaces and wood stoves don't make the grade.

One good thing about the law is that this is a tax *credit*, not a tax deduction: That means it's an actual reduction in your tax bill. It also applies to renters as well as to homeowners.

The credit applies only on your principal residence. (This will only confuse those with summer and winter residences.) It also doesn't apply to landlords. The tenant can make such improvements and get the credit, but the landlord can't.

The second part of the new law covers renewable energy-source improvements. This immediately brings to mind solar energy, and includes windmills that use wind power to produce residential energy. The credit under this section is 30 percent of the first $2,000 and 20 percent of the next $8,000 for a maximum of $2,200.

Now maybe you don't think $300 is a lot, and maybe you've already figured that the $2,200 credit requires you to spend $20,000—which you haven't got. Remember that the $300 isn't the most important part of that section. The most important part is that you'll save on your out-of-pocket utility bills. The rates aren't coming down, so you have to cut usage. On solar and other alternate sources, I really think it's wise to wait until more research and development come up with better ways that are more economically practical.

Whatever you do, be sure to save your receipts to get your tax credit. And here are some miscellaneous ideas that may save you a buck or so, or at least make you more comfortable.

HEATING AND COOLING TIPS

We've already talked about the extreme importance of proper maintenance as an energy saver. Here are some other ways to help.

● Put sheets of reflective aluminum foil behind radiators to reflect more heat out into the room.
● A few minutes before I start a meal, I close the vent into the kitchen. This means that the heating system keeps its heat for other parts

of the house. The heat generated from cooking keeps the kitchen warm, but I don't burn up any more. I'm saving energy and my patience.

● Here's a source of *free* heat for your home. After you've taken your bath, don't pull the plug and let all that hot water go down the drain. You've paid for the heat, so don't send it down to warm the sewer pipes. Let it cool in the tub until it's down to room temperature. The warmth it lets off in going down 30 degrees will be approximately 10,000 BTUs, enough to heat the average house for about an hour. If you prefer showers, close the drain during your shower and use this same heat source.

● When it's party time in the winter, set the thermostat back a few degrees and let the body heat from your guests warm the room.

● The fireplace damper should be closed except when there's a fire. Otherwise, all the expensive hot air your heating system has produced can be updrafted right out the chimney.

● Placing a TV set under the thermostat in the den was a mistake. The set throws off so much heat that it caused the thermostat to "think" the room was hot, so the air conditioning was running constantly to keep up.

Summer or winter, you should make sure your thermostats aren't being affected by any outside influences. TV sets, lights, drafts, or cold air from inside the walls could confuse the "brain" and maybe waste energy. While it's wrong to continually fiddle with the setting, it's wise to lessen the requirements when you retire and when you'll be gone for several hours during the day.

● An outside awning or shade will do a much better job of keeping the heat from direct sun out of your house than inside shades or venetian blinds. Air conditioning experts estimate as much as 50 percent more efficiency is attained if the sun doesn't hit the glass.

APPLIANCE ENERGY SAVERS

● A freezer is more efficient when it's packed full. The frozen foods help to retain the cold. In the refrigerator part, however, leave enough space for air to circulate.

● Like many apartment kitchens, ours is very compact. This is fine except I soon realized that having the built-in oven right next to the refrigerator was wasting energy (and since I pay the electric bills, my money). The heat from the stove cut way down on the refrigerator's efficiency. I think I've helped the problem by wedging insulation batts into the space between the two units. To cover the edge of the insulation that shows, I constructed an L-shaped wooden frame and painted it to match the trim in the kitchen. The landlord likes the idea, and has put in the insulation every time there's a vacancy.

● While my wife was ill, I discovered an energy saver that cuts down on the electric bill. The dishes in an automatic dishwasher are dry long before the last drying cycle is finished. By doing a little experimenting, I found out how long it took. Now we turn off the washer at that time in the drying cycle, saving that much electricity.

● A home economist told me that shiny pans use less heat for cooking than dirty ones. Soot or dirt requires more heat.

● A friend who's a home economist tells me that many people waste energy by sneaking a peek at whatever is cooking in the oven. She ran some tests and found that every peek lowers the oven temperature from fifteen to twenty-five degrees. That is quite an energy waste. So unless there's a glass door on the oven, keep your peeping down to a minimum. Spy on the neighbors instead of the roast.

● The best time to set a self-cleaning oven to do its thing is *after* cooking, since the heat will already be up near the high temperature needed for cleaning.

Unclassified, but helpful:

● The amount of electricity used in an average home workshop for an evening is less than the amount you use in watching TV for the same period of time. In fact, one tool company says that the current for an evening of tube watching would provide enough power to drill all the holes needed in building an average house.

● When it snows, look upon it as a blessing—a time to check for areas of heat loss. Look at your roof and see if there are spots where the snow melts long before the rest of the roof has lost its covering. Check next to the walls outside to see if there are spots where heat from inside has caused premature melting. It's good to find something useful about snow before you have to shovel it off the drive and walks.

● Our cold basement doesn't bother us too much because it's strictly for storage. However, I discovered that the area around the basement door was cold. Rather than weather-strip, I bought a damaged storm door for next to nothing. The damage was to the frame and strictly cosmetic, so it made no difference to the items in the basement. It was easy to install and did a better job than if I'd tried to weather-strip and put in a threshold on the regular door.

● A locked window is usually tighter shut, and therefore holds the heat in the house better. It's a little thing, but will make your house a lot snugger.

● Our son is a fresh-air fiend and always sleeps with a window open. This used to cool off the entire house and make our furnace work overtime to keep the rest of the house warm. By the simple installation of weather stripping on the door leading to his bedroom, we now keep the cold air out of the rest of the house. It's made a big difference in our heating bills. (Might cut down on the noise from a snorer, too.)

● Your column carries some good energy-saving hints for which all of us here at the utilities company thank you. One other hint that many people don't think about is the heat that can be derived from the sun. When the sun is shining, all windows facing the sun should be free of drapes, blinds, and shades to let the heat in. Additionally, the sunshine will provide more light and preclude having to burn lights. Keep up the good work.

● Our bathroom always seems a little coolish and drafty in the winter, and I finally figured out that there was cold air coming in around a built-in medicine cabinet. I removed the unit and placed insulation between the studs all around the hole, and now we're a lot warmer. Maybe others haven't thought of this as a source of cold.

8.

Floors

Since floors always seem to be underfoot, it's not surprising they're such troublemakers. We'll try to bring forth some help, and hope some of the unusual ideas will floor you.

SQUEAKY FLOORS

You've tiptoed out toward the kitchen for a forbidden midnight snack, or you're coming home late after an evening out, or the baby has finally gone to sleep, and you're creeping in to be sure ... then you step on that one spot in the floor that squeaks. And at that time of night, it doesn't squeak, it *screams*.

Maybe you can cure it. All squeaky floors are the result of movement, usually two boards rubbing against each other. The first thing to do is locate the squeak. (That's not hard to do—you found it last night!)

If the flooring is hardwood, there are several easy tricks you can try. One is to dust talcum powder into the cracks. Sweep it back and forth so as much powder as possible goes in. If the powder covers the parts of the boards that are rubbing, this can stop the squeaks.

Floors have to be repowdered every so often as the powder sifts on down or is sucked up by the vacuum cleaner. (Substitute powdered graphite. It lasts longer than talcum powder.) Another method is to flow liquid floor wax or all-purpose glue between the cracks. Either of these lasts longer than powder.

● Rubbing a bar of soap across the cracks stops noise.

Other readers suggested salad oil or liquid detergent.

Another way is to place a block of wood over newspapers and tap sharply with a hammer. Move it around over the squeak and an area about two feet on all sides of the squeak. This will often reseat loose nails that are allowing movement.

These ideas are all easy ... but sometimes more permanent

repairs are needed. If the floor is exposed underneath, as in a crawl space or basement, this is the place to attack. To locate the squeak from underneath, you need an accomplice to step on the squeaky spot. You can usually see movement in the subflooring. If you can't, a magnet right above the squeak and a compass below will help locate the trouble spot.

Sometimes you can drive a wedge between the joist and the moving subfloor boards. This pushes the boards up tight and stops movement. Shingles make good wedges.

● For wedges, I flattened the sides of golf tees on a grinder wheel. They were then easy to tap in place.

● Good wedges can be had by using the wooden pieces from spring-type clothespins.

● Drill a hole in the subflooring. Then insert the nozzle of a caulking gun into this hole and squirt caulk in. This cushions the two layers of floor and prevents them from rubbing against each other.

If this isn't possible or doesn't work, a wood screw may be inserted through the subflooring and on up into the hardwood boards above. The screw will draw the two together. Drill a pilot hole for the screw, but make sure the screw isn't long enough to go all the way through both layers, or you've created a new problem.

If you can't get underneath hardwood floors, there are permanent ways to attack from the top. If you ascertain that the squeak is caused by the hardwood boards rubbing each other, drive 6d nails in the crack between the squeakers. A pair of nails five to ten inches apart and at slight angles may do it. If not, try another pair in each adjoining crack. Drill a pilot hole, and when you near the surface, use a nail set to drive them. Then countersink and cover with wood filler.

If the squeak is between the joist and subflooring or between the two layers of flooring, and if there's no way to attack from the underside, you must use longer nails. They should go through both layers and into the joist, if possible. Try to locate the joist by sound. Tap along the floor with your ear to the ground, and you should be able to detect the hollow sound between joists. Toenail these 10d finishing nails. Use the same procedure of pilot holes, nail set, and countersinking mentioned above.

If your squeak is under carpeting, vinyl tiles, or some other covering over subflooring with no way to attack from underneath, there's no magic trick. With carpeting, try driving finishing nails through the carpet at an angle. Use a nail set to put them below the carpet. Usually the pile will hide the nail hole. Resilient floors? Sorry—you either have to remove the top covering or learn to live with the squeak. Once the covering is off, nails or screws can usually pull the subflooring tight against the joists. (The subfloor will probably be of plywood, so there won't be as many joints to worry about.)

Stairs can also squeak. Try this:

● Get under the staircase and squirt caulk into all the cracks where the different wooden parts meet. The caulking gun has enough pressure to get the stuff in there, and it stops the noise.

● Use metal shelf brackets under the noisy stairs. Wood screws will pull the bottom of the step and the back of the riser tightly against the braces, and there can no longer be any rubbing together of wood because there's no more movement.

RESILIENT FLOORS

One thing that seems to go wrong with resilient floors is that the adhesive sometimes lets go at the seams. It's not always going to work, but sometimes this will solve the problem:

● Place a piece of heavy paper or aluminum foil over a loose seam and run a moderately hot iron back and forth across the area. The heat will often reactivate the old mastic. However, you must put some weight on the seam for a few hours, and I find that a set of encyclopedias does well here.

If that doesn't work, you may have to add new glue. Before you do, warm the flooring to make it more flexible, then bend it back to let you scrape away all the bread crumbs. Then use new adhesive sparingly. You'll still need the weights while the mastic sets up. Put waxed paper over the seam just in case there's any squeeze-out. (I don't have a hint on removing floor mastic from encyclopedias.) An even better way is to use a chemical seam sealer, available for many newer types of floors.

Handle loose floor tiles the same way. If you've gouged or otherwise damaged a tile, however, you can replace it. No matter how many seams have come loose, you'll find it's not that easy to actually remove a tile. Knowing these tricks will make it easier. Heat from a propane torch or a heat gun will soften the mastic and let you pry and scrape the tile up. If you'll cut a gash in the center of the tile to be removed, you can start working with both the heat and the scraper there and avoid the edges, and thus not damage the surrounding good tiles.

● To pry out the tile before the mastic hardens again, I take my plumber's friend and stick the suction cup in the middle of the tile. Then I lift up on the plumber's-friend handle, and the tile comes right out.

● If you don't like the hazard of a flame, a heat lamp will also do the job. Put the lamp in a clamp-on photographic light holder and clamp it to a chair leg. Position the bulb about a half inch from the tile, and pretty soon the mastic will soften. It's not as fast as a flame, but certainly a lot safer.

● The edges of a floor tile came loose,and the tile curled up. I put the heating pad over the tile so the heat could soften the edges. Then I placed a stack of books over the heating pad to weigh the edges down. The heat even softened the adhesive so the edges stuck down again.

Another—and seemingly opposite—way to remove these tiles is with extreme cold. Dry ice, available from the Good Humor man, placed over the tile will make both the tile and the mastic very brittle. If you don't have dry ice, a bucket filled with ice cubes plus some water and rock salt will do. After about five minutes, hit the tile with a hammer blow, and it should shatter. Then you can use a putty knife or scraper to remove the material. Tap and scrape as you go.

Clean away the old mastic before gluing down the new tile.

A new resilient-tile floor is well within the realm of most do-it-yourselfers. The various makers of this flooring put out some really good instruction sheets.

● Here's a tip when laying floor tiles. Open up all of the boxes of tiles and work alternately out of each box as you go along. This will compensate for any variations in color often found from one batch to another. If there are such variations, having all the tiles mixed in together keeps you from ending up with a solid area looking different.

● When you lay a floor of resilient tiles, always buy a few extra squares. Sometime you'll have to replace one that's been damaged. That's when many people discover that the pattern they bought is no longer being made. Also, don't pack these extras away. Place them out in the room under a piece of furniture or someplace where they won't be seen. When you do have to replace a tile, the replacement will have weathered and aged just about like the ones on the floor and will blend in much better.

● If there is any pattern to the tiles, be sure they're placed in the same direction. Look at the back and see if there are any arrows. If so, you won't make a mistake if you use them. If not, run a felt marker across the ends on one side and face all the marks in the same direction.

● If you heat the bottom side of each asphalt tile square before putting it down, it smooths out the bed of mastic and also lets the tile better conform to any irregularities. Heat slightly softens the tile, but won't harm it. I keep a heating pad and let one tile heat while I set the previous one.

● The easy job of installing vinyl floor tiles goes even faster if you have a child's wagon around. Stack the tiles in the wagon and roll it along with you as you lay the tiles. It's easier than sliding the box they come in.

● Baseboards often fail to be flush with the floor when you're nailing them in place. If no base shoe molding is used, then there's an unsightly gap. If you lay a two-foot-long scrap of board on top of the base and kneel on it, the baseboard will be forced down against the floor until nailed in place.

Most spills on resilient floors can just be wiped or mopped up. Some, however, require special attention. The very best special attention is to consult the printed material you got when the floor was installed. Different types of floors require different treatments. But if you lost the sheet, maybe these hints will help.

● To remove fruit juice, coffee, or mustard stains from the kitchen floor, make a compress soaked in hydrogen peroxide. Leave it on for a few minutes, and the stain will be gone.

● I found that spraying ink stains with hair spray will remove them from vinyl flooring. [Rubbing alcohol on a compress also works on some inks.]

● Heel marks are often too stubborn to respond to my kitchen spray cleaner. When that happens, I use superfine steel wool (0000) dipped in liquid wax and lightly rub away the heel marks.

After any of these treatments, you should probably wash the surface and use your regular floor polish or wax to bring it back to the proper sheen.

● My old surefire low-cost method of cleaning is to use very hot water with a mild detergent, and the secret ingredient called elbow grease. Enough scrubbing will remove all the wax, and give me a good workout.

● To move an appliance or any piece of heavy furniture without damage to resilient floors, stick a throw rug under it. Put all of the rug under except a few inches. Then lift up the other end and scoot the rug back so the entire appliance is on the rug.

● When we moved our freezer to the utility room, I discovered it had left big dents in our vinyl kitchen flooring. I filled them up by pouring clear shellac into the dents. This made the floor level again without hiding the pattern, as that much wax would have done.

● Vinyl flooring is great for withstanding most anything—except a three-year-old boy. Our junior handyman gouged several holes in my kitchen floor with some of his tools. I hid the holes with a wax crayon to match the color of the vinyl. By holding a lighted match to the crayon, it melted and dripped into the hole. When it set up, I scraped off any excess and made it even with the floor. When waxed over, the patched places can't be found. (Neither can my son's play tools.)

CARPETS

Carpeting is also now a do-it-yourself undertaking. You may need to rent some equipment for the tacked-down installation, but for the type that goes in the bathroom, all you need is a pair of scissors and some of the double-faced carpet tape. You do need to make a pattern—for this, tape heavy brown paper together or even use newspapers (Figure 34). When you have the pattern cut and taped, and know that it fits perfectly, be sure to label it so you know which side is the top. Then be sure you turn it face down over the carpet—which is also face down—before you make the first cut. Tape the pattern to the back of the carpet and mentally check to be sure that when you cut the rug and flip it over, the opening for the toilet isn't going to fall in the middle of the room. Now you're ready to trace the pattern and cut.

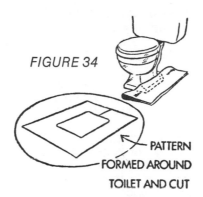

FIGURE 34

PATTERN
FORMED AROUND
TOILET AND CUT

Care of carpets is important. Spills should be attended to immediately. First blot all spilled liquids with a cloth or cleansing tissue and scrape up any solids. Then you're ready for cleaning. However, *never* use any cleaner on the carpet until you've tested to see if it does any damage to either the fibers or the color. If you've saved scraps, you can test on them. If not, try a spot under a couch or in some out-of-the-way area. If you have a scrap, you can even spill some of the same junk on it and see if the cleaner will do any good.

When working on the spot, it's best to work from the outer edges of the stain toward the middle. No matter what the cleaner, avoid overwetting. Here are some specific cures for specific stains:

Acids: These need to be diluted and neutralized quickly. Club soda does both, as does baking soda and water.

Blood: Never put hot water on a new stain, as that will set it. After you dab and blot to remove, use a dry-cleaning solvent.

● I found that a teaspoon of salt to a half cup of cold water will loosen bloodstains that would otherwise remain in a carpet.

Butter: see *Grease.*

Chewing Gum: Put an ice cube in a plastic sandwich bag and hold against the gum. The cold makes it brittle for removal by scraping with the end of a spoon.

Coffee and Tea: Blot and dilute with plain water. Then spot clean with shampoo or dry-cleaning solution.

● If you don't have any carpet shampoo, use Woolite or other mild cleaners made for delicate fabrics.

Crayon: Although this is wax based, I don't suggest you try the

methods suggested for wax later on. Sometimes they work, and some-
tims they don't. Scrape up any excess, and then use a dry-cleaning
solvent.

Grease: A dry-cleaning solvent is your best bet.

● I have found that after I've scraped up all the grease that I can
from a carpet, I can lift most of the rest up by putting cornmeal over the
spot. I leave this overnight, and then vacuum it up. It absorbs and lifts the
grease out of the carpet.

● Use a rag with mineral spirits paint thinner to rub over greasy
carpet spots, being careful not to get the carpet too wet. Then sprinkle
table salt over the damp area, and the salt will lift the rest of the grease.

● Ground-up corn cob is an excellent absorbent for grease spots
on carpets, upholstery, or drapes.

Ink:

● Hair spray will help to remove some types of ball-point ink.

● Sprinkle some table salt on ink stains and let sit for a few minutes
before brushing away.

Lipstick: Use a dry-cleaning solution.

● I dropped my mother's lipstick on the rug while the tube was
open. My aunt suggested rubbing gently with an art-gum eraser. It took up
the lipstick, and mother never knew.

Liquor: The alcohol can attack some dyes, so wipe up and
dilute booze stains as soon as they happen. If it happens to be red
wine, cover it with table salt. As the salt absorbs the wine, vacuum it up
and apply more. You may still have to use a dry-cleaning fluid or a
carpet shampoo.

Mud: This is one spot you don't have to get after immediately
because it is best removed after it's dried. Then you can brush it loose
and vacuum up the dirt.

Pet Stains: Blot spot up as soon as it happens. Club soda will
remove the spot and also help remove the odor. Another home remedy
for these boo-boos is to use equal parts of white vinegar and water.

Wax: You can use a blotter and iron to melt and absorb wax.
However, candle wax may leave color that needs a dry cleaner.

● If you have taken some of the color out of the carpet, you can
sometimes replace it with artist's pastels. They come in just about every
color. When the touch-up is done, use hair spray to hold the color in place.

● Judicious use of felt markers can replace color to a patterned
carpet. I wouldn't try this unless you have some artistic ability, but it does

work, and these markers come in so many different colors that you can match just about any that a carpet would have.

For carpet burns, just snip off the charred fibers with a pair of fingernail scissors (Figure 35). If the char doesn't go down to the backing, that may be all you need to do, as this one low spot probably won't show. However, if the burn went through so the backing shows, clip some fibers from a carpet scrap or from under the couch. Put a small amount of white glue on the exposed backing, and when it gets tacky, carefully place these fibers into the glue. If this is done right, you'll never know there was a burn there. If the burn goes through the backing or over a large area, you will probably do well to cut out this place and put in a patch. With a shag carpet, you'll never know; and even with other types it can be done with good results. Just be sure the nap on the patch and carpet run the same way. Use double-faced carpet tape to hold the patch in place.

FIGURE 35

SNIP...DON'T PULL

● The legs of heavy furniture often leave dents in the carpet. To remove them, just use a steam iron. Don't actually touch the surface; just get the iron close enough for the steam to come out against the rug. Right after steaming, rub across the dents with a coin. The nap will raise up like new, and you won't be able to even see where the furniture was.

HARDWOOD FLOORS

With all the super new types of flooring and floor coverings, hardwood flooring took a back seat for a while. People got caught up in the newer no-maintenance types. The beauty of a good hardwood floor is worth the little bit of care required.

The key to keeping a great-looking wooden floor is to keep it well protected. Assuming it has a good finish on it, waxing is your way to give added protection. Depending on how many kids you have, you'll need to wax two or three times a year.

● When I was very ill, my husband took over all the housekeeping. I hobbled into the kitchen one day as he was waxing the floor. He was using a paint roller with its extension handle to apply the wax. He had poured the wax into the paint tray. It went on fast and smooth, and now that I'm well, I use his method. Sometimes it just takes someone who isn't bound to the old methods to come up with a better way.

● It's a good idea to remove the brushes from an electric floor buffer between uses. The weight of the buffer resting constantly on the brushes tends to push them down, and eventually they're ruined.

● After the floors are done, my method of removing wax from the floor polisher is to put the brushes up on a table and cover them with a paper towel. Then go over them with a hot iron. The wax melts and is absorbed by the paper towel.

Between waxings, it's very important to keep dirt and grit off the floor, so either dust-mop or vacuum regularly.

Get after spills as soon as they happen. But don't wet-mop them up. If you have to use a wet rag, use it sparingly, and then wipe the floor dry. The all-around best cleaner for spots is mineral spirits paint thinner. With that and some 0000 steel wool, you can rub away water marks, heel marks, grease spots, white spots, dark spots, and maybe even ink spots. Sometimes you may have to use a not-so-fine steel wool. The key is the wax job you did, because all those spots are probably on the wax. After you give the spot the brush-off, rewax the area.

Gouges and scratches have to be doctored. If the scratch is just in the finish, you can often hide it with rewaxing. If the scratch or gouge is into the wood, you may have to patch and also add stain. There are putty sticks and furniture melt sticks that fill and add stain all at once.

● Rolling heavy furniture with casters across hardwood floors can leave scratches and streaks. Before you roll, coat the rollers with floor wax. Coat the part you can see, and then roll it a little to expose more of the caster until the entire roller is coated with the wax. Wait until the wax dries to do the moving.

Sometimes you have to replace a single board in a hardwood floor. This can be done by either setting your circular saw to the depth of the floorboards and sawing lengthwise down the middle; or by drilling holes in the center. Then, with either method, a chisel is used to split the entire length of the board. With that done, you can pry up the board without damage to adjacent pieces. Since these boards are usually tongue and groove, you just have to remove the lower lip on the groove side (Figure 36), and angle the board into place. When it's in position, you nail it in for good, and it's ready to be finished.

● Installing new wood flooring is the kind of job you don't do very often, so you want to give it every chance to be the best possible. Many folks don't allow the flooring to become acclimatized to its new surroundings. Allow the wood to stay loosely stacked in the room for several days so it can gain the same moisture content as that of the

FIGURE 36

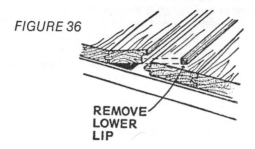

**REMOVE
LOWER
LIP**

house. It is best to have the heat about the same as normal house heat would be. Also be sure to avoid bringing the flooring in right after plastering or tiling, as the moisture content will be unusually high at that time. A few days' wait will result in a much tighter floor when installed.

● I don't know what carpenters do when putting in a hardwood floor, but I created a helper. I soon found that nails in a regular carpenter's apron weren't easy to get to from the crouching position. I found that when I was nailing, my right knee was on the floor, and my left knee was up. I made a nail pouch that I tied around my left leg so it hung at my shin. This meant that the nails were always within easy reach.

Here are some more floor tips:

● Here is a lesson I learned the hard way. I refinished our hardwood floors, and since the sandpaper kept tearing, I thought there was something wrong with the floor-sanding unit. Finally I figured out that many of the nail heads weren't countersunk enough and were therefore playing heck with the paper. After I went over the floor with my nailset and hammer, there were no more protruding heads, and no more ripped sandpaper.

● When refinishing floors, it's almost impossible to tell if the floors are uneven by just looking. Use a flashlight and a long, straight board. Place the light behind the board, and then move the light and board around on the floor. A high spot will raise the board and allow light to show under the board next to it.

● If you've ever varnished floors, you know how hard it is to avoid a few skipped places. I place the trouble light down on the floor in one doorway. With the light on and aimed into the room, I start putting on the finish at the lighted door and work away toward the other side assuming there's a second door on the other side of the room. The light shines along the floor and lets me see any skips immediately so I can cover them and still be working against the wet edge.

● I recently rented a floor sander to redo our floors. Before returning the machine, I took it out to the shop, climbed up on my workbench, and smoothed up a badly beat-up bench top. I removed the vise and just walked the sander around as if it were on a floor. It did the job in no time, but to do it with a hand sander would have taken a lot longer.

● Save old carpet when it's taken up and cut a piece to fit inside the trunk of your car. This lets you put things in there without their getting scratched up. Also cut a piece to fit over the deck between the back seat and the rear window. This looks much better than the plastic that's often there.

● A strip of carpet in front of the workbench is easier on the feet.

● Staple carpet scraps to the garage wall where your car door hits.

● Protect your work from scratches by carpeting part of the workbench and sawhorse.

● A scrap of leftover carpet can cover the wastebasket so that it matches the rug. Glue it in place.

● New carpet should usually be accompanied by new padding. The old pad can be cut to fit under area rugs. It can also be used to pad sawhorses or workbench tops, to cushion ladder steps, and as runners in the shop where you do lots of standing.

● We've made throw rugs feel much more expensive by putting a free 'pad' underneath. We placed several layers of newspaper under the rugs. It's amazing how much more luxurious the walk is.

● The inside of a rolled-up rug or carpet can be very attractive to rodents or insects. It's very easy to seal off the ends by just slipping a large paper bag over each end and taping it in place.

● I don't know how the pros do it, but when I put in my brick floor, I devised a way to get even mortar joints. I decided on the joint size I wanted, and then cut scraps from plywood of the proper thickness to act as spacers. These scraps were long enough to stick up between the bricks. I laid out the entire floor in the bed of mortar, using the spacer scraps. Then I went back and put in the mortar for the joints, removing the spacers as I did so.

9.
HEATING AND COOLING SYSTEMS

With the energy crisis, people have become much more aware of their heating and cooling systems. Anything costing you that much money just has to be noticed. While most breakdowns are best handled by a pro, any homeowner can do many things to make the units operate free of trouble and with greater efficiency.

Unless you really know what you're doing, I suggest you have a pro check central systems at the beginning of the season. However, be sure to get a reliable guy, or you could be victimized. Once you know such a system is safe and ready to go, you can keep it going with routine maintenance. In these systems—as with almost every type of heating and cooling—cleanliness is the key word.

If your unit has a filter, you should either clean or change it about every month during operation. Permanent filters can be vacuumed, washed, and dried. They stop dust better if sprayed with a filter coating, available at heating-supply houses. The throwaway type are very inexpensive. Just be sure you see that the arrows on the filter point in the direction of the air movement when the filter is installed.

● Each time I replace a filter, I enter the date on a strip of masking tape on the furnace front, and I can tell at a glance how long the old filter has been there.

There are other places to clean, too. If there's a blower fan, it should be cleaned also. Most are of the squirrel-cage type shown in Figure 37. There are lots of fins to catch lots of dirt, and when there's too much dirt involved, the fan doesn't move enough heated or cooled air out into the rooms. The blower isn't always easy to get to: You may have to remove a plate that's attached to the unit. The fan is probably going

**EACH FIN ON BLOWER
SHOULD BE CLEANED**

FIGURE 37

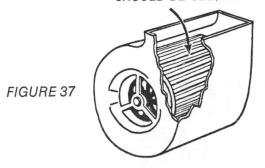

to be on a track held in place by sheet-metal screws. After you remove these screws, the cord may not be long enough to let you slide the fan out to get to.

Don't let these obstacles stop you, because cleaning it will make the unit work better and save you on utilities. Be sure to cut the electric current while you're working on the fan, and be sure not to let it drop on your foot when you pull it out. Cleaning is best done with an old toothbrush, brushing both sides of every blade. Then get in there with your hose-type vacuum cleaner to get all the dirt and dust you've loosened.

Lubricating the blower motor is also important. Look for oiler caps. Even a heating-unit motor with sealed bearings that "requires no oiling" can get a little thirsty after a while. If you have such a motor, several years old, it might be wise to oil it. A few drops of oil around the shaft will go into the housing and be absorbed by the felt pad, and maybe this will help it keep its cool a little longer.

With a central unit, you also need to clean all the vents with your vacuum cleaner.

If your central unit is also an air conditioner, there are a few other parts to be cleaned. There are evaporator coils inside the house, and condensor coils outside. Both must be kept clean or you may lose your efficiency—and eventually your very expensive air conditioner.

The inside coils are located just beyond the fan, where air is blown over them. If you keep a clean filter, you may never have to clean them, but it's good to check them regularly. To get to them, you'll have to remove a metal access plate, but the screws holding it in place may be hidden under tape and insulation. Be sure to save these to reseal the area. While you have the unit open, pour a cup of laundry bleach into the tray below. This tray catches the condensation and sends it through a pipe to the outside. Sometimes the pipe gets clogged from a fungus that can build up inside. The bleach will kill the fungus and keep the pipe running free. A clogged system can pour lots of water out onto the wrong things, and if this ever happens, you may have to put several cups of bleach down to get it unclogged. Or:

● Take a hand pump for bike tires, and it will usually fit right into the clogged tube. A few blasts can usually clear out the tube.

The outside coils need the air drawn across them for cooling. Block the air and the compressor has to work harder and can burn up, costing you lots of dollars. Some service people use a brush to clean dirt from between the fins, while others use a blast from a hose. If you use a hose, be sure you cut the current, and let the unit dry off before you turn it back on. Sometimes dirt isn't the problem. Vines or grass growing against these fins will shut off the air flow, so keep them trimmed back.

One of the most important things you can have—whether you have gas, electric, coal, or oil heat—is the owner's manual. Most will have troubleshooting tips to tell you what to look for when there's no longer any warmth in your relationship.

● The outside compressors for air-conditioning units usually come with a schematic. If you leave it with the unit, the weather usually fades it by the time something goes wrong. If you take it inside, it gets lost. I solved the problem by placing the papers in an airtight jar. The jar is placed in a corner inside the compressor housing where it won't be in the way. Air and moisture can't get to the papers, but if anything goes wrong, I can.

THERMOSTATS

A thermostat is the brain center for almost every type of heating system except the wood fire. If the room is too cool, it sends a command to the heater to fire up. What happens if the brain goes loco? It could call for heat when you don't need it, or not call for it when you do. That's why you need to give it a checkup.

Put a thermometer that you know is accurate up on the wall next to the thermostat. Tape it there, but don't let it actually touch the wall—you want the temperature of the air, not the wall (Figure 38). Give it about fifteen minutes to stabilize, and compare the readings. If there is more than a couple of degrees difference, you need to do something.

First, check to see that the unit is clean and that it's level. With the face plate off, blow away any dust with your breath. If that doesn't correct the difference, you can either learn to compensate in your mind or have the thermostat replaced. Some can be recalibrated, but this probably has to be done by a pro.

● If your thermostat has never quite controlled your heating the way it should, you may be getting a false reading. Did you know that cold air

THERMOMETER
TAPED TO WALL

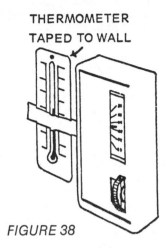

FIGURE 38

inside your walls can be attacking the thermostat from the back? Check the opening where the wires come through to the unit. If it's a big hole, this may be your problem. Caulk or putty around the wires to close up the hole (Figure 39), and your thermostat will now be governed only by the air in the room. Also, make sure the thermostat isn't too close to a localized heat source such as a TV, a vent blowing directly on it, or a large light bulb—that would throw it off.

　　● Before you throw away a thermometer just because the liquid has separated, leaving a gap in the column, try this: Tie a string around the unit, making sure it is securely fastened. Aim the bulb away from the end where the string is tied. Now swing the thermometer in a circle above your head, and the centrifugal force will usually bring the two sections back together.

FIGURE 39

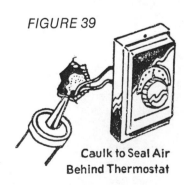

Caulk to Seal Air
Behind Thermostat

PILOT LIGHTS

Many heating devices that use natural gas have a pilot light to provide instant heat when needed. These include central furnaces, space heaters, water heaters, clothes dryers, and ranges. The owner's manual for the appliance is your best guide for lighting and maintaining its pilot light. But if you've lost that, here are some general rules.

For lighting the pilot, most appliances have a metal plate with instructions. Usually there is a gas cut-off valve that has three positions ... "on," "off," and "pilot." Unless otherwise suggested, the valve should have been in the "off" position for at least five minutes before lighting the pilot. With the setting on "pilot," hold a lighted match to the pilot. Most units will have a red reset button. This must be held down for thirty seconds while you light the pilot.

If the pilot won't light at all, then you know that gas isn't getting to the flame. There's probably an obstruction in the tiny orifice. If so, it should be cleaned.

If the pilot light stays on until you release the red button and then goes out, you either have a faulty thermocouple or the pilot flame isn't hitting the thermocouple properly. What is a thermocouple, you ask? This is a safety device. It's a sensor that tells the gas valve that there is a pilot burning so it would be safe to send gas to the burners when needed. The sensor is a tube you'll see right next to the pilot light. The pilot flame should bathe about the top half inch of this tube. If not, loosen the bracket nuts and reposition the thermocouple.

If the pilot won't stay lit, and you've determined that there's no breeze to blow it out, the thermocouple may be faulty. Sounds ominous, but you'll be surprised to find that a thermocouple is inexpensive, and replacement is within the realm of most home handypersons. When you purchase a new unit of the same type and with a lead-in tube of the same length, you'll see that there are replacement instructions on the back of the card. In fact, read these before you buy to be sure this is your cup of tea.

When the replacement is done, the pilot flame should be steady, blue in color and hit the thermocouple rod as described above.

FIREPLACES

Most fireplaces are very inefficient as far as heating goes. Not only don't they do a good job of heating a house (much less the room they're in), they often suck out heat created by the furnace. You have to have the chimney to carry out the smoke, but the updrafts can also take out your heat. However, I like a roaring fire; and if you do too, look into the new devices that help throw more heat out into the room. Also consider a glass screen to help better control the updrafts.

● When first lighting a fireplace, it sometimes doesn't draw until hot air currents start up the chimney. If this happens, quickly make a torch from a rolled-up newspaper. Light it and hold it as far up the chimney as you can. This will form a heat current that will start the fireplace smoke going up, and will also suck in the smoke that has already escaped into the room. It has to be done quickly, though, before the smoke in the room has strayed too far away.

● To remove the smoky spots on a wooden mantelpiece, spray starch over the smoked area. When it dries, use a soft brush and brush starch and smoke spots away. A damp cloth does the final cleaning.

● Make a paste of cream of tartar and water to remove smoke stains on brick.

● Add enough household ammonia to powdered pumice to make a paste. Cover the smoked areas and let the paste dry completely. Then use hot water with detergent to scrub it away. Rinse, and you're ready to start smoking it up again.

● Mix two parts baking soda and one part each of pumice stone and table salt. Add just enough warm water to form a paste. Rub this over the smoky regions with a stiff brush. After a good rubdown, let the paste dry on the brick. Then take a dry brush and remove the dried powder. In most cases, the smoke stains will be gone.

If you have a fireplace with a smoking habit, it may be an indication that the opening is too high. You can determine exactly how far down it must be lowered by using a large piece of corrugated board wide enough to screen off the top. For lots of smoke, light a fire of damp newspapers. Now gradually move your screen down until the smoke quits coming out. Mark this, and you'll know how much to either lower the opening or raise the bed.

● To get smoke out of the house, wet a large towel, wring it out, and then swing it around over your head.

● Our fireplace has a gas jet to help get the logs started. However, it's far enough back that you burn your fingers getting a regular match back there. Those long matches are fine, but they cost more than they're worth. I rebelled and made a holder. I glued a tiny alligator clip to a length of coat hanger wire with metal-mending epoxy (Figure 40). My holder clamps down on the match. I light it, and the holder reaches all the way back, with my fingers away from the flame. I also use this for lighting charcoal in the outdoor grill.

FIGURE 40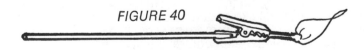

● Form a loop in a wire and insert a small scrap of rolled paper in the loop. Light the paper to reach the jet.

● A paper drinking straw can be lit and can allow you extra reach. And so, believe it or not, can a long strand of thin spaghetti—uncooked, of course!

● A kerosene-soaked brick is a great fire starter. Keep one soaking in a container outside. After the brick has soaked for at least 12 hours, remove it from the container and allow it to sit until the surface is dry. The soaked brick can then be wrapped in aluminum foil and kept until ready to use. When ignited, it will burn for a long time, starting even the toughest logs. Be sure to wash your hands before striking the match.

● Most fireplace grates have spaces so wide that when you really get the fire going, the coals drop down into the ashes. By cutting a piece of expanded metal mesh or hardware cloth to fit over the base of the grill, you can keep the coals active longer and allow a better draft. Bend the mesh to conform to the shape of the grate. If the mesh starts to get clogged, a few taps with the poker will cause the residue to fall down through.

The fire does produce ashes. Please remember that even though the ashes look dead, there may still be live coals hidden underneath when you clean out the fireplace. I learned the hard way. I placed the ashes into a grocery bag, and before I got around to taking them outside, the bag caught fire. Fortunately we caught it before it did much damage. Now I use a metal bucket for the ashes, and I get them out of the house as soon as I shovel them out of the fireplace. I then dump them into a metal garbage can with nothing combustible in with them, or use them on the flower garden, lawn, or compost heap. Here are some other ash-hauler tips:

● For those who are nagged by their mates to clean out the fireplace after each fire, here's some good news: A layer of ashes actually makes the next fire start quicker and easier and makes the fire warm the room quicker. The ashes act as insulation over the cold hearth.

● To clean out the ashes in your fireplace without stirring up that soot that seems to float all over the house, fill a spray bottle with water. Use the type bottle that mists. Line a corrugated box for the ashes with newspapers. Spray the papers. Next spray the ashes—just a mist is all that's needed. Moist ashes won't dust up. As you dig down, you may have to spray several more times. When you're through, place a moist newspaper over the top and haul your ashes out. You'll be pleasantly surprised at the lack of dust.

● Wad up a piece of newspaper, place it over in a corner of the fireplace, and light it. The updraft from the fire will carry most of the dust you're raising back into the fireplace and up the chimney.

● Cover soot marks on carpets with dry table salt. After an hour, the salt and soot vacuum up.

● Clean glass fireplace doors by spraying them on the inside with oven cleaner.

● Fireplace ashes are good for many things. Use them on icy walks and in a compost heap. However, if you burn lots of scrap lumber with nails, 'mine' the ashes before using them. Use a very strong magnet to remove metal from the ashes. It doesn't take that long to do, and is much better than getting a flat tire or stabbing your hand when digging in the dirt.

The chimney that's caked with soot can be a fire hazard and can also not work properly. Cleaning it is something you can do, although it's not on the top ten list of thrills.

First thing, seal off the fireplace coming into the room. You can tape a sheet of vinyl over the opening. Be sure it's a good cover-up, because if it isn't, you're liable to have soot floating throughout the house. Then you need a burlap bag stuffed with wadded newspapers or straw with a brick in it for weight. Tie this securely to a rope so it can be lowered down the chimney. The idea is to let this bag rub against the surfaces inside to loosen the soot. After this has been done on the entire inside surface, wait a half hour or so for the soot to settle. Then you can start cleaning out the fireplace. You will have to reach up through the damper opening to a place called the smoke shelf and remove the soot that's piled up there. Wear gloves for soot handling. After you're through, use a mirror and flashlight to look up the chimney and see if you've done a proper job.

● Since it's fireplace season again, I've once again cleaned out my chimney using an old folk remedy passed on by my grandpappy. When I build the first fire of the season, I toss a handful of rock salt into the fire. As this burns, it cleans away the soot. I also do this a couple of times during the year and once toward the end of the winter.

● A few potato peels tossed into the burning fire each week keep the chimney soot-free.

Others claim citrus peels do the job.

When it's time to close the chimney up until next winter, take a few extra minutes to clean the soot that's collected on the hinges of the damper. This stuff can eventually cake up so bad on these hinges that the damper won't open or close all the way. Therefore, you lose cool air in the summer, and in the winter your fireplace doesn't draw properly.

FIREWOOD

Every year, thousands of people are royally clipped by some of the people who sell firewood. The price is high to begin with, but some people just don't deliver what they are supposed to. Most homeowners don't really know what a cord of wood is. When they come out and see the giant stack in the backyard, they take the guy's word that it's a cord.

If it is, it should be roughly 128 cubic feet. Measure the wood pile lengthwise. Then multiply this times the width times the height. If it's close to the magic number 128, go enjoy your fire. If you measure before it's unloaded, you may save a lot of trouble later on. Also, a mixture of sizes (to include some small sticks) yields more wood. Here are some tips to make cutting and splitting your own firewood a little easier.

● This trick is a big help in splitting logs for firewood. As a holder for logs to be split, I use a couple of old auto tires stacked one on the other. The log is held upright inside the ring of tires (Figure 41). This is a big safety factor because if you should ever miss, the tires catch the ax blow.

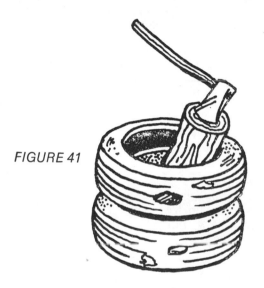

FIGURE 41

● After cutting firewood, I ended up with pitch and other dirt on my hands—and this ended up on my steering wheel when I started home. Now I have a traveling washroom. In addition to my thermos of coffee, I carry a thermos of hot soapy water and a bottle of plain water.

● If you're stacking split firewood outside, it's best to stack it with the bark facing up. The bark will repel water, and the logs will be much drier when you get ready to use them.

● Each year, the bottom layer of leftover firewood next to the ground picks up bugs. Then these varmints are carried in, and before the fire starts, a few of them get away into the house. This year I put down a row of bricks and stacked the wood on them. The wood is held up off the ground and protected from bugs as well as moisture. The bugs will have to find another way to be carried into our house for the winter.

● We don't have a protected area next to the house to keep firewood, so I devised one. I bought a garbage can on sale and find that it holds enough wood for a couple of fires. So that I don't bring bugs into the house, I keep one of those pest strips inside the can. Now we have dry, bug-free wood right outside the door . . . if I remember to fill the can after each use.

● A child's sled really comes in handy for bringing in fireplace wood on winter days.

● I made a log tote from a section of an old tire. The section is only about six to eight inches long. Handholds are cut out of the edges. One big log or several little ones rest in the tire, and I can carry it at my side without getting the logs against my clothes.

● Scrap lumber used as fireplace wood will burn slower and last longer if you nail several boards together. Three or four pieces of one-inch-thick lumber will make a good "log," as will a couple of two-inch scraps. The nails can be sifted out of the ashes and used again for this purpose.

● Buying firewood by the bundle and toting it home so we can have an occasional fire on our hearth is extravagant, but what the heck. The one problem, other than carrying the firewood home in a cab, was where to store the logs we couldn't put in the fireplace right away. I covered a large metal potato-chip can with Contact paper to blend into the decor of the apartment. This holds exactly the amount from a bundle that won't go into the fireplace. The logs are stored on end and stick out a few inches but don't look bad at all.

Fireplaces are great to watch. However, some folks aren't content with the natural flame colors, and I'm often asked about how to create technicolor flames. The following chemicals will create the following colors: salt—yellow, borax—green, barium nitrate—apple green, copper nitrate—emerald green, copper chloride—blue-green, calcium chloride—orange.

Want to make fireplace logs from old newspapers? The key to longer-burning paper logs is to make them as big around as possible and to roll them very tightly. Each log should be at least six inches in diameter.

Some people then twist wire around the log to hold it tight. Another way to hold it is to place the roll on a fully spread-out double sheet of newspaper and roll it around the log diagonally. Then tuck in the ends to keep it from unrolling. One of these paper logs is ideal as a bottom log to get the fire started. However, if your community recycles old papers, it's best to use 'em that way rather than burning. Colored inks in paper are thought to produce cancer-causing smoke.

MISCELLANEOUS

Here are some miscellaneous tips to make your heating and cooling systems do their thing without costing you so much.

● For greater comfort, the fan on a central air conditioner can be left running all the time. This works because the movement of air makes you feel cooler even when the compressor isn't running—the old wind-chill factor. If you live in a high-humidity area, however, or if your house is very humid, you'll do better to leave the fan on automatic. This way, the moisture on the coils will have a chance to drip off and go away instead of being blown into the house. If you do have such humid conditions, of course, you may have a dehumidifier, and leaving the fan going all the time again makes sense.

● A jar of that liquid that kids use to blow bubbles is good for detecting leaks in Freon lines. It also works for finding any kind of gas or air leaks.

● With a forced-air furnace in the basement, I can use my heater to cool the house. The basement is always cool, so I opened the furnace panel to expose the blower fan. With the heater turned off, the fan can still run, moving the cool basement air to the house up above.

● If you have window air conditioners and also central heating, you may be sending some of your cold air out through the heater's fresh-air return vents. These are usually located at floor level and can have a nice draft going through them. Even if they aren't the kind that can be closed, it's an easy matter to remove the grill and block these vents off until next winter.

● If you have central heat and air, you may like this idea. With the changeover from heat to air conditioning, turn the registers upside down. When heating, the flow of air should be aimed down; and when cooling, the air should be aimed up. This takes advantage of the fact that warm air rises and helps keep the flow going against Mother Nature's flow.

● If you ever have to cut into metal heat ducts, try using the old-time can opener with the hooked blade that is punched into the can and lifted up and down to cut.

● Want to have a nice-smelling house all the time? If you have central heat and air, keep a wick- or solid-type room deodorizer inside the return air vent. The blower will pick up the scent and carry it through the ducts to every room in the house.

● If the holes in a gas furnace's burners start to clog up, the efficiency of the heater is impaired. About the best thing to use to clean these holes is a pipe cleaner.

● Pilot lights on heating units are situated so that there's no draft, and so they're hidden from view. To check to be sure you have a proper flame, you may have to slither on the floor to see the pilot. You can usually position a hand mirror to make it easy to see the flame from a more comfortable position. In fact, if you're the kind who checks very often, you may even want to glue the mirror in place.

● A clean radiator is much more efficient than a dirty one. However, getting those devils clean is something else. After I've brushed them, I hang a wet towel behind them. Then I insert the vacuum cleaner hose into the blower end and turn the stream of air on the radiator. This blows all the dust and dirt out the back against the wet towel. The moisture holds it on the towel, and I haul it out.

● Each fall I repaint our radiators, but I can never remember how much paint it takes. I called the paint dealer, and he gave me a magic formula. Measure the front area of all the radiators in the house and multiply it times seven. This gives you the total area to be covered; then it's easy to figure out how much paint you need to buy to cover that area.

● Many radiators have a sort of metal shelf over the top. Since the shelf doesn't get too hot, many people use the shelf as a place to put all sorts of things. Problem is, all the stuff you put on the shelf acts as insulation and prevents a lot of the heat from rising from the radiator and doing its thing. Use it as a shelf in the summer, but not winter.

● In the spring and summer, floor furnaces are nothing more than dust catchers. I made covers for ours that keep the dust out and even look nice, too. I cut a piece of Masonite to fit the opening. Then I got a carpet scrap that matches our carpets and attached it. In the kitchen, I used vinyl tile to match that floor.

● Rather than spend money on covers for the turbine vents on my roof, I took plastic trash bags and put one of these over each vent. Then I used wide waterproof duct tape to attach the bags securely to the vents. Next spring, I'll be able to take the trash bags off and use them for garbage, so I've really done the covering with no investment.

Did you ever feel a chill and go over to turn up the thermostat, only to find out the temperature's already in the upper seventies? Other times you can be perfectly snug with a lower reading. The difference is the humidity. If the air in your house is too dry, you'll feel cold; and unless you already have a humidifier, you'll do well to add moisture to the air. Of course, if you add too much moisture, you end up with condensation and all the other problems excess moisture can cause.

The happy medium is somewhere slightly above 40 percent humidity. Before you decide what kind of humidifier to add, find out for sure if you need one. An inexpensive humidity indicator will be a good investment and will let you know. Proper heat and proper humidity equal comfort.

● A container of water on top of space heaters evaporates to add humidity to a dry house.

● The same mister used for houseplants can fog the air when it's too dry. Aim it upward. The moisture is absorbed into the air and doesn't hit the floor.

Quite true—unless you have hard water in your area. Any minerals in the water will fall to the floor as a fine white powder. Use distilled water, or even rainwater, in any humidifier to keep the house clean and prolong the machine's life.

10.
HOUSEHOLD APPLIANCES

If I tried to cover all the repairs for individual appliances, you'd probably have a 26-volume set of books. However, I can tell you that right now, 3.2 people are forking over a handsome fee for an appliance-repair man to come out and do something anyone could do. Even if you haven't the foggiest notion how an appliance works, there are a couple of things to check before you call for help:

  1. Is it plugged in? Don't laugh. Maybe a kid or a cat came through and tripped over the wire. Is it worth twenty-five dollars to have someone plug in your TV?
  2. Is there any power to the unit? You might have a tripped circuit-breaker switch or a blown fuse, or the wall outlet could have gone bad.
  3. Is the cord or plug bad? Remember, with the unit disconnected, you can easily replace either of these without danger.
  4. Let's say you have examined all these things and can't find anything wrong. At least take a look inside to see if you spot a loose wire or some other obvious problem. Here again, with the appliance unplugged, you'll be safe with all but a few electronic devices that store current. (Unfortunately, the TV set can still shock until this stored power is discharged.)

  The best advice is to hang onto the owner's manual, plus any other material you get when you buy a new mechanical monster. Include warranties, guarantees, and the sales slip. In fact, one reader suggests putting all this material in a loose-leaf notebook. Then you'll have a guide that will help you at least make an effort to care for a problem. Many owner's manuals will have a troubleshooters' guide and a parts list.

● I liked the idea of a loose-leaf notebook to keep track of warranties and instructions on all the appliances, but around our house one of the children would probably use the binder for school. So I put these papers—as well as any others regarding a particular appliance—in a large envelope, and taped it to the back of the appliance. If anything goes wrong, the necessary documents are right there, and I don't have to form a search party to find them.

● You've sold me on the value of doing it myself, but if an appliance is still under warranty, be cautious about making any repairs. In some cases, doing even simple minor repairs can void the warranty.

● How many gadgets do you have that won't work without extra muscle power? How many make strange noises? Often, all the help they want is a drink of oil or appropriate lubricant. The use of the proper lube won't only stop the noise and ease the strain, but can often prevent great, sometimes fatal, damage to the gadget. The best guide to the proper lubricant is the printed material you got when you bought the thing. If you didn't keep it, use common sense and give the gadget a shot of something.

Here are some general appliance hints:

If you're like most of us, you've had the experience of fixing some gadget, getting it all back together, and finding you still have one small part left over. Sometimes it's a part that isn't vital, but usually not. You may avoid this by making a simple organizer and parts holder. Just take a sheet of white typing paper and fold it accordion fashion, creating peaks and valleys. As you disassemble, place the tiny parts in order in the valleys. Don't overcrowd. When you're ready to put the thing back together, reverse the order; you'll not only get all the parts back in, but know which goes back in first. Then you won't have to have a container in the shop marked "Leftovers." (Incidentally, I have several such containers, but I mark the cans "Spare Parts" rather than admit what they really are.)

● When disassembling a small appliance, I use a calendar to help me keep track of the sequence in which the parts are removed. It's last year's wall calendar, with big squares for each day. I put this down on the workbench, and the first part goes in the first square, etc. When I get ready to put the thing back together, I start backwards. It makes reassembly a lot easier. If a part's too big to fit in a square, I put it at the top of the column and leave that square blank. Maybe this will help others who always end up with a few leftover parts.

● When repairing a small appliance, a good way to keep track of all the parts is to use a magnetic knife-holder bar. Just place it next to your work area, and as you remove parts, let the magnet hold them for you. This also lets you keep track of the sequence in which they were removed so you can get everything back in place in the proper order.

● Many small screws and parts that come out of appliances look so much alike that when putting the thing back together, you have to resort to trial and error. You can do away with this fiddling around if you draw a rough sketch of the parts, then place each part at its proper place on the diagram as you take it off.

• When you are taking an appliance apart, a blackboard eraser is an excellent organizer for small parts. The parts can be poked down between the sections in the order in which they are removed. They are organized and can't roll away. The soft eraser material also doesn't scratch up anything.

• When I take an appliance apart, the biggest problem is getting all the wires connected back where they belong. As I dismantle, I mark each wire and its connection with a different colored crayon (lighter colors on dark wires and vice versa). Connecting parts can also be color-coded with crayons. They will mark on practically anything and come in a wide variety of colors. For the few things that won't hold wax markings, I use felt markers as you once suggested.

• Groups of wires in appliances usually need a harness to keep them from getting all tangled up. Instead of using tape on small wires, I cut one-inch lengths of plastic drinking straws. These are slit and then slipped over the wires at points where harnesses are needed. They are easier to use than tape and do a neat job.

• Like most apartment dwellers, I don't have many tools. However, I have learned that getting appliances level is most important to their efficiency. Since I didn't have a level, I improvised, using an ice tray. I filled it almost to the top of the partitions, which made it very easy for me to see whether the surface I placed it on was level or not. It's actually easier to tell at a glance than with a regular level.

• Do people still eat off of TV trays? We don't, but when you're taking a small appliance apart, a TV tray is an ideal work table. It's a good height. All the parts can be kept right together, and the tray won't let anything roll off and get lost. The only hazard is a kid on a trike who might run into the tray. This causes parts to scatter into a minimum of three rooms.

• The vibration from a motor-driven appliance often causes a screw to get loose. Sometimes this can cause trouble and even stop the appliance. About every six months, I get out my screwdrivers and go all around the house and tighten screws. Just for fun, I kept track of how many had worked loose. I actually tightened thirty-eight. At the same time I'm tightening, I have a chance to see if anything else looks wrong.

• Did you ever carefully reach into the back of an appliance with your screwdriver and accidentally touch the wrong thing? *Zap!* You knew you should have unplugged it. However, why not make yourself a plastic screwdriver that won't cause the fireworks? Just take an old toothbrush and grind or file down the end into a screwdriver tip. It's easy to do. Then use fine sandpaper to smooth it. The brush end is also handy for brushing out dust without shorting anything out.

• If some appliances such as a refrigerator or freezer are accidentally unplugged, it can be disastrous. I've rigged a simple lock that keeps the plug in place in its outlet. I twist a strand of insulated wire around the neck of the plug, leaving a pigtail of a few inches sticking out.

Then I trim the wire so it's long enough to reach the screw in the middle of the cover plate. I strip off the insulation at the end, and with the plug in place in the outlet, I use the tiny screw to anchor the wire end to the plate. Now there's no easy way to disconnect accidentally.

● Several small appliances and tools come with suction-cup feet so you can anchor the gadget wherever you're going to use it. When you put it up on the shelf between usings, however, the suction cups have a way of sticking to the shelf. I slip plastic sandwich bags over the suction cups to prevent this. No big idea, but it can save a little aggravation.

● In recent years, most appliance colors have a code number. Sometimes there'll be a plate on the back with the code number. If not, check with the dealer and see if he has a record of your purchase. With that number, you can order a touch-up paint to match exactly. Otherwise, you'll have to try to match by sight.

● Ever try fine soldering on an appliance only to find the wire solder is too big? If you are going to use wire solder at such times, take your tin snips and slice it in half lengthwise. Fold one half back out of the way. This'll give you a smaller wire to work with.

CLOCKS

Most electric clocks have all the works inside a sealed unit, so there isn't much you can do to either tinker or lubricate. However, here are a couple of off-the-wall ideas you might try:

● Sometimes a noisy electric clock can be silenced by simply turning it upside down for a few hours and letting it run that way. I think it allows lubricant to be redistributed to the dry parts. It won't cure all clock problems, but it's worth a try before taking the thing apart.

... or even weirder:

● I fixed a noisy electric clock by putting it in a slightly warm oven. (Be sure it's not hot enough to melt the plastic case.) After about fifteen minutes I took it out, and it worked fine. The warmth softened the lubricant, which must have been holding dirt, and redistributed it so there was no longer a strain to cause the noise.

● After I inherited an old clock we had in the house, I found that a few months in the workshop did it in. When I took it apart, I found the reason. It had picked up a lot of floating sawdust. After I cleaned it, I sealed all the seams with paraffin and put masking tape around the openings from the stems on the back. Now no sawdust can get it. It was doing fine for about a year until I knocked it over.

COFFEEPOTS

Morning coffee should be at its best. Maybe these hints will help:

● After a vacation, you'll drag out the old coffee maker and probably find it doesn't make coffee as well as you remembered. Coffeepots need regular TLC, because even though they look clean, a residue can build up on the metal parts that makes the coffee slightly bitter. The best way to clean it is to brew a full batch, using baking soda instead of coffee in the basket. Let this go all the way through the brewing cycle, and then rinse it out, making sure you remove all the soda. Then your coffee won't have a bitter taste—except at the checkout counter.

● To avoid residue, odor, and bad flavors in an electric coffeepot, leave the pot full of water after you clean it, until the next time it's used.

● When a drip filter-type coffee maker makes coffee but won't keep it hot, remember there are two heating elements: One makes, the other warms. Probably you'll only have to replace the warming element to fix it. Your owner's manual should tell you where this element is and how to get at it.

TOASTERS

One thing that happens to all toasters is that crumbs fall off the bread. If yours has a crumb tray, be sure to empty it regularly. Also check the elements for particles. Never stick a knife or fork into the toaster to remove particles or to retrieve a piece of toast while the unit is plugged in. That's a deadly way to convert your toaster to a curling iron.

● This is probably not very orthodox, but I repaired a faulty toaster this way. It wouldn't work, so I looked inside and spotted a resistance-type heater wire that had broken. After trying several unsuccessful ways to rejoin the wire, I clipped a small section of hollow metal tube from inside an old ball-point pen. I fitted each end of the broken wire into the tiny tube, then crimped it tight against the wire ends. When I plugged in the toaster, I stepped back to avoid any fireworks, but to my surprise and pleasure, it worked.

● If your toaster works only on one side of a piece of bread, it means that an element on the untoasted side has burned out. Don't bother trying to repair the element, as this repair will probably be very temporary. Replace it. You may have to order the element from the factory.

APPLIANCES FOR HAIR

The first key to using any of the several types of electric curlers, blowers, dryers, and stylers is to follow all the directions and suggestions in the owner's manual. Never use them while bathing, and keep them away from water. If you should ever drop one into a basin, don't try to pick it up until the cord is disconnected. Other than that, keep 'em clean.

Don't use a curling iron on wigs made of synthetic hair. Don't use hair spray until after you're through curling, as the spray can clog the steam vents.

All types of blowers and dryers have to have free air flow. Be sure that your curly locks haven't fallen out and clogged the places where the air goes in.

● The plastic hose on a hair dryer is one of the most vulnerable parts, because most are made with wire rings that give the hose its rigidity. A size-ten foot on the hose can bend the wires. You can look like a hero with your wife or daughter by straightening out the hose. All you need to do is insert the end of a broom handle in the hose to the smashed point and force the bent wires back out. They can be reformed with your hand around the handle. Then next time, watch where you step.

● When my daughter's hair dryer gave out, I rescued the plastic hose and attached it to the sawdust-discharge spout of my radial-arm saw. With it in place, the sawdust is carried away from the table top and doesn't get in my eyes or all over the work.

REFRIGERATORS

The refrigerator is about as dependable as any appliance you have. It can continue to serve you for years without too much maintenance *if* you keep the word "cleanliness" in mind. If you let dirt and dust collect on the evaporator coils (a series of tubes usually on the back) the dust makes the compressor work harder. Use a hose attachment on your vacuum cleaner to clean the evaporator as well as the dirt and dust around the motor and compressor (Figure 42). Here's proof it works.

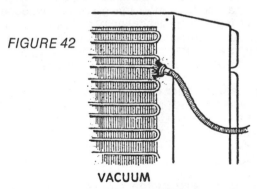

FIGURE 42

VACUUM
CONDENSER COILS

● The efficiency of our refrigerator had gone way down. I decided to take a crack at seeing what was wrong. When I opened up the compartment below where the works are, it was so covered with dust and grime I told my wife she'd have to vacuum it before I could tell anything about it. She did. Somehow, I didn't get around to looking at it right away, but a few days later my wife complimented me on fixing it. My buddies at the plant seem to think the thick dust wasn't allowing it to work at peak efficiency. So if any husbands are faced with the same task, try this first. What have you got to lose?

Also, check the pan under the unit. This has a tube that drains condensate from inside. The tube must be positioned so it drains into the pan. Should it become clogged, this condensate water will end up inside the box, and you'll have a mess. Fungus is often the cause for clogging, and this can be poked out with a wire or dissolved with a few drops of liquid laundry bleach. Keep the pan clean or you'll have an odor problem.

Another reason for water inside the box is that air from the house is getting inside. This could be because you spend too much time with the door open. Families with kids or with a beer-drinking brother-in-law often have this problem; or that air could be coming in around a bad gasket or because of loose hinges.

● In case you think the value of the dollar is nil, that one skinny dollar can save you lots of money. Many refrigerators allow cold air to leak out around the gasket on the door. Close the door with a dollar bill inserted between the gasket and the box. With the door shut, the dollar bill should require a tug to remove. If it comes out easily, you probably don't have a seal tight enough to keep in the cold, and the gasket may need replacing.

● A bad seal of the gasket around the edge of the refrigerator door costs you money. This isn't always caused by the rubber gasket going bad, however. Dirt and crumbs can also create this problem. Particles that get behind the gasket or on its surface can prevent a proper seal. Also, grease and dirt that collect on the surface of the box can prevent a tight seal. None of you would have dirt problems, of course, but maybe you could pass this along to some of your messier neighbors.

● The gasket strip around the refrigerator door can lose its bounce when it gets old, and may not stick up far enough to seal in the cold. It's easy to replace, but sometimes you have to wait a while for the new one because they don't always have all models in stock. Until you get the replacement, cut up a shirt board, making little strips the width of the space behind the gasket. Poke the cardboard behind the gasket, and it will usually push it out enough so your refrigerator doesn't lose its cool.

● The magnetic door latch on a refrigerator might have ceased working because the house settled, and the unit is no longer level.

● Most noisy freezers or refrigerators aren't sick. The noise is usually caused by vibration. Check to see if you can spot any loose parts, loose motor mounts, or contact from any outside objects. Also, make sure the unit is level. This can cause noise and also puts a big strain on the motor.

● For years our refrigerator made noise, but I didn't know what to do. Then Uncle Charlie came to visit. He said the copper tubing that brought the water to the ice maker was vibrating against the wall when the motor ran. He placed a slit section of garden hose around the tubing at the point of contact, and there's no more noise. We're almost glad Uncle Charlie came.

● My refrigerator, not the automatic-defrosting kind, used to take half a day to defrost. Then I tried an experiment that works great. After a defrost, I sprayed the freezer compartment's interior walls with some of the vegetable-oil spray that keeps things from sticking to pans. The next defrost was done in about forty-five minutes because the frost just slid right off with no chipping, gouging, or cussing.

● For repairing the molded plastic shelves in your refrigerator door, there is a new epoxy that's just what the doctor ordered. It will work without your having to remove all the food for a day to let the refrigerator warm up. This epoxy is the kind that dries in five minutes. The quick-drying element also allows it to harden in below-freezing temperatures. It won't harden in five minutes in colder temperatures, but it will solve your problem.

● Thanks to an overly smart builder, the only place in our kitchen for the range and refrigerator is side by side. That is certainly convenient but we soon found our refrigerator had to work overtime because of the heat from the range. I got a piece of acoustical ceiling material that also has good insulating qualities. This material is only one-half–inch thick, the exact space between the appliances. I taped a layer of aluminum foil around one side of the material and wedged this between the stove and refrigerator with the foil side facing the range. This really has taken the strain off the refrigerator.

● Copper tubing used as fuel and water lines to such add-ons as ice makers can easily be bent to fit into place. However, the bending is usually trial and error, with time wasted holding the tubing in place after each bend. If you take a piece of heavy wire and bend it to form a pattern, you can then bend the tubing to the exact shape against the pattern. Saves time!

● A power failure can be disastrous to a locker full of frozen foods. If the power is off long enough, the food could spoil. Then when the power comes back on, it will refreeze, and you might not know until you prepare it. If you're away on vacation, how are you going to know if there has been such a failure? No sweat. Put an ice cube in a glass container. If it melts, it won't refreeze in cube form, and so you'll know the power's been off.

● I know there are new paints for the enameled finishes on kitchen appliances, but we live out in the country, and nearby stores don't carry them. So when our refrigerator got chipped, I resorted to an old technique that my father used before those new paints existed. I covered the chipped place with crayon to match, and kept rubbing until enough crayon was on to level the surface. The I put a piece of cellophane tape over this spot and pressed it with a hot iron. This smoothes the surface and melts the crayon so it bonds to the surroundings. It is an excellent cover-up, seals out moisture so no rust gets started, and won't come off unless hit with something sharp.

● If you've bought a new refrigerator and have kept the old one, go out right now and remove the door to that empty unit. These things are very attractive hiding places for kids, and are usually fatal. The door can be put back on when you move the appliance out to your lake house or wherever. Even if you're storing a box temporarily while living in a furnished apartment, kids get in to play in community storerooms even though the areas are locked. Do it now! Most communities have laws against leaving empty boxes around without some means of protection.

● Here is a useful way to get rid of the old death-trap refrigerator. I made mine into a worm bed, where I grow the most fantastic fishing worms in the whole state. I dug a pit big enough for the box to go in lying down with the opening facing up. Once I had it in the ground, I filled it with rich dirt, and added coffee grounds and table scraps. An old window screen covers the opening. I also added beet juice, and the worms have a reddish look that really attracts fish.

DISHWASHERS

Time was that the dishwasher was a member of the family. Another member dried, and even though everybody griped about doing the dishes, it provided time to converse. Now the dishes are thrown into a mechanical monster; if it doesn't run right, the owner's manual should have some troubleshooting steps for your particular brand.

However, all types should be checked periodically to be sure the drain is clear. Undrained dirty water can result in less-than-squeaky-clean dishes. Remove the bottom dish rack, and you should be able to see how to get to the filter over the drain. You may find that missing piece of silver, a piece of aluminum foil, or maybe just food particles. Clean the filter with a stiff brush and detergent. Also check the sprayer arms to be sure the small holes aren't clogged. Use a wire or ice pick to clean them, as a toothpick often breaks off in the hole, and you'll spend an extra hour on the job.

● Our dishwasher was doing a lousy job, and my wife kept changing detergents. Finally, she was about to call a serviceman when I figured out the problem. The hot-water heater was so far away from the dishwasher that we weren't getting any hot water until toward the end of the cycle. There was a single solution: I just turned on the hot water at the sink and let it run until it was hot. Then when I turned on the dishwasher, it started off with hot water. Now the dishes look like those in TV commercials.

● The drain hose on our portable dishwasher began to leak at the connection. A quick check revealed that the washer was going bad. Knowing that my husband would procrastinate on getting a new one, I used an old trick to repair the connection temporarily. I took the washer out and reversed it. This put the chewed-up side down in the hose and left a new good side to seal the connection. I know this is strictly temporary, but it should last just about as long as it will take my husband to remember to bring home a new one. (It's not like he has to go out of his way; he works at a hardware store.)

WASHERS AND DRYERS

The clothes washer and dryer are two entirely different appliances, but are in the same room. Let's talk about how to care for them.

The most common problem with a dryer is overheating, which causes the unit to cut off. Nine times out of ten, the cause is a clogged lint filter. This should be cleaned after every load. A partially clogged filter can cause slower drying, and thus larger utility bills. Another place where you could have a clogging problem is in the exhaust system. Check it with a flexible hose to see if the exhaust hose has developed a sag, and be sure the vent is free.

Both washers and dryers work better when level. Sight your level on these units; most have adjustable feet. If not, put shims under the legs until the surface is level.

Most washing machines also have a lint filter, and it too should be cleaned after every load. There are also small screens at the point where the water goes into the machine. These can become clogged with particles from the water supply and can cause the machine to fill slowly or not at all. Remove the screens and use a brush and vinegar to solve this problem. If they clog often, add a second set of screens at the other end where the hoses attach to the faucets.

● A washing machine that's ripping your clothes up could have a rough spot inside. First check the agitator and see if there is a broken spot. Then take an old nylon stocking and run it all around the inside. After you have found the snag, you should be able to remove it or smooth it over. Another cause for ripped clothes is a zipper left down. The teeth plus the movement can cut up your linens. Keep your flies zipped.

● Spring-type hose clamps aren't always easy to use, because you have to hold the two tips apart with one hand to widen the opening while you install with the other. When the hose is in some out-of-the-way place, like behind a washing machine, the chore becomes next to impossible. If you wrap wires around the tips to hold the clamp open, you've freed one hand. When the hose and clamp are in place, then reach down and snip the wire so the clamp can close tight.

● I have always believed that constant water pressure against the mixer valve in an automatic washer will cut down on the life of the valve. Therefore, I've suggested that my wife reach back and turn the two faucets off after each washing. In our new home, however, the cutoffs are too low to be easily reached. I found there is an in-line cutoff designed for use on a garden hose. By coupling the hoses and the washing machine with a pair of these units, my wife can reach this cutoff easily and thus remove the pressure.

BLENDERS AND MIXERS

● Electric mixers are great, but at times a rotary hand beater is more practical. Only trouble is, these gadgets are hard to dry, and eventually the gears get rusty. I oiled mine, and the next cake I made was ruined by the oily taste. Then I got smart and used cooking oil as a lubricant. I oil the gears regularly with this. No rust, and no disasters because the cooking oil has no taste.

● You have suggested vegetable-oil lubrication where the appliance is used for food preparation to avoid getting any oily taste on the food. I've found that you can also use glycerin as a lubricant. It won't ruin food and does a good job of making gears work better.

● Many of your readers seem to delight in sneaking items out of the kitchen for use in home handyman chores. I pulled a switch on this when my electric mixer went on the blink. I went out to the garage and borrowed my husband's electric drill. By inserting a mixer blade into the drill, I was able to finish the cake without having to blend the ingredients by hand. I hope you'll point out to other wives that two can play the same game.

● We discovered that each time my wife turns on her electric mixer, it causes static on the radio down in my basement shop. Rather than try to fix it, we use it as a signal for her to let me know when I'm needed upstairs.

RADIOS AND TELEVISIONS

These electronic gadgets usually require more technical expertise and often more exotic test equipment than we average folk will have. And going into even an unplugged TV set can be dangerous. There are components that retain a charge. Also, more than a few tinkerers have done more damage to the set than there was before they started. Many times, however, TV problems are caused by the antenna or lack of proper adjustment. Read the owner's manual and find out how to adjust. Here are some electronic tips from the column:

● Other than yelling her lungs out, how does your wife in the house let you know that your adjustments of the TV antenna on the roof are right? We ran my trouble light out the window and into the the yard, where I could see it from the roof. My wife had the plug inside. When the picture began to get better, she plugged it in and out, causing the light to flash. Longer flashes meant it was improving. When it was perfect, she left it on. It was sure a lot better than running to the window.

● With an insulated handle, there's not much danger to you when using a screwdriver to work on a radio, TV, or other electrical appliance. If the blade accidentally touches the wrong thing, however, it can short out something and do damage. I wrap all but the tip of the screwdriver with electrician's tape and remove that problem.

● Your TV reception will be much better if you replace the entire length of antenna wire and have no splices. And when you put in the new wire, use only as much as you need—don't try to coil up any excess in the walls. The antenna and its wire are very important to good reception.

● Recently I was attaching some wires to my radio for an extra speaker. When I got ready to solder, I found the tip in my solder gun had worn out, and I didn't have any more on hand. I remembered my wood-burning set and found that the burning tool would do the same job as a solder gun, plus it's really better for getting into tight spots.

● The speaker on a small radio developed a crack, and the result was a rather fuzzy tone. I discovered that the speaker cone was a sort of paper, and so before sending it to the shop, I decided to see what I could do to patch it. I put a piece of tissue paper over the cracked place and cemented it down with nail polish. The fuzzy tone is gone, and the radio sounds like brand new.

● Not long ago I opened up the back of a radio to see if I could spot a tube that had gone out. I noticed there was an accumulation of dust all over the wiring and other parts. I reasoned that this wasn't helping, but also figured that trying to brush it out would probably disconnect some vital gadget. I got a drinking straw and was able to blow the dust out of the tight spots and really got the insides pretty clean. I also found the burned-out tube.

● The biggest drawback to our apartment is that our neighbors below complain about my stereo, and I've had to go to headphones for my evening listening. When they're not being used, I keep the headset on a cheap plaster bust of Beethoven I bought at the variety store. This keeps the headset in easy reach, yet it is up where it cannot be damaged. Besides, it's a conversation piece when I have company.

STOVES

Here are some thoughts to make your home on the range a little more pleasant:

● If you want to save some money, quit buying expensive oven cleaners. Just fill up a large, flat dish with household ammonia and place it in the oven in the evening. If the oven door doesn't seal tightly, tape around the door with masking tape. Leave this overnight. The vapors work on the oven all night long and loosen the residue. The next morning, use a sponge with more ammonia on it, and all the baked-on guck will wipe right off.

● In a gas oven the thermocoupler, next to the pilot light, is a little rod that sticks up and is bathed by the flame. Oven cleaner can damage this rod, so it's a good idea to protect it during the cleaning. Wrap it and the pilot in aluminum foil, and you won't have to be so careful. This preventive maintenance will save you a possible repair job later on.

● Our kitchen exhaust fan is used for only a few minutes a day. The rest of the time it sits there, causing a draft, letting cool or warm air escape, and making a little clanging noise as wind moves through the vent. By gluing magnets on a piece of vinyl flooring cut to fit over the outlet, we make a cover that stays in place and closes the outlet. The vinyl is left over from the kitchen floor, so it looks right at home. The air we've cooled or heated can no longer escape, and the noise is gone. When my wife uses the vent, the cover is easily removed, and sticks to the metal hood with the magnets.

● Our house has an island range in the center of the kitchen with a hanging hood and cabinets over it. I installed a clock in the cabinets that is a real conversation piece. The clock was an old one that had a broken face. I removed the hands and drilled a hole in the cabinet for the center stem to fit through. The works went inside the cabinet. The hands were reinstalled outside on the end of the cabinet. We glued tile dots to indicate the three, six, nine, and twelve o'clock positions. I spliced into the wiring for the vent fan so there are no exposed wires.

● Most people realize the importance of clean filters on air-conditioning and heating units, but do you know that exhaust fans have filters too? An exhaust fan in the kitchen takes away a lot of steam with grease in it, and this collects on the filter. After a while it can become a fire hazard, plus cutting down on the efficiency of the fan. In most kitchens, cleaning this filter every week isn't too often. Most can be washed in the dishwasher or with warm water and detergent. The fan will do a better job and last longer.

● The heater coils unplug on most electric ranges, so it is a simple matter to order a replacement and install them yourself (Figure 43). The units are interchangeable, so to be sure the problem is in the unit, try one that works in the place where the nonworking one has been. If that isn't it, then check the wiring. Be sure to shut off power to the range while you're messing around in it.

FIGURE 43

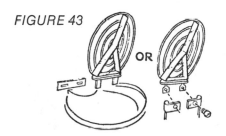

● You once urged us to make sure motor-driven appliances are level, since being out of kilter puts a greater strain on the motor. I'd like to suggest also that a level be used on kitchen stoves. I love to bake, and when we moved into a new apartment, my cakes began to look not as perfect as I liked. Finally I figured out that all the layers were a tiny bit lopsided. Sure enough, the range wasn't level. By correcting this, I'm again the champion of the culinary arts.

VACUUM CLEANERS

● While I was cleaning up for my bridge club, my vacuum-cleaner belt broke. No time to go get a new belt, so I tried a rubber ring I had left over from some home canning. Voilà! It lasted until about a half second before I was through, and I got my vacuuming done in time.

● There's nothing more frustrating to a housewife than to find the extension tubes on a tank-type vacuum cleaner stuck so tightly together that they can't be separated. Rather than wait for the strong man in your life to put brute force to work, try holding the stuck connection over a burner for a few moments. The heat will expand the outer tube, and you'll be able to twist it off. Be sure not to get your fingers too close to the spot you heated, or you'll burn 'em. Also, don't let the heat affect the tubing. Just a little quick warmth will do the job.

WATER HEATERS

The water heater is another champion that just keeps on working. Most carry good, long warranties, and you can get even more life from the unit with a little bit of care. First of all, in most homes you don't need the setting on Hi. Even the automatic dishwasher will require water temperature at around 140 degrees F or less. The higher setting will create much hotter water and may even make steam that causes noisy rumblings in the tank. For most purposes, you temper the water with cold, so it's a waste of energy too.

Another heater problem is that the water contains chemicals that become solids. This sediment settles to the bottom of the tank and can cause rumbling in a gas-heated tank or whistling in an electric one. It also cuts way down on the efficiency of a gas-fired water heater. To remove the sediment, you need to drain water off the bottom of the tank.

Your unit will have a drain cock that looks sort of like an outside hydrant. Attach the hose and lead the water to a sink or outside. Drain off just a little to see if there is sediment in the water. Then continue to drain until the water runs clean. The best time to do this is usually in the morning, before anyone has used any hot water. Therefore, all the sediment will have settled to the bottom, and you'll get rid of more of it. In some areas the sediment is so bad you have to drain almost once a month. In others, you just need to check it once a year.

If you've never used the drain cock, it may be hard to turn. If so, don't play King Kong. You'll be better off with sediment than with water gushing out from where the drain cock used to be. Sometimes after a water-heater drain is opened, it will drip. Rather than try to replace the washer, just go to the hardware store and purchase a hose cap. It screws onto the tap and seals the leak.

A pilot light that won't stay lit on your gas unit may need a new thermocouple. We discuss this in chapter 9 in the section on heating systems.

● Most gas appliances have a shutoff valve right next to the unit. Some have a handle and are easy to shut off; others have a rectangular knob that requires a wrench to turn. In an emergency, you may have to waste too much time finding a wrench. Why not buy several cheapies from the bargain bin and tie them to the pipe so they hang there ready in case of emergency. If the gas meter also has this type of cutoff, hang one there too. If the meter is outside, however, encase it in a plastic bag. Otherwise, the wrench may become too rusted to use.

● Here's a hint for those with an electric hot-water heater. (Why do they call it a hot-water heater? Isn't that redundant?) I put a timer on mine to turn it off at night and then back on in the morning in time to have hot water when we get up. Then, since we both work, I have the timer turn it off when we leave and back on before we get home. On weekends we leave it on during the day. It has saved us quite a bit.

Here's the rotten way to approach appliance problems:

● I'm the most unhandy husband in the country. However, I have carefully built a reputation by every so often sneaking in and removing a part or undoing a wire to one of our household gadgets. When my wife discovered the thing didn't work, she would ask me to take a look. I would drag out my tools, fiddle around for a respectable length of time, and then, presto! When I say we need to call in a pro, my family knows it is in really bad shape.

11.
OUTDOORS

For the do-it-yourselfer, the great outdoors is more than just a good-looking green lawn. "Thank goodness for that," say I. Not being blessed with green thumbs, I've had to depend on fences and patios to find much to crow about outside. As you'll see later on, however, I have learned some tricks to make my brown thumbs seem a little greener.

ROOFS

Let's start at the top of the outside world. Everyone spends a lot of money to provide a roof overhead, and yet few do very much to care for the roof itself. What can you do? Well, for one thing, keep all trees from touching the roof. Branches can rip off shingles as wind blows through the trees. Trees (or any vegetation) also hold moisture against the roof, which can cause rot and fungus. Vines that grow up the side of the house and onto the roof may grow under the shingles and heave them up. Trim back trees and vines, and make sure they are checked regularly.

What about leaks? When a roof leak occurs, many people assume that wherever the water shows up on the ceiling inside the house is directly below where the leak is. If you get up on the roof and patch away, you may be surprised when the next rainstorm comes and you still have a waterfall in the living room. Often the water from a leak will run as much as several feet down a rafter before it drips off.

Best time to track down a leak is when it's actually raining. Get into the attic and spot the point of entry. During a rainstorm is the *worst* time to get out on the roof for repairs, however, so put out buckets, or do some temporary repairing—and wait until the roof is safe to work on.

● Water that runs down a rafter and drips off into the bucket you've positioned will suddenly change its mind and drip at a point farther down the rafter. Control the drip by tacking a string to the rafter, across the stream of water. Run the string straight down into the bucket—it works.

Be sure you mark the spot within the attic so you'll repair the right place. If you don't want to wait for rain, you may be able to spot water stains in the attic that will let you know where the flood is coming in.

● In most cases you can temporarily patch the leak from inside by covering the hole with asphalt patching compound. Then when the weather is better and it's safe to walk on the roof, you can fix it right.

● Cover a scrap of plywood with a generous coating of patching compound. Press this against the underside of the roof (Figure 44) with the hole centered on the scrap. Use a precut two-by-four to wedge between the patch and the attic floor. Make it a tight fit, and the patch will stay in place—and the water will stay out.

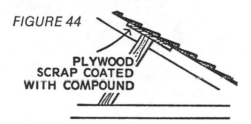

FIGURE 44

PLYWOOD
SCRAP COATED
WITH COMPOUND

After you've pinpointed the trouble spot on the inside, here's what to look for on the outside. Flashing is one of the chief breakdowns. Flashing is used to seal a junction between the roofing material and another surface or in valleys between different slopes. Metal is often used. On a composition roof, composition strips are often used. Holes in the flashing are easy to spot and can be treated with asphalt roofing compound (the same's true for seams that may be taking in water). You can buy this in bulk for application with a wide-bladed knife, or in a cartridge for use with a caulking gun. When in doubt, I always run a bead of the roofing-cement compound along all the seams in the flashing.

● New nails driven into metal flashing on a roof should have a dab of asphalt roof-patching compound over each nailhead. I didn't have any, but used plastic metal solder. Just a dab spread thin over each nail, and they are waterproof. Also, they sure look a lot neater than with that black guck.

Wood shingles sometimes curl when they dry out. This can cause splitting, and if the split is over a space between two shingles or over another split, it can result in a leak. Sometimes you can put a piece of building paper or a piece of metal under the split shingle and stop the leak. Any exposed nails used in securing the patch or in nailing down a loose shingle should be covered with a dab of "black guck." Badly warped shingles can sometimes be nailed down, but often the effort to nail them down will split them. A damaged wood shingle that can't be repaired should be replaced.

● To raise up shingles for roof repair, a long flat shovel is a very good tool. The blade will easily slip under the shingle without damaging it. Then when it's in place, a gentle step on the handle acts as a pry bar to raise the shingle without splitting it. This leaves both your hands free to work under the shingle.

Since the nails are hidden, in removing the bad shingle you must be careful not to wreck more of the roof. There's a tool that'll slide under the shingle to cut the nails holding the bad shingle. However, most of us don't have this tool and wouldn't want to buy it for a single replacement. A hacksaw blade removed from the saw frame can do the job.

Just raise the shingle slightly, and often you'll be able to wiggle it back and forth without disturbing the adjacent good shingles. Usually the wiggle will split the shingle at the two points where the nails are holding it. If the nails are still in place, they'll be in the way of the replacement.

Slide the new shingle in place until it hits the nails. Push the edge so the nails will leave an imprint on the edge of the shingle. Then remove it and saw a line at each imprint to form nail slots that'll allow the replacement to slip in all the way. You can't blind-nail the new shingle, of course, so when you've secured it, cover the nail heads with roofing compound.

● Did you ever try to shingle a roof with the wind blowing? If you don't watch it, about half of your bundle of shingles will blow away. I solved this problem by merely draping a tire chain across them. This weights down the shingles, and still lets me pull out one from the bundle without having to move my weight.

One of composition shingles' biggest problems is that they tend to curl up at the edges and allow a leak. Blobs of roofing cement under the corners can hold the tips down. To avoid breaking off the tips, however, it's best to bend composition shingles when they are warm and pliable, so do this on a warm, sunny day.

● Put a heat lamp on an extension cord, and with a few moments of heat, composition shingles are softened and again pliable. A dab of mastic under the corners will flatten them out permanently.

Remove a damaged shingle by lifting the edges of overlapping shingles to get at the nails holding the bad guy. Again, don't try to bend a cold shingle or it will snap off. When securing the new shingle, you'll end up with exposed nails, so cover the heads.

● I had some roofing cement left over, and since the last batch hardened in the can, I decided to experiment with a new way to store it. Since it wasn't a water-soluble mixture, I poured in enough water to cover the surface. Next time I needed to use the material, I just poured off the water, and the stuff was as soft and pliable as the first time I had opened the can. Maybe this same principle will work on other materials that aren't water soluble.

● If you or any of your neighbors are replacing a roof with new composition shingles, be sure to latch onto a few leftover strips of the roofing. Stash them in the trunk of your car. When you run into an icy or wet spot where your car won't do anything but sit and spin its wheels, place the strips under the rear tires. This will give you excellent traction and get you going again.

Leaks in the valleys of any roof are usually from holes. Before replacing the valley, try to patch the hole with roofing cement.

The built-up or flat roof is often a problem because there's very little slope to carry the water away. Usually it's fairly easy to find the leak, however, because it will usually be just above where it shows up underneath.

There are sometimes low spots where water collects. In a flat roof, blisters often indicate a trouble spot. These are easy to repair. First remove the gravel over the blister, if any. Then use a utility knife to cut a slit in the blister (be careful not to cut into the layer of roofing below). Now use a putty knife to fill under the blister with asphalt roofing compound.

Use roofing nails to nail down the material on both sides of the slits. Put a dab of the asphalt cement over each nail head. Next, cut part of a composition shingle or a square of tar paper that covers the area and extends beyond the slit by several inches. Coat the area with roofing cement and then nail down the patch, again using flat-headed roofing nails. Cover these with roofing cement, and then cover the seam around the patch.

For a bigger damaged area, it's best to remove the top layer and cut a patch of the exact size and shape. A rectangular patch will be easier to match. Use cement and nails just as with the patch above. Then add an oversized patch to cover and extend beyond the first.

If the whole roof has problems, remove all the gravel and use asphalt roof paint. This is similar to the black guck, but easier to spread—with a special roof brush. Start at the high point and work toward the edges. Be sure to leave a path to work from; come back and cover it when the rest has set up. While the paint is still wet, spread the gravel back on. Gravel reflects heat which could shorten the life of the roof paint.

● When nailing into corrugated metal roofing, special nails with washers under the head are suggested to prevent leaks. Not having any of these nails, and not wanting to drive thirty-seven miles into town to get them, I made my own. I put beads of silicone seal around under the head of the nails. After this cured, I had nails that were self-sealing when driven against the metal.

● When reusing metal roofing material, the old nail holes never end up where the new nails go. After I installed such a roof on my tool shed, I sealed all the old nail holes with fingernail polish.

GUTTERS AND DOWNSPOUTS

After water runs off the roof, it should go into gutters or eave troughs. Gutters collect not only water, they often collect leaves. You should keep them clean so that water can run off. This often requires removing the debris physically. Use a whisk broom or kitchen scraper and wear gloves. After the debris is gone, flush the gutters out with a blast from the hose.

● To clean the fall leaves out of the gutters, rather than doing my death-defying balancing act, I borrowed my wife's tank-type vacuum cleaner. By putting all of the sections together, and with a curved attachment on the end, I was able to reach up and into the gutters while standing on the ground. At times, large leaves stuck to or in the tube, but it was still easier than climbing up and moving a ladder—and much safer.

Or,

● Put the hose in the blower end and blast 'em out. [A shop vacuum is stronger and better.]
● I made a gutter rake that I like. I attached a loop, made from an old auto fan belt, to a long pole. The belt loop is flexible enough to conform in shape to the gutters, but firm enough to scoop out the leaves. The pole allows me to do the job with both feet on the ground.
● Rather than climb up on a ladder to inspect my gutters, I have a tool that lets me check them out from the ground. I taped an old auto rearview mirror to a broom handle. The mirror can be adjusted so I can see right in the gutters. That way, I only have to climb the ladder where there is a problem.

You may find that leaves have gone into the downspouts and have clogged them. If so, blasts from the hose at the top may clear them. If not, try a plumber's snake from the bottom. Then flush with the hose.

While you're cleaning the gutters, also look for low spots, rusted areas, or loose supports. A low spot can be found when you're flushing out the cleaned gutter with the hose. Normally, a sag is caused by a loose support—or just not enough supports. With most types of guttering, there should be supports about every three feet.

There are three basic types of supports used. One is a gutter spike, a long nail driven through a metal sleeve into the edge of the roof. If it's just loose, tap it back in. When it comes loose, however, it's often because the hole has become enlarged, so to anchor the spike, you may have to remove it and put some sort of filler in the hole. Epoxy putty does a good job there, but any of the exterior fillers will usually hold.

Another hanger is a strap nailed under the shingles. You won't be able to renail under the shingles in most cases, so when you renail through the shingle, cover the nail heads with guck.

The third type of support is nailed to the fascia under the gutter.

If it's not accessible, install a second bracket right next to the first. Both the bracket type and the support held by a strap may be specially designed for the guttering you have, but if you'll take a look, you'll see what's causing the sag—and some types can be adjusted.

Rusted areas should be treated immediately, before they become holes. Use a wire brush to remove as much of the rust as possible. Then put on a chemical rust remover; or sand down until the metal is clean. Once the rust is gone, cover the bare metal with paint or asphalt roofing cement. If the gutters are galvanized, there's a good spray-on galvanize.

If your sanding or brushing went all the way through the gutter, or if you discover a hole, here are some patching ideas. If rust was the cause, clean it away. Then cut a scrap of metal to cover the hole. (Be sure your patch is of the same type of metal so no electrolytic action starts to cause corrosion.) Clean both the gutter and the patch with a solvent. When they're dry, apply a generous amount of roofing cement around the edges of the hole, then press the patch firmly in place. Next, coat the patch with a thin layer of the cement, feathering it out from the edges.

If the hole is large or in a curved part of the sides, you may find it advantageous to cut a patch that follows the contour of the entire gutter at that point. It's best to make a paper pattern. Then when the pattern is made and the metal cut out, you can bend the metal in the shop or on the kitchen table. If you don't have sheet-metal bending aids, you can often close a door against the metal. The door holds it like a vise and allows you to bend in a straight line. But make it a door in the shop or someplace where a few marks on the door won't cause regrets.

When the piece is roughly formed, use the same technique for sticking it in place. Help it conform completely by crimping it around the edges with pliers. Paint the exposed side of any metal patch to match the old finish.

Almost any type of gutter can develop leaks where sections join at the seams. Sometimes metal guttering can be soldered at the joints, but the easiest way to repair is to seal with caulking or plastic metal.

● Most downspouts are composed of a number of sections. Often the edge of one piece is crimped to allow it to fit snugly into the adjoining one. If the fit isn't right, you probably have a piece that falls off every other week. Pop rivets can be installed from outside even though there is no access to the other side. All you have to do is drill a hole through both pieces, and join them with a pop-rivet tool. It's not an expensive tool, and after you've fixed the downspouts, you'll find lots of other ways to use it.

If you don't have gutters and downspouts, you should consider them. The rainwater may be falling directly off the roof, too close to the house, and be the cause of foundation problems. The water can also ruin flower beds or wash away your soil. Guttering is made for the do-it-yourselfer, and most home centers and hardware dealers that sell the components have printed instruction sheets that tell you how to plan for the installation, how to estimate your needs, and how to install the gutters and downspouts. The new plastic gutter systems may appeal to you because they are so nearly maintenance-free.

I'd be remiss if I didn't remind you that rooftop work can be dangerous. You're high to begin with, and then in most cases you'll be walking on a sloping surface. Play it safe, and you can do the job without having to suddenly learn how to fly. Never go out on a damp roof, which includes the early morning dew. If you have vision or inner ear problems, you have the perfect excuse to let someone else do it. A certain feeling of caution is good, but if you can't get over an abnormal fear, stay off the roof.

Wear sneakers or crepe-soled shoes, of course; but even so, test them for traction because not all shoes hold well to all roof surfaces. And be sure the laces are tight and aren't going to trip you.

● My old sneakers were so slick they didn't give me sure footing on the roof, so I made me some roof shoes. I glued scraps of indoor-outdoor carpet to the soles of an old pair of shoes, and cut the scraps to fit. This gives me the best traction I've had, and I feel safe even on a damp day.

● Slick-soled sneakers on a rooftop are almost as bad as cowboy boots as far as traction goes. Rather than take a chance, I put across the soles a few strips of that carpet tape that's sticky on both sides. It takes a few steps to get used to walking with these, but they have really great traction.

Don't wear clothes that are too bulky or too tight, as they could restrict your agility (if you have any). Watch out for power lines and for cables bringing electricity into your house. If there's any wind blowing, wait until it's calm; also, be sure there's no electrical storm in the offing. Some roofs have enough slope that it'll pay you to wear a rope harness anchored to the chimney or to something on the ground on the other side of the roof. There are devices that anchor a ladder to the ridge, which gives you very sure footing.

Always work low to the roof and scoot and crawl as much as possible. If you get overly nervous, sit down for a few moments and then scoot back to safety.

Splinters can be another hazard of roof work.

● Hold an ice cube against the hand (or knee, or thigh) where the splinter is embedded. After several seconds, this will deaden the area and allow you—or the amateur surgeon—to extract the spear with fewer screams. Even seems to make the splinters come out easier.

Roof work can be unsafe for those below, too, if you drop things on their heads. Maybe these ideas will help you keep things up there in tow.

● An old tire can act as a holder for your tools and materials. Unless the roof is very steep, the tire will stay in place; and your materials can be put in the ring and will stay. If there's any doubt, tie the tire to the chimney or something else, and you can be sure it won't slide. [Or use a swim float ring.]

● When you're working on the roof, a cigar box filled with sand becomes a dandy tool holder. Poked into the sand, tools will stand upright and be easy to reach. The sand gives the box enough weight so it won't slide around, but just to be sure, I put rubber bands around the box to make it nonskid.

● The minute you lay a hammer down on the roof, it goes sliding off. I solved this problem by gluing a pair of carpet scraps to each side of the hammer head. The carpeting makes it almost slip-proof.

● As an extra precaution, I put slide-proofers on the tools I carry up on a roof with me. I stick a few thumbtacks through the sticky side of a strip of masking tape. Then I wrap the tape around the tool, and the points of the tacks stick out all around (Figure 45). When the tool is put down on the slanting roof, the tacks keep it from sliding. Every tool has some place where tacks can be put so neither they nor the tape is in the way.

tools made
slide-proof by
tacks in tape

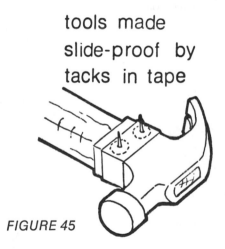

FIGURE 45

● I never got on the roof for any fix-it job without running out of nails or screws just before the job was finished. That meant a trip back down, and then back up. Now I keep an old tennis ball with a slit in it. By squeezing the ball, the slit opens, and a good quantity of small hardware goes in. When I'm on the roof and need something small, I yell for my wife. She fills up the tennis ball, and with the accuracy of a Tom Seaver, she fires it up to me. (Don't run for it if your pitcher isn't accurate.)

● The biggest problem to painting on a sloping roof is to keep the bucket level. You can't set it down on the roof unless it's half full, and then it's liable to slide off. I rigged up a wooden box with sand in it. I put the box on the roof, then spread the sand so it's level. The bucket then rests on this level surface. To prevent the box from sliding off, a series of small nails driven through the bottom act as spikes to keep it in place. This allows you to use both hands instead of having to carry a bucket in one hand.

● When you want to find the angle of a roof without climbing up there, stand off from the structure and hold up your zigzag ruler at arm's length. Sight along the ruler and line it up with the wall. Then fold the first section so it lines up with the roof. Now place this angle against a protractor, and it will show the angle of the roof.

For roof work and other outside chores, most of us use a ladder to get high. Be sure you remember all the safety rules in the Workshop chapter.

CONCRETE REPAIRS

Concrete is subject to cracks, and once a crack starts, it can soon become a canyon if you don't take care of it. Moisture gets in, and temperature changes expand and contract the masonry until that hairline is big enough to swallow your Volkswagen.

The easiest way to patch a small crack is with the type of concrete patch that comes in a cartridge for use with a caulking gun. There are also patching compounds of vinyl, epoxy, and latex that work well. Just be sure to follow the directions.

Preparation before patching is important. It's best to actually widen the crack with a chisel and hammer. As you do, undercut— making the crack wider under the surface than it is on the top (Figure 46). This gives the patch a better shot because it has something to hold

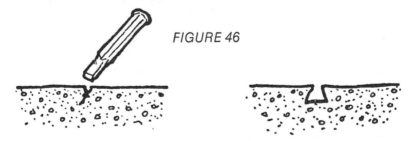

FIGURE 46

onto. (Always wear safety goggles when chipping concrete.) Use a wire brush to remove all the loose material, and then use a water or air hose to blast out what's left. If the crack goes all the way through the slab, pour in sand and tamp it below the surface. Leave the surfaces damp, but don't allow any standing water. It's best to use a bonding agent—a chemical that helps the new concrete adhere to the old. This can be bought where you buy concrete; be sure to follow directions. Tamp the patch into the crack with your trowel and be sure to remove any air pockets. When you have smoothed the patch to conform with the surface, keep the new concrete from drying out for about six days to let it cure. Cover it with a tarp, straw, burlap, or plastic sheeting. It should be examined each day, and if it's drying out, wet it down with a fine mist from the hose (big drops will pit the surface).

Breaking up a slab of concrete can be dangerous because the chips fly out. In addition to wearing protective clothes and goggles, I always place a large section of heavy screening down over the concrete. While sledge-hammer blows will eventually split the screen, it will hold up long enough to get most of the job done. The screen doesn't block your view, but where possible should be staked or tied down to the ground.

● Filling hairline cracks in concrete can be difficult, and a trowel usually isn't very helpful. One good way to do this is to put on a rubber glove and let your fingers do the spreading. You will do a much better job of getting the patching compound into the cracks and smoothing the finish as you go. Keep the finger wet, and the compound won't stick to it.

● Last winter I noticed small cracks in our concrete patio. I didn't want to chisel them out and mix up mortar to fix them properly, but I also didn't want to leave them for winter to damage. I had some leftover auto-body filler compound and reasoned that this would resist winter and should last until warmer weather. The compound is gray, so it doesn't look bad; and so far, all the cracks are still fixed.

● The plastic patching concrete that comes in caulking-gun tubes is much more expensive than mixing it yourself. Empty tubes can be reused, however, if you take care in removing the moveable bottom cap. Then refill the tube with the less expensive home mixture, and the convenience of the spout and gun can still help you in filling cracks.

● With all the handy ways to patch concrete, it may seem useless to come up with a substitute unless you live thirty-seven miles from the nearest source. I patched tiny cracks in our concrete barn floor with a mixture of two parts table salt and one part alum dropped into a small amount of boiling water. Keep adding until a thick paste is formed. This mixture can then be troweled into the cracks and forms an excellent patch.

Sometimes the surface of a large slab will start to flake off. After a rain you may discover birds bathing in the low places. Patch with the sand mix. It's also best to use the chisel and undercut around the edges. Matching the patch to the old part is more important here because the difference will be more apparent. Use of a bonder is a must because otherwise the patches will not adhere. When all the chiseling is done, use the same steps of wire brushing and hosing out the cavity. You're more likely to have standing water in this repair, so remove it with a sponge. Also give this repair the six-day cure.

The edges of steps and curbs often get chipped. Undercutting, bonding, matching, and curing apply here too. However, take a look at Figure 47 for the easy way to provide a form for this repair. Also, leave

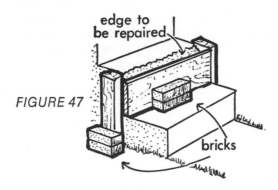

FIGURE 47

edge to
be repaired

bricks

the forms in place throughout the curing so some clod doesn't step on your work before it's cured.

Here are some tips for drilling into concrete.

● When a power drill can't be used, I attach the star drill to the head of my hammer with a large rubber band. This gives me a comfortable handle that relieves my hand of the shock of the constant pounding to drill the hole. It also moves my hand far enough away so I can't whock it if my aim gets bad. Yet I still have a solid hold and can rotate the drill back and forth.

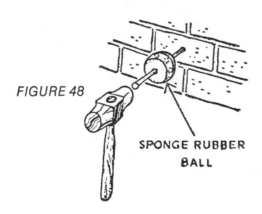

FIGURE 48

SPONGE RUBBER
BALL

● If you have ever used a star drill to make a hole in concrete, you know the perils of a misdirected hammer blow. Why not hold the drill with a pair of vise-grip pliers? Lock them to the shaft, and this will allow you to hold far enough away that a badly aimed shot won't get your hand. You'll also find the pliers make it easy to rotate the drill back and forth as you tap away. Or use a sponge rubber ball as shown in Figure 48.

● To know when a star drill or masonry drill starts to drift, draw a pair of lines at right angles to each other, crossing at the center of the hole to be drilled. Now you immediately see when the drift starts and can correct it.

● Drilling in concrete is certainly a lot easier with a power drill. It can be more accurate if you make a pilot hole with a masonry nail. Now the drill bit will start doing its thing without skidding away from the spot before the hole is started.

● Rather than take the drill out of the hole being drilled in concrete to dip the bit in water, I use a water pistol. I just stop the drill every so often and pull the bit out slightly. This lets me shoot the water into the hole and get the bit at the same time.

CONCRETE MIXING AND FINISHING

Somewhere along the line, you'll want to pour a patio, drive, or walk. It's often hard work, so you want it to be done right so it won't have to be done over. There are three basic ways to provide the concrete mix. One is to buy bags with all the dry ingredients premixed. All you do is add water. Or you can buy sacks of cement, plus sand, plus gravel, and mix everything yourself. The third way is to have a company deliver the concrete already mixed and pour it from the truck into your forms.

In most cases, the size of the job will determine which method you use. Setting a fence post, pouring a few stepping stones, or making a splash block for the downspouts could be done with premixed bags. But a small patio, a walk, or setting a bunch of fence posts could cost quite a bit if you don't buy the ingredients and mix them yourself. Sometimes you can't order a small load of sand and gravel; and if you end up with a pile of either in the middle of your lawn, you may decide the little extra you spend for the premix is worth it. For the really big jobs like a driveway or the foundation for an addition, the already-mixed from a truck is the best go.

Just how much concrete is needed? Most concrete requirements are referred to in cubic yards. The cement packages usually have free charts that help; and if you give the dimensions of your project to the guy at the home center, he'll take the square footage of the area and multiply it by the number of inches of thickness. (I know—you can't multiply feet times inches, but trust me on this one.) Now take the answer, divide it by 324, and the result will be the number of cubic yards.

The small job done with premix is easy because all you have to do is add the right amount of water and mix—in a wheelbarrow or on a vinyl sheet on the driveway. A hoe is a good mixing tool. As you start mixing, it will seem like you don't have anywhere near enough water, but use only the amount called for on the bag, *no more*. Keep mixing, and it will work out. Too much water will weaken the mix. If you'll only be using part of the bag, mix the dry ingredients while they are still in the bag because the heavier parts tend to separate to the bottom. (Do this carefully or you could break the bag.) When mixing with the water, have each pebble and every grain of sand coated with the cement. When it's all gray, the mix is OK.

When mixing the dry ingredients yourself, you can mix small batches in the wheelbarrow or in a mixing box made of wood. Or you can use a cement mixer that you buy or rent (for the average home-owner, renting a mixer makes more sense).

When concrete folks talk about how much of each of the ingredients go into the mix, they use numbers like 1:2:3. The first number stands for parts of cement, the second for parts of sand, and the third for parts of aggregate or gravel. The 1:2:3 ratio is a good rule of thumb for most home projects.

Since a bag of portland cement is exactly one cubic foot, there is an easy way to measure. It requires that you make a bottomless box—a cube that is one foot high, one foot deep, and one foot wide (Figure 49). The box is open at the top and bottom, and you can lay it flat on the mixing surface and pour or shovel in the sand or gravel. When the box is filled, you have a cubic foot of the material. Just lift the box and move it over to fill again for another cubic foot.

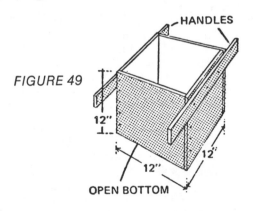

FIGURE 49

HANDLES

12"

12"

12"

OPEN BOTTOM

If you're mixing by hand, mix the dry ingredients with the hoe first. Then measure out the maximum amount of water to be used—never more than six gallons per bag of cement, and less if the sand is damp. Very wet sand can cut down by a gallon. Then try to use less than the maximum. Add a little bit of water at a time and mix. If you can get the batch mixed with a little less water, you'll end up with a stronger mix. Remember, it may look like the amount of water isn't enough, but if you'll keep mixing back and forth, it can bring about the right blend.

In colder areas, where the concrete will be subjected to freezing, ask your dealer about an air-entraining additive. This adds to the concrete microscopic cavities that help to compensate for con-traction and expansion. Now you're through with the mixing.

● If you have a bad back or are just a little lazy, you probably don't want to carry a ninety-four–pound sack of cement from the garage to where you'll be mixing it. No need to if you have a snow shovel or other big-mouth scoop around. Slip the shovel under the bag and pull the sack to the job. The shovel will slide across almost any surface, with much less back strain.

● I created a super-easy groover tool for my driveway. I cut a two-by-four the width of the drive. Then I cut a quarter-inch metal rod the same length and attached the rod to the board with screws. By placing the board across the wet concrete at the proper places, all I had to do to make grooves was to tamp it down even with the surface. It really cuts down on finishing time.

● I found a quick way to trowel off a large, rough concrete area such as a drive. After screeding off the top, I put a long pipe across the entire expanse of concrete, then roll the pipe back and forth over the area. The smooth metal acts as a trowel and leaves a quick, smooth finish. A hose will keep the pipe wet and clean for better results.

● When you need a tiny amount of concrete, put the needed ration of cement, sand, and gravel in a heavy paper bag. Hold the top closed and shake the bag up and down to mix. Now you can dump this into a pan and add the water. Most of the mixing has been done, so you'll be able to finish with just a hand trowel to make sure all the sand and gravel is covered with the paste.

● When I poured new concrete steps, I decided to add texture so the steps wouldn't be slippery when wet. While the concrete was still wet, I pushed a section of a rubber door mat, cut to the size of the steps, into the mixture. When I removed it, a uniform crisscross pattern was left in the concrete that rendered the steps slip-proof.

● Want an inexpensive, long-lasting, good-looking paint for concrete? Mix white portland cement into skim milk. When it reaches the consistency of paint, it's ready to go. It is applied with a brush, pad, or roller. Once it dries, it has a strong, long-lasting finish.

Forms and other preparation must be done before you start mixing. There is nothing worse than to pour and smooth a big concrete

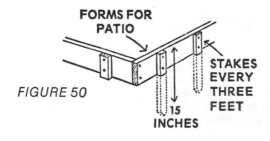

FORMS FOR PATIO

FIGURE 50

STAKES EVERY THREE FEET

15 INCHES

job, then hear the pop of a nail and the crack of boards, and see the concrete oozing out of the recently burst forms. Be sure that the forms are well braced, because concrete has lots of weight. Lots of braces and stakes will make for sturdy forms. A walk or patio should have stakes at least a foot long about every three feet (Figure 50). Try to build the forms so their top is also the top of the slab. This way, you can lay a two-by-four across the forms to strike off the concrete.

● I use those two-headed nails when building forms. They can't be driven all the way in, so are easy to remove when the forms have to be taken away.

● Before pouring the concrete, coat all forms with old drained crankcase oil. This makes them let go much easier and also prevents the wood from absorbing too much water from the mix.

Curved edges can be made with forms of sheet metal, hardboard, or even gypsum board. These flimsy forms must be very well braced. Even dirt piled up against the back of such forms will make them secure. Sometimes the forms are not made, but dug. If the slab is to be flush with the surface, just dig down and let the dirt serve as the form.

Part of most forms is the excavation done underneath the slab. In addition to the depth of the slab, most projects should also allow for a bed of sand or rocks. Tamp the sand to compact it as much as possible. You can make a tamper by nailing a two-by-six to a two-by-four handle to form a T-shaped tamper. A layer of tamped sand of about three or four inches will be fine for a drive or patio in most soil conditions.

● To rig up a tamper for compacting sand or dirt, I nail or screw a floor flange to a wide board. (A floor flange is a metal piece threaded to accept a threaded pipe.) Then I screw in a five-foot scrap of pipe for a handle. This provides an easy-to-hold handle. When the tamping is done, I dismantle the tamp and have all the pieces for other uses.

● A spare tire from the trunk of the car is a bouncing good tamper.

● When pouring concrete steps and porch, it's better to add the wrought-iron railing after the concrete is set. I left places for the ironwork by setting glass jars in the concrete while pouring the porch. Then after it set up—and I was ready to do the railings—I broke the jars, cleaned out the biggest pieces of glass, and had holes just the right size and depth for my ironwork.

● A metal garbage can lid makes an excellent instant form for concrete stepping stones. If the handle prevents the lid from resting on the ground, place it in a bed of sand. Coat the inside of the lid with old crankcase oil so the finished stone comes out easily. Also put in a scrap of chicken wire or a couple of wire coat hangers to reinforce the concrete.

After all that, it would be a shame to end up with a patio or walk that didn't have a good finish. While the finishing process does require a certain amount of finesse, most of the time when there is a bad finish, it's because a step was skipped or was done at the wrong time.

After the mix is poured into the forms, you don't want any large pieces of the gravel at the top. An easy way to force them down is to tamp lightly with a rake. This also helps remove any air pockets. But don't overdo this or you'll send all the large aggregate to the bottom, leaving little strength near the top. Many folks also spade the edges, which moves large aggregate away from the very edge. To do this, insert a flat spade between the form and the wet mix.

The next step is to strike the top surface (Figure 51) by raking a straightedge across it. This levels off the top of the concrete. After striking, a special long, wooden tool called a darby does just a little better job than the board. However, you don't ever want to overwork concrete, and if the straightedge leaves an even, level surface with no hills or depressions, that's all you want at this stage. If you do darby, stop as soon as a water sheen appears. This is called bleed water, and you cannot do any more finishing until this disappears. Some folks use another wooden tool called a float for this. There are hand-held floats and a large type with a handle called a bull float. Many times a wood float is enough to give the surface as smooth a finish as you'd want. But be sure to stop any action as soon as the water sheen appears.

If you want a glassy smooth finish, use a metal trowel next. However, each time you go over the surface and bring up that sheen, you are bringing water to the cement surface, and too much leaves you with a weakened slab.

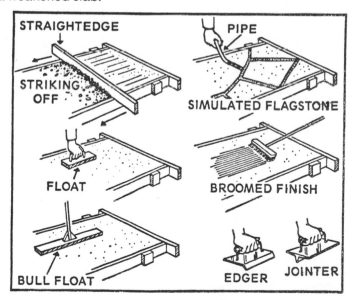

FIGURE 51

If the slab is too big for you to work from the edges, place knee boards down on the wet surface and work back toward the edges so you can smooth away the marks left by the boards and your weight. If curved edges are desirable, there is a small tool called an edger. Large slabs often require control joints, a tooled line in the slab done with a special tool called a jointer.

Special finishes and textures are easy to come by. A good nonskid surface can be made by running a broom over the wet surface. A push broom gives you better control. Do this soon after you've floated. If the bristles cause the concrete to come up in small blobs, it's a little too soon. If you have to press hard, it's almost too late. Pull the broom toward you from one edge to the other. Pounding the surface with a stiff broom gives a stippled effect.

In warm climates, rock salt is often embedded in the surface, and after the concrete sets up, the remaining salt is dissolved by water. The result is a pattern of small cavities that make for an interesting texture. Just scatter the salt, and then press it into the wet mix. If this is done too soon, the salt sinks down out of sight. In a cold climate, these cavities collect moisture that could freeze and do damage.

Leaf impressions are interesting. Place real leaves on the surface and trowel them in so they are below the surface to leave a good impression. They will decay and leave their design.

Raked joints can be made to resemble flagstones. Just press a piece of pipe into the wet surface as you draw it along. Almost anything with an interesting shape can be pushed into the surface, as you'd use a cookie cutter on dough. You could even write your initials or make imprints of your hands or feet.

After all the work of finishing, you want the concrete to last, so be sure to give it at least a full six days for curing. To prevent the slab from drying out too fast, keep it covered with a tarp or vinyl sheet, and if it needs more moisture, use a fine mist from the hose daily. Curing will help your project to be well finished ... not done for.

BRICKS AND MORTAR

One of the most common problems with mortar is the cracking of the joints between bricks. Loose or crumbling joints should be replaced, or else moisture can enter, enlarge the crack, and damage material inside the wall. The process of replacing these joints is called "tuck-pointing".

The first step is to remove all the loose joints with a cold chisel and hammer. Always wear your safety glasses when doing this. Chisel out the stuff to a depth of a half inch or more. It seems to work best to do the vertical joints first and then go after the horizontals. When your chiseling is done, brush out the loose material and then hose out the cavity. You're now ready to put in the new mortar mix.

Concrete crack-filling materials, available in a cartridge for use with a caulking gun, would be the easiest way to fill these cracks. However, the color of the old and the new would probably not match, so if looks count, you'd want to mix your own mortar. Also, if there is considerable tuck-pointing, it would cost less to mix your own. If you do use the cartridges, be sure to follow the manufacturer's directions.

● When mixing a small batch of mortar, a metal garbage can lid is ideal. With the lid upside down, pour in the dry mix and add water. Use the trowel to mix with. The handle of the lid allows you to carry your mortar to the job and hold it right where you need it.

● If you need to mix just a small amount of mortar, a plastic garbage pail can come to your rescue. When the proper ingredients are put in the can, tilt it at about a forty-five–degree angle and roll it back and forth. This gives the same action as a cement mixer, and before long, the mixing is all done.

You can buy a sack of mortar mix that has all the dry ingredients already mixed—all you do is add water. Be aware, though, that the wet mix looks much different from the way it will look when it sets up. If you want your new joints to match the old, make a test batch and then place a small blob of the mix on a piece of corrugated cardboard. This material will quickly drink out most of the moisture so you'll know about what the dry mortar will look like. If you need to have a darker look, add lampblack. If you need a lighter tone, add chalk dust from white blackboard chalk. If colors are needed, there are powdered dyes made for use with mortar. Play around until you get the right shade. When the cardboard has the right look, you'll know about what the wet mix should look like; mix the entire batch to match.

● I recently had trouble trying to match pink mortar and pink brick. I finally tried adding some chalk dust from a piece of red blackboard chalk. This mixed easily with the mortar, and I ended up with a perfect match.

Dampen the joints, but have no standing water. Fill the vertical joints first and poke the mortar in with your trowel, making sure to not leave any pockets. After the joints are filled and before the mortar sets up, you must rake the joints to shape them to match the old joints. In hot or windy weather, you may have to hurry. Use your trowel or a special tool made for this. After you've sculpted the joints to match, wait until the stuff sets up and clean the face of the brick with a stiff brush.

Replacing an entire damaged brick or a loose brick is done about the same way. Since you have to remove all the mortar around the brick, take a masonry bit and your electric drill and make a series of holes in the joints. With the holes almost touching each other, chiseling away of the mortar joints will be easy. When the brick can be removed, chip away all the remaining mortar in the cavity and use a wire brush if need be. If you're going to replace the same brick, remove all the mortar from it. The replacement brick needs to soak in a bucket of water, and the cavity needs to be damp, but without standing water. Mix and match the mortar the same as with tuck-pointing. Lay a bed of the mix onto the cavity floor. Now shake off the excess water from the brick and butter it with the mix along the top and on each end. Ease it in place and line it up with the other bricks. You'll have to poke much of the mortar back in with your trowel. Clean away any excess and rake the joints to make 'em match.

● I use a children's old wagon to haul bricks. You can load quite a few in there by stacking them. Then you can roll the supply along as you put the bricks in place.

PATIOS

Now that you know a bit about brick and masonry, maybe you'll want to make your own patio. One of the easiest is a mortarless brick patio. No mortar means no back-breaking mixing. Really, the only manual labor is the first step, which is to excavate for the patio. You need to dig out an area deep enough for a layer of bricks plus at least a two-inch bed of sand. You should also have a slight slope to the area for drainage (Figure 52).

With no joints, the square footage of the area will easily tell you how many bricks will be needed to cover it. It's best to use bricks graded SW (severe weathering).

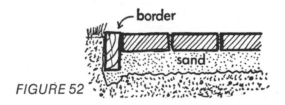

FIGURE 52

● Our neighbors were getting ready to make a patio, but to be sure it would be big enough, they held a prepatio party. They invited as many people as they ever expected to entertain outside, and set up the patio furniture and outdoor grill on the grass. They had staked out the patio and ran strings between the stakes to show the size it would be. As it turned out, the area they had marked off wasn't big enough, so they enlarged it right then by moving the stakes and strings. We had a good time, and several of the guests volunteered to help build the patio. It was a pretty smart idea.

With the digging done, pour sand onto the ground and tamp it down. Dampen the sand with a fine mist from the hose as you tamp, and compact it as tightly as possible.

● Make a tamp for compacting dirt or sand out of a gallon paint bucket into which is poured some leftover concrete mix. Then insert a five-foot-long section of pipe into the concrete. When the concrete hardens, you have your tamp (Figure 53). It's heavy enough to do the job, is easy to handle, and has a nice broad base.

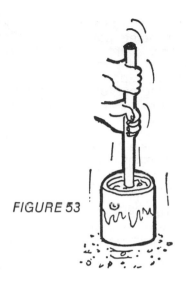

FIGURE 53

The bricks can be laid in any pattern you wish. They are butted together; and as you go, look for any that might be unlevel. Take these up and adjust the level with the sand. Start in one corner and work out.

With this type patio, it helps to have some sort of border to act as a retaining wall to keep the bricks from falling away along the edges. A moisture-resistant wood border of two-by-sixes or just some more bricks standing on edge can do this. If you'll have such a border, dig a trench for this as you excavate. Plan for the border to be level with the patio. By actually installing it after the patio is done, it can be made to butt right against the patio.

With the bricks down and level, and with the border in place, sprinkle dry sand over the entire surface. Then take a broom and start sweeping the sand back and forth. Even though the bricks are abutting each other, sand will go into the cracks. Sweep off the excess and take the garden hose, set to the finest mist, and wet down the patio. This causes the sand in the cracks to sink down. When the patio is dry, sprinkle more sand, sweep, and mist. Keep doing this until you almost have the cracks filled to the top, and then sprinkle a mixture of half sand and half dry portland cement. Sweep and mist this.

This easy patio will last for years, and one of the beauties of it is the ease of repair if ever needed. If the ground below shifts and a section sinks, just dig it up and adjust the level by adding and tamping sand, and then replace the bricks.

This same procedure will make a great walk. Instead of bricks, you can use concrete stepping stones or even round sections of big logs sliced off with your chainsaw. The logs need to be at least an inch thick and should be treated with a wood preservative.

A concrete patio need not be all one big slab. A good way for the weekend worker to make a concrete patio is to build forms that allow you to mix, pour, and finish one square at a time. This way, you set your own pace. If you make forms out of a rot-resistant or treated wood, the forms stay in place and act as expansion joints, giving the slab an interesting pattern. After digging out for the patio, including a bed of tamped sand or gravel, lay wire mesh on sand for reinforcing. Don't forget to slope the forms for drainage.

● If you have a concrete-slab patio, you can break up the monotony. Before painting it with patio paint, I put down strips of masking tape in a crisscross pattern forming two-foot squares. I painted over the area, and when dry I peeled off the masking tape. This left a very interesting look of a tile floor.

● Recently I was out on the painted concrete patio, antiquing some furniture by splatter-dashing. As I ran a stick across the toothbrush loaded with black paint, I did a beautiful job on the furniture, but lots of flecks of paint got on the patio. It looked interesting so, using a bigger brush, I splatter-dashed the entire patio. It looks super, but the big advantage is that it doesn't show dirt and cuts down on sweeping.

● I made a patio out of large flat stones, and rather than strain my back, I slipped two lengths of iron pipe under each stone, to help me roll it into place. If you have to move it a long distance, use three pipes (Figure 54). As one section of pipe moves toward the back of the stone, slip another in at the front. With a little practice, you get to the point where you can steer them into tight spots.

FIGURE 54

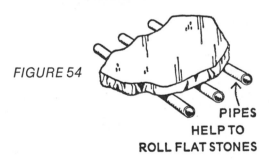

PIPES
HELP TO
ROLL FLAT STONES

● My new concrete patio slab butted up against the house, and I didn't have a trowel that would curve the concrete up to look the way I thought it should. I found that the bottom of a beer bottle smoothes the edge out and makes a uniform curve up against the house.

● I heard starching a patio makes it more dirt resistant. Since we eat out on the patio, and someone slops occasionally, I had to try it. The idea is to use a fairly thick mixture of starch and mop it on right after you've cleaned the surface. After it dries, you're ready for more sloppy eating that can just be swept off, leaving no stains.

Here are some hints for walks:

● When a section of sidewalk sank to one side, I used the bumper jack from my car to raise it. Next to the walk I dug a hole big enough for the base of the jack to fit into, and deep enough for the jack to get under the concrete. When I got the slab back up level with the rest of the walk, I put sand and rocks in to fill underneath, so when I removed the jack, it stayed level. I never could have lifted the slab by hand.

● After pouring stepping stones, the big problem was getting them out without tearing up the forms. I lined the form with a plastic sheet from a dry cleaner's bag. The film of plastic makes it easy to get the forms off.

● I misfigured and ended up with several extra redwood fence posts. Rather than have them in the way in my garage, I made a garden walk out of them. I sawed them into three-inch-thick blocks. With the four-by-four squares facing up, I set the blocks on a bed of sand. To keep them in place, I put a two-by-four border along each side. It really looks neat.

A patio is nothing at all without outdoor furniture, an outdoor grill, and all the other accessories. They require a few do-it steps, too.

● We finally got rid of the old chrome dinette set. The chairs have been converted into a pair of lawn benches that look great. I removed the seats and backs, then cut slats of redwood about five feet long. Three slats form the bench seat, and three form the back. I drilled holes in the metal frame and in the slats so the bench could be held together by nuts and bolts (Figure 55). They are sturdy, comfortable, and good-looking. The dinette table now is used as a work table in my shop.

FIGURE 55

● Want to give your outdoor furniture a special extra-heavy-duty waxing? That hard paste wax meant for cars works on either wood or metal furniture.

● The new material I used to recover our patio chairs wasn't waterproof. I remembered an old technique I had learned for use on tents when I was in the Boy Scouts. Using a potato peeler, I shaved a quarterpound block of paraffin into thin slivers. Put these into a quart of turpentine, and place this container into a larger pan containing very hot water. The heat helps the wax dissolve faster, but without the danger of heating over an open flame. When the paraffin is melted, brush the mix on the canvas. When completely dry, the fabric is waterproof and will last much longer.

● If you have any wooden porch or deck furniture without glides on the feet, why not drive nails through bottle caps to attach them to the bottoms of the legs? They will make the furniture easier to move. More important, the bottle caps will raise the wood up off the deck and prevent moisture from going to work on the wood.

● Your column suggested using a crumpled wad of aluminum foil to clean aluminum lawn chairs. I always used petroleum jelly to clean and protect them. I tried dipping a wad of foil instead of a rag into the petroleum jelly. It works great. The furniture was pitted and dingy, but with our collaboration treatment, it now shines. I left a thin film of the petroleum jelly for protection from Mother Nature.

● While rewebbing some patio chairs, I found that the plastic webbing had a bad habit of unraveling at the ends. Hold a lighted match and run the ends of the webbing quickly back and forth through the flame. The webbing melts at the end and the loose strands fuse so there can be no more unraveling.

● Contoured metal patio chairs with solid bottoms have a big disadvantage: water that collects in the seat can't run off. This standing water can eventually do damage to the chair. I solved the problem by drilling a series of tiny holes in the low places on the seat. Now the water can run out, and the holes don't ruin the looks of the chair.

● Our lightweight aluminum patio chairs used to blow over in the slightest breeze until I poured slurry cement mixture into the tubular legs. They aren't so heavy that they can't be carried, but they don't blow over anymore.

● We noticed the aluminum arms of our patio furniture had begun to leave grayish marks on clothing and skin. I cleaned the metal with steel wool; but after a few weeks, it turned dark and again started leaving its mark. The next time I cleaned the metal, I applied a coat of thinned shellac. Now we have no more problem.

● About every year, the old outdoor barbecue grill needs a new paint job. Last year, instead of using regular metal paint, I reasoned that some automobile-engine paint would be made to withstand high temperature and might be better. This year it still looks good, so I didn't have to repaint. It must be a good idea.

● I'm really proud of my roll-around outdoor grill—an old wheelbarrow with a metal bed. I found a grate that would lie across the top, drilled some holes in the bottom for better air flow to the charcoal, and painted the wheelbarrow to match the patio furniture. Now I can roll it down by the pool or up on the patio, or if it's raining and we want to cook out, I can roll it into the garage out of the rain.

● As a backyard chef, I could never keep the meat from being charred. When drippings melted off the meat and fell on the charcoal briquettes, they caused flames that often burned the meat on the outside.

Now I keep a section of window-screening material cut to fit over the bottom of my outdoor cooker. When I get the coals glowing, I place the screen over the coals before replacing the grill. The flame still appears when the grease falls on the coals, but won't rise above the screen. Thus it doesn't reach the meat.

● If you'd like to have some rustic hooks for a patio fence, use an adaptation of an old Boy Scout trick. I selected tree branches about three to four inches in diameter. By cutting a section of branch that has a limb angling off, I could fashion my hangers. I used about a six-inch section of the main branch and about a three-inch stub of the limb. Then I sawed lengthwise through the main branch so there was a flat side to be nailed to the wall, and left the stub sticking out and slightly up (Figure 56). This makes a nice hook for hanging plants and all sorts of paraphernalia.

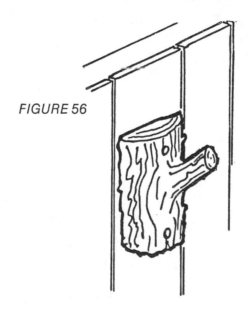

FIGURE 56

● At the last moment before a patio party, my husband created some very unusual candle holders for exotic outdoor lighting. He gathered up all the clay flowerpots we had and placed them around where we needed light. Then in each pot he placed a candle short enough so the pot protected the flame, using the drain hole in the bottom to anchor the candle. They looked super.

● I bought a bunch of cheap flashlights and use them as yard lights around the backyard. They create a stunning effect. I used a hand trowel to dig holes, and the flashlight goes into the ground up to where the cut-off switch is. I attached others to trees and fence posts. They're easy to hide and waterproof, so can be left outside. It's not as convenient as flipping one switch, but they cost very little. They can also be easily moved to change the effect.

GARAGE

Even though the garage isn't always outside, the driveway leading into it is.

● We have an attached garage and were constantly forgetting to turn out the garage light. To check, we had to open the door and look. Then we installed a viewer that lets us look through the door. Not only can we check the light, but recently we heard noises in the garage and were able to see an intruder without letting him know. The police arrived while he was removing the tape deck from our car.

Garage doors have a way of causing problems. Most raise up to open. When they reach near-hernia stage, most people want to adjust the tension in the spring or springs. While the spring could be at fault, more often there's something else. Many doors are in sections, equipped on each side with a series of rollers that travel in tracks. If the tracks are clogged or dirty, bent or not plumb, the rollers may not travel easily. Clean the tracks with a degreaser and actually swab them out. Then use a level to check for plumb. Most tracks are held in place by brackets, and by loosening the brackets, the tracks can be adjusted. If the tracks are clean and OK, lubricate them with grease. Then lubricate the rollers with machine oil or spray lube. Make sure each roller will turn.

Check over all the hardware to be sure it's tight. That includes hinges, brackets, and tracks, as loose ones can cause balkiness. Be sure the door itself doesn't bind against something as it's moved.

The door may not work well because it's too heavy. The weight gain can be brought on by moisture. If the edges or other surfaces are not sealed, a door can absorb several new pounds of moisture. After the wood has dried out, paint or seal the edges and back (Figure 57).

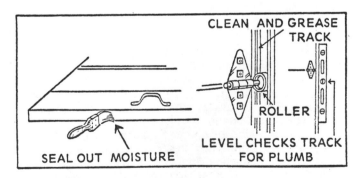

CLEAN AND GREASE TRACK

ROLLER

LEVEL CHECKS TRACK FOR PLUMB

SEAL OUT MOISTURE

FIGURE 57

If everything else is all right, then maybe you could suspect the springs. If your door has a torsion spring in the center above the door, I'd suggest that you get a pro to adjust the tension: I've known people to get hurt when the spring got away from them. If you have the type with springs on the side, many times you can adjust the tension by moving the hooks to another hole or by shortening a cable.

● Those heavy garage-door springs have a way of getting a little loose after a while and need to be moved to the next hole. However, the spring is next to impossible to stretch by hand. Move the door so it stretches the spring to its fullest. Then with the door set in that position, insert nails between the coils. Put them in opposite the side where you'll be so if the spring kicks out, a nail won't get you. With the nails in place, the spring won't go back all the way. Put in enough nails so the spring is long enough to hook into the next hole.

Metal washers or coins could do this job, too.

● If garage-door springs held in place with an S-hook ever slip off the hook, they can be dangerous. Even if no one is hurt, getting them back on can be a chore. I added an ounce of prevention, putting a second S-hook next to the other, but facing the opposite way so it forms sort of a figure eight. Now there is no way for anything to come loose.

Installing an automatic garage-door opener is very easy—in most cases it requires only simple tools, and the makers of most openers include easy-to-follow directions. Now that we have ours, I wonder how I could have been so unkind as to have my wife, Jean, open the door by hand during rainstorms. Now I just have her push a button. Here are some other garage-door thoughts:

● When the wind blows from the north, our garage door used to rattle like a bucket of bolts. I found the cause for the rattle is the gap between the roller and the track in which it rolls to open and close. By tightening a C clamp down against the roller and the track when the door is closed, the door is held steady against any wind.
● I broke the key off in our garage-door lock. I tried several methods of extracting the broken end from the lock. Finally I magnetized the tip of the part I had and inserted it in the hole. By gently pulling it out, the broken piece came out with it.
● I cut a wedge to use as a doorstop for the garage door. Each week it got lost, and I had to cut another. Finally I got smart and attached a new wedge to the door with an old screen-door spring. Screw eyes hold the spring to the door, and the wedge to the spring. When not in use, the wedge hangs up out of the way. When needed, the spring stretches and lets the wedge be placed under the door.
● To attach discarded garden hose to a garage door for weather stripping, I cut pieces of waterproof duct tape long enough to go around the hose and leave a half-inch tab where the two ends stick together. I put

these tabs every foot or so along the hose section, then stapled the tabs to the door.

Parking your car can mean all sorts of spots on the garage floor. To fight oil and grease spots, saturate the spots with either an auto degreaser or with paint thinner. Then cover this with an absorbent like cat litter, cornmeal, sand, sawdust, or dry portland cement. I like cat litter best. Wait overnight and sweep away the spots. If there's still some there, mix a TSP (trisodium phosphate) solution and scrub.

● To remove all the oil drippings from the garage floor, use washing soda (different from baking soda). Put it on dry over the spots, and let it stand overnight. Next day turn on the hose and use a stiff brush to scrub away the soda and oil spots. On tough spots, the process sometimes has to be done more than once. These spots will come out much easier if you get on them as soon as possible after the car drips.

● New oil stains on concrete can be lifted by scrubbing the spot with a paste of lemon juice and salt, using a stiff brush. Then the oil can be hosed away. After the oil has been there for a while, it takes something stronger.

● I had some rust stains on the concrete floor of our garage. One of your readers once said a paste of turpentine and salt removed rust from a kitchen sink. The sink remedy didn't work at first, but I tried again and used a stiff brush to scrub the stain with the paste. Most of it came off after several tries.

Some people have a unique way of knowing when the car is far enough into the garage—they just drive until the front bumper hits the wall. Everyone's heard of the trick of hanging a rubber ball on a string so that it just touches the windshield when the car is in the right place. Padding the wall where the bumper hits with foam rubber or a section from an old auto tire is also a help. Or ...

● To let my wife know when the car is in far enough, I used some leftover concrete mix to set a stick in a coffee can so it sticks straight up, higher than the hood of the car. I placed this gadget on the garage floor. We now drive the car in until we see the stick start to tip, and then we stop. No more banged-up garage walls.

Not everyone has a garage.

● Our new home has a carport, where we have to hide all the tools and junk we used to store in our old garage. Then my husband made a screen on wheels that's the same material and color as the back wall of the carport. We roll the screen out of the way to get out a tool, and then roll it back in place to camouflage what would otherwise be an eyesore.

● It used to bug me to get home and find someone else parked in my carport. Then I rigged up my fake barricade. I used epoxy to glue a block of wood to the concrete in the center and at the entrance. To that, I hinged a two-by-four about eighteen inches long so that it can stick straight up, but will fold toward the rear of the carport. I used some reflector tape to stripe the upright to let people see it even at night. I set the post up when I leave each morning, and when I return at night, my space is still vacant. I ease the bumper of the car against the post, it folds back, and I drive on in.

FENCES

Fences are put up for protection, privacy, decoration, or all three. Since there are so many different fence materials and even more designs, I won't try to cover all the ins and outs of fence building. However, be sure to consult the local building code because many communities have restrictions as to the height and positioning of fences as regards property lines; some even dictate the types of materials and style.

Whatever type fence you build, it will probably rise or fall by the way you install the posts. Most posts are best set in concrete. All the posts should be set first, and then the fence built or attached to them. So lay out your fence with stakes and strings and then stake out the position of each post. Normally they should be six to eight feet apart, but the purpose of the fence, the terrain, and the type of fence may govern the spacing. Even though you will be using a rot-resistant wood, the underground part of the posts should be treated with a preservative.

● Fence posts last much longer if you apply roofing cement to the part that goes into the ground. Let it dry before putting the posts up. This worked better than other preservatives I used in the past.

Metal posts should be coated with paint to prevent rusting.

How deep should the posts be set? About a third of the total height of the fence should be underground. Make sure that at least those posts at corners and at gates are set that securely; if there's to be any fudging, make it on posts in between. Dig the corner posts first, then run a string along between corners. This will make it easier to line up all the other posts.

If you have a bunch of posts, I'd suggest you rent a powered posthole digger or contract with someone to do this step. After the basic hole is dug to accommodate the post, dig down about an extra two inches—for a layer of small gravel to aid in drainage (Figure 58). Also take a few minutes and bell out the bottom with a spade so that the concrete blob will have additional holding power.

Use a level or plumb bob to be sure the post is perfectly straight in the hole. Mix only enough concrete for one post at a time. Use a regular mix if you buy the premix in bags. If you mix it yourself, use a 1:2:3 with the aggregate being only medium-sized gravel. As you shovel in the mix, use the shovel to poke down and eliminate air pockets. Use enough concrete to come above the surface, and then use a trowel to slant it down from the posts on all sides. This lets water drain away from the post. After all the posts are set, it's best to wait six days before erecting the fence so the concrete is fully cured.

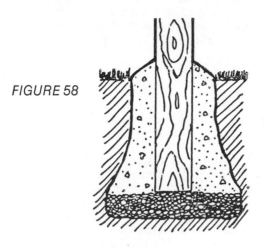

FIGURE 58

● One extra step will make your fence last longer. Drive two large nails into each side of the post where it'll be below the concrete. Leave about three inches of nail sticking out (Figure 59). When the concrete is poured around the post, these nails will act as anchors for the concrete to hold to and will make sure the post never comes loose.

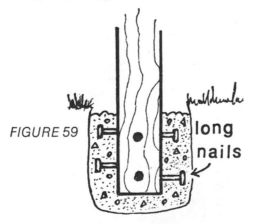

FIGURE 59

long nails

● To make metal fences or clotheslines more solid, drill a series of holes in the bottom of the metal post. When the concrete mix is poured around the post, the mix will squish in the holes below ground and lock the pole both inside and out.
● To make wooden fence posts more solid, nail scrap strips on the bottom of the post. The scraps form underground ridges around the post that allow the concrete better holding power.

● Another way to help a wooden fence post stay in place is to drill holes through the post down below ground level. Insert pipe scraps through the post so they stick out on all four sides. The concrete is poured all around the pipes as well as inside them, and there is very little likelihood that they will ever become loose.

Leaning fence posts are also a problem.

● Rather than remove the post and reset it, sometimes it can be straightened. I create a mire of mud around the post by using a root feeder attached to the hose. By moving this around the post, the ground soon becomes so muddy that I can push the post back straight. Then fill around it with dry earth to keep it straight. It won't always work, but you can try.

● Hollow metal fence posts should be capped to keep them from filling with water. But metal caps cost money. Stuff some rags or paper down in the post as a base and leave enough room for a couple of inches of leftover concrete mix on top. Level it off, and the post will be sealed against the ravages of moisture—and you don't have quite as much concrete left over.

● To keep water from getting into a wooden fence post, I cut leftover scraps of asphalt roofing shingles into squares to fit the post tops and stuck them in place with roofing cement.

● Because my driveway gate was so long, it began to sag. I installed a caster on the end, and now the gate rolls over the drive.

● One reason my picket fence looks so good is because the picket spacer I devised allowed me to get all the pickets the same distance apart and level, without having to use a rule and level for each one. First I cut a scrap board the exact width of the proposed space between pickets, then I trimmed it to the same height as the pickets. On each end of this, I nailed parallel boards, sticking out from the main board in opposite directions to form a sort of Z shape (Figure 60). The top horizontal piece rests on the

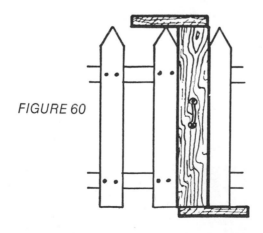

FIGURE 60

picket just installed. The main board is against this picket. The new picket goes right up against this, and so is properly spaced, and rests on the bottom horizontal piece so it's the same height as the other picket. A screen-door handle let me place and hold my spacer easily.

● When replacing sections of a weathered cedar or redwood fence, new boards stick out like a sore thumb. I discovered through careless gardening that an application of chelated iron from the garden shop will weather the wood almost overnight. Just mix according to directions and apply with a brush.

● Before spray painting a fence, go to an appliance store and get a spare corrugated packing crate for a big appliance. Place the crate behind the fence to act as a shield for the spray to keep it from getting on everything in the neighborhood. As you move along, it can be moved too.

LAWN

Now for the secret of how I developed a green thumb. Get one can of crab-apple-green latex enamel and dip in both thumbs.

12.
PAINTING

Few do-it-yourself undertakings offer as much saving to you, the homeowner. Doing painting yourself saves the biggest part of the price of having it done—the labor. Also, painting can make a dramatic change in the way a room, a piece of furniture, or even the entire house looks. It's something almost anyone can do, and many paint jobs go very fast after you get the knack.

The first key to any paint job is preparation. If the surface isn't properly prepared, you're probably going to have a failure. It's not the end of the world to have to do it over, but it's not all that much fun, either. Be sure to follow all the preparation steps before you begin.

INTERIOR PAINTING

I suggest you start with your first paint job inside. Then if you make a fool of yourself, nobody'll see you.

The first thing to do is go over the entire room looking for protruding nails, cracks, holes, and gouges. These have to be taken care of (and you can find out how to do it in the chapter on Walls). However, here are a couple of hole-filler tips:

● Sometimes when you patch up a crack or hole in wallboard, it still shows after you've painted over it, and you have to come back with another coat. To mix the spackling compound, I use thinned paint that matches the walls. When the patch is done and dry, it needs only one coat to be hidden. In fact, the patch is almost invisible.

● As a quick way to patch nail holes before painting, I just rub a bar of damp soap across the holes and wipe away the excess. It dries almost immediately, so I paint right over it.

● When you're in the middle of an inside paint job and find you didn't patch all the holes in the wall, you don't want to drag out the patching compound and then have to wait until it sets up before painting over it. You don't have to if you'll use my quickie patch. Pour out a few drops of paint, and add enough cornstarch from the kitchen to mix a paste of putty thickness. Work this into the holes, and then you can immediately paint over the patch. Because the patch is already the same color that you're using, there won't be any coverage problem either. This same patching material can be used to patch a hole when you don't want to have to touch up the patches.

As you go along, also look for loose or flaking paint. It must be removed!

Next is maybe the most important step—that of cleaning every surface to be painted. Paint will not stick to dirt, dust, grease, or chewing gum. In some rooms, maybe just dusting will do; others require a cleaning solution. Kitchen walls are often coated with an invisible layer of airborne grease from cooking. It's best to just assume it's there and attack the walls with a cleaner.

● In cleaning the walls before painting, always start at the bottom and work your way up. This way, any water that runs down the wall will run across clean surfaces. If it runs across a dirty surface, it could leave streaks that show through your paint job. Keep this in mind whether you're cleaning for a paint job or just because the walls are filthy.

Enameled woodwork will probably have a glossy surface. Any surface with a gloss should be deglossed. This can be done by sanding or with a liquid deglosser available at the paint store.

● When you're sanding down a wall for painting or sanding the floors, the dust goes all through the house. To keep the mess down, of course, open the windows and close the door. Block over any return air vents. Now you'll find that the cracks around the door will let out so much sanding dust that you'll still have a problem. What to do? Dampen a bed sheet. Make sure it won't drip. Tape or tack it over the door and around the frame. It stops the dust and actually helps keep it down some within the room. (Just as soon as you have yourself blocked into the room, the phone will ring.)

In most cases your intent will be to paint the ceiling, walls, and woodwork—not the floors, furniture, piano, or panes of glass. The best thing to do is move everything out of the room. If that's impossible or impractical, however, evacuate as much as you can and cover the rest. Plastic drop cloths are supercheap, or invest in better drop cloths that you can use over and over.

● Plastic drop cloths on a slick floor—such as hardwood or resilient flooring—can be dangerous. If you're not careful when you walk across them, they may slip out from under you. This is especially bad if you happen to be carrying an open can of paint at the time. Canvas drop cloths are safest for the floor. Then use the cheap plastic jobs over furniture and on nonslippery floors.

● Many folks put down newspaper on the floor when painting. If it happens to be on a hardwood floor or on a slick vinyl, this too can be dangerous. As you walk across, the newspaper has a tendency to slip, and you're just liable to land on your ear.

● Even though I put protective covers over everything, I still manage to get paint splatters on things. Now I wax the floors and furniture before I start painting. I use a heavy coat of paste wax, but don't buff until after the painting is done. Any paint that gets on the wrong thing is really only on the wax and buffs right off. It also forces me to wax the floors, which I might put off otherwise.

Next, use masking tape next to the paint areas to protect anything you don't want painted. Even if you'll be painting over electric outlets and light switches, take off the plates and paint them separately, or they'll require a jackhammer for removal.

Sometimes it's best to remove a light fixture. You must be sure there's no current to the fixture when you start to mess with it. Some fixtures will be light enough that you can merely loosen them to hang down from the ceiling. Even with the fixture away from the ceiling, enclose it in a plastic bag from the cleaner. Sometimes you can even get by with the plastic bag and masking tape and just leave it in place. Have plenty of rags on hand while painting for wipe-ups.

● Here's a trick to keep track of your paint rags. Use an old screen-door spring to form a holder around the paint can. It will stretch around the can and hook together. In addition to corralling the rags, the spring will also hold a putty knife and other small items.

● My paint-rag holder is a jim-dandy. I use a shower-curtain ring to hold a paper clamp to my belt loop. The clamp then holds the paint rag. If I use a long rag, I don't even have to remove it from the clamp to wipe. If the rag does have to be removed, however, it comes out and goes back into the clamp with no trouble. When not painting, I hang the rag holder from a hook on my shop wall.

● I keep several mousetraps in my shop because their spring clamps are good holders for many small items. The other day, I was going to do some painting. I taped a mousetrap to the side of the paint can. This gave me a holder for a paint rag, the one thing I misplace just about the time I need it. This time, the rag was trapped to the side of the can.

● Need a paint-rag holder for use up on a ladder? A shower-curtain ring and a spring-type clothespin will do the job. The clothespin holds the rag (Figure 61). Then slip the end of the shower-curtain ring through the coil spring of the clothespin. The ring fits perfectly around the rung of a ladder, and you're in business.

● I used to always have to look around for my paint rag when I needed it. Then I put a rubber band around my paint can. When the rag's not in use, I tuck a corner of it under the band so it's never lost.

Next, you'll want to protect *yourself*. Many stores will have free painter's caps. If not, a paper bag with the sides rolled up will keep the flecks from your locks. One reader just borrowed his wife's shower cap.

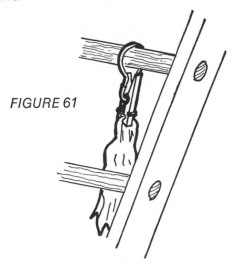

FIGURE 61

If you wear glasses, protect them from the splatters of ceiling painting with a small square of Saran Wrap over each lens. When the spots get too bad, strip off the plastic and put new patches in place. If you don't wear glasses, how about this:

● In rolling paint on the ceiling, I didn't get tiny droplets in my eyes because I wore my son's swim mask.

● Just because rubber gloves spring a leak and are no longer good for the many chores they were intended for, don't toss them away. They're still great for several handyperson chores, including painting. You can get the job done without getting your hands all covered with paint. They are fine for concrete work and for using other such mixtures where the idea is to just keep your hands from contact. Even my husband likes this idea.

● When painting a ceiling with a brush, the paint runs down your arm, and if you have a lot of painting to do, will cover your entire body. I solved this messy problem by putting a strip of foam rubber left over from an upholstery job around the brush at the top of the bristles, held in place by a rubber band. The foam rubber caught all the drips and kept me clean.

● Form a cup from aluminum foil. Crumple it around the handle to catch dribbles.

● Half of a hollow rubber ball can catch paint drips. Cut an X in the ball ball and slip it over the handle.

● To keep your face from getting speckled during painting, smear it with cold cream—and have a beauty treatment during the work.

● If you rub your hands with linseed oil before you start, any paint you get on your hands will come off much easier after you have finished. Soap and water will get all the paint off. I've found that linseed oil doesn't harm my skin in any way.

Wear your oldest clothes, of course. However, if you don't have any old clothes or don't want to sacrifice them to painting, for inside jobs you can just go bare. Nude painting is wildly accepted in the fine-arts field.

Some people wear old sweat socks to protect their shoes. They'll stretch to pull right over the shoe. However, this makes for slippery footing on some floor surfaces, so be careful.

You also want to protect a few things in other parts of the house. If you're really sloppy, have a path of newspapers to lead you from the paint job to where you'll go to clean up. Have the cleanup supplies already out. Put plastic sandwich bags over all the doorknobs in other rooms that you might touch. And remember the phone. You know it'll ring about the time you're up to your elbows in paint. Tie a rag or a sock to the receiver, and try not to think about how silly you look in case somebody should drop by.

● As a drip catcher, I rip off a piece of waxed paper from the kitchen and wrap this around the bottom of the paint can. I put a rubber band around the can to hold the paper in place. Then, just above the rubber band, I flare out the waxed paper. Any paint that drools down is caught in the trough formed above the rubber band and can't get down to the floor.

● When I paint, I use a paper grocery bag as a drip catcher. Fold down the top of the sack until the top is lower than the top of the can. Then place the paint can inside the sack. All the drips are in the bag. When the can is empty, unfold the sack, and both the mess and the can are tossed away.

● Almost every household has an old bookend in the attic. I found one and discovered that it was excellent as a holder for a paint can. Taping the bookend to the can provides a base that's practically tip-proof.

● Here is my drip-catcher idea for painting. I get a corrugated box big enough for the paint can to fit into, but shallow enough to leave easy access to the paint. With the top of the box cut off, I place the paint can down in the center. Then I take crumpled-up newspapers and stuff 'em in good all around the can. This holds the can in place and catches all the drips.

● After I got through stirring the paint, I put the paint paddle down on a newspaper. Later, when I wanted to stir again, the paddle was stuck to the paper. After I got the paint and paper cleaned off, I just left the paddle in the paint bucket. So it wouldn't be in the way, I held it against the side by simply clamping a clothespin to the paddle. It stands ready until I need to stir again.

● Using a small paint can with no handle is no problem if your children have a sand bucket. The can rests in the sand bucket and is easy to carry by *its* handle. Of course, you look a little ridiculous with a bucket painted all over with duckies, but who cares?

● With a quart paint can, there's no handle, and therefore no way to hang it when you're painting from a straight ladder. I keep an empty gallon can on hand and place the smaller can in this. Then I use a plain old wire coat hanger to hang the two cans from a ladder rung. With the hook part stuck through the handle, the wide part of the hanger can't go through and rests flat against the bucket handle. No bending of the hanger is needed.

● What do you do when you're painting from a stepladder and want to put down your brush without cleaning all the paint from it? I rigged up a holder that I clamp in place on the top step. It's just a stick with a cutout tailored to hold the brush handle at its smallest part. I position the holder so it is directly over the bucket. The brush slips in place in the holder and can drip right back into the bucket.

● Your book mentions aluminum foil as a good liner for a paint-roller tray. I prefer a piece of plastic from a dry cleaner's bag. Just lay it over the tray and let it hang over the sides. When you're through painting, remove the paint in the tray by bringing the corners of the plastic together and lifting the whole mess out like a bag. The tray is left spotless, and the plastic and paint go into the garbage can. It's easier to use and costs a lot less than foil.

● I am the handyperson around our house, and when painting, I found that putting down the roller either made a mess, or flattened out the nap, or both. Then I clipped a spring-type clothespin to the side of the paint tray. The V of the clothespin holds the roller frame, and the roller is placed upright in the tray. Drips go back into the tray. Even my husband thinks this one is worth sending to you.

● Sometimes you need to hold some odd-shaped small item at a strange angle for painting. When normal methods won't work, maybe the old bean bag will. Put enough beans in a plastic bag and close off the top. Form the bag around the work and see if it won't hold it. Those big bean-bag chairs will even hold *my* odd shape, so you know the idea will work. With the price of food up where it is, dump your holder in a pot when the work is done. Sorry I don't have a bean recipe.

● Painting small objects on newspaper usually results in the edges of the object sticking to the newspaper when the paint dries. I stick thumbtacks up through the bottom of a shirt board. The small object to be painted rests on the points of the tacks, and there is nothing for the paint to stick to. But be sure to put enough tacks to give the object a solid base.

● When I set a full gallon of paint on the fold-out shelf of my ladder, it folded on down. We now have an apple-green floor as well as the walls. Tell other home painters to be sure to check that part of a ladder before using it. Since mine wasn't used very often, it somehow got broken without my knowing it. It sure would have been a simple matter to check it beforehand.

● To assure that a can of paint on the top step of my ladder can't be knocked off, I made a wooden turn-button on the end of the top step. It's just a six-inch scrap of wood with a hole in the center. Through the hole, insert a screw and place a washer between the wood and the ladder, and another between the wood and the screw head. When I want to anchor a can of paint, I flip the turn-button up and tape the can to it (Figure 62). When not painting, the turn-botton is down, out of the way.

● For small paint jobs, I use a cardboard soft-drink carton as a handy tote. The sections hold the small cans of paint, thinner, rags, brushes, and whatever else I'll need for the job. I can carry it all with one hand, keep it all together, and not have to worry about drips.

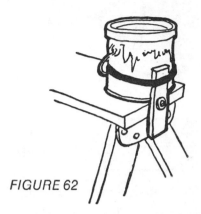

FIGURE 62

● When you set out to paint, do you end up having to make several trips to get all your equipment to the site? If you've got a large plastic bucket, put the can of paint in the middle. Then place your brushes, scrapers, rags, and whatever else you'll need around it in the bucket. This is particularly good when you are going to have to climb a ladder, since it leaves a free hand for holding on as you go up.

Now you're ready to start the paint job. Even if you just bought the paint this morning, be sure to mix it well. The method most painters use is called boxing—that is, pouring it back and forth from one bucket to another. Then as you go along, keep the paint mixed by stirring.

● The best mixers for paint and shop chemicals are wooden mixing spoons. I snuck one out from the kitchen one time, but when my wife discovered the theft, she just went to the variety store and bought me a half dozen. They really do a great job of stirring and mixing.

● I'm sure all your readers have tried to pour paint from a can. The lip on the can makes it impossible to pour accurately; and when you stop pouring, the ridge in the rim fills up and makes paint dribble down the side. Not with my solution. I slightly bend a cardboard shirt board and stick it all the way down into the can. The curve fits against the rim. This acts as a spout to pour from that gives accuracy and keeps paint off the sides and out of the rim. The paint on the spout drains back into the bucket, and then the cardboard is wiped clean on the inside of the can.

● Ever try to pour all of the paint out of a gallon can only to find the rim around the lip won't let it all come out? Punch a hole in the side of the can with a punch-type beer-can opener. Just hook the opener on the rim with the point on the side, and it will go through (Figure 63). Lets you drain out every drop.

● I read in your book about drilling holes in your paint paddle to make mixing go faster. I never owned a paint paddle, but for years I have

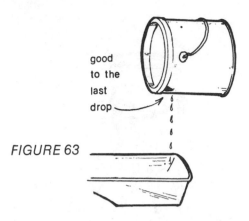

good
to the
last
drop

FIGURE 63

used a strip of Peg-Board to stir with. It already has the holes and the paint flows through them as I stir. It's better than a regular paint paddle because it's wider and does the job faster.

● When I'm going to paint, I turn the paint can upside down the night before I plan to start. When I start to mix it the next day, there is no danger that I'll leave any pigment unstirred in the bottom of the can.

The accepted sequence is to do your ceilings first, walls next, and woodwork last. The roller or large pad with an extension handle does best for the broad areas, but won't get right up to the edges. For this, use a brush. This first step is called cutting in. When this is done, start with your roller or pad right next to the cut-in stripe and work with back-and-forth strokes on the ceiling, all the way across the width of the room. Keep working with the same technique, all the way across the room, always painting against the wet edge of the stripe you just painted. If you paint against a stripe that has dried, it's liable to show up with a streak. Therefore, arrange to finish all walls and ceilings once you start. Resist the urge to paint dirty words over the surface before you start. Some folks reason that since they'll be painted over, nothing will show. Then one day when the light is just right, and the preacher comes to call, you'll look up and see all the painted-over words. Here's another streak causer:

● Did you know that adding new paint to the roller tray can often mean a definite different shade at that point in your paint job? Even with the cleanest wall, your roller picks up some dust as you go along. This mixes with the paint as you reload the roller. Airborne dust also settles in. Then you add pure new paint, and it can leave a streak. Always plan to start with enough paint to finish that wall. On big surfaces, that means a big plastic bucket instead of the tray. There are hook-on grids to remove the excess paint from the roller, so the bucket works out just fine.

After you've cut in a wall with a brush, start with the roller in a corner. If you're right-handed, start in a left-hand corner. Start at the top and work all the way down.

● I found a much better way to paint with a roller than to use the conventional roller tray. A plastic garbage pail is better because it holds so much more paint. I found one that's wide enough to let me put the roller grid into the pail. The grid stands at an angle and allows me to remove the excess paint as the roller is brought out of the pail (Figure 64). The pail has a handle, so it's much easier to carry around than is a tray, and the extra capacity lets me keep on painting longer. When latex paint is being used, the plastic can easily be hosed out.

FIGURE 64

● Even if you're not ambidextrous, you'll find you can paint with both hands. It'll prove much less tiring if you switch hands every so often. Some people just hang in there with one hand until it's ready to fall off. You may not want to use your weaker hand for very exacting work, but for spreading paint on a big area, it'll do just fine.

Paint woodwork with an enamel for easier cleaning. You can usually get the same colors in enamels as in flat paints, if that's what you want. But as mentioned earlier, you must remove the gloss before painting. Brushes work best for most woodwork because the areas are too small for most rollers and pads. However, there are special rollers and pads for special areas, and when you buy the paint, you might want to take a look at what all there is. Start with baseboards, then windows, and then doors.

● Lots of people think that since no one will see the bottom of the door, it doesn't need painting. You're painting it to seal out the moisture and not for looks—unless we're invaded by Lilliputians. A paint pad without the holder will slide under the door and give the door bottom a good coat.

● Our son outgrew his tricycle, but Carrell's Law is "Don't throw anything away." I found it to be an ideal roll-around stool for painting the lower parts of rooms. I just sit backwards on the trike and move it with my feet. Sure beats bending over to get down to the floor.

● When it comes to painting the molding on baseboards, you have a problem taping down floor covering to protect the carpet. If you tape to the carpet, it pulls up nap, and if you tape to the molding, you can't paint it at all. If you don't tape, you risk getting paint on the carpet. I have found that folded newspaper can be slipped under the molding if you use a piece of stiff plastic. A cheap place mat works for me. By placing the plastic in a fold of the newspaper, the paper can be slipped under the molding, and the plastic pulled back out, leaving the paper in place.

● When painting baseboards, you have to be careful to keep paint off the floor. A good paint shield that can be easily moved along as you paint is a dustpan. It has a straight edge, a handle, and is lightweight. Also, it doesn't make any difference if you get paint on the dustpan . . . they always look cruddy anyway.

● Using a dustpan as a masker to keep the paint from getting where it's not supposed to be is a good idea. I have adapted it for my housework. When I wash baseboards or door frames, there's always the problem of getting detergent on the wallpaper. I use your moving-masker idea and can slop all over the dustpan without ruining the paper.

● A metal venetian-blind slat is a really keen movable masking shield when painting around baseboards, trim, or other straight parts you want to protect. When you're through, most of the paint wipes off, and the slat can be hung on the wall until the next paint job.

● When installing new molding of any sort, you can make the first paint job much easier by premasking around it. Cut strips of newspaper about three inches wider than the molding. Then, when nailing the molding in place, insert the strips of paper under the molding. The molding will hold the paper in place. When all your carpentry is done, you can paint the new wood without worry of getting paint on the area around it. After your painting is dry, you can pull out all the strips of paper. Next time you paint, when you have to mask and be so careful, you'll see how much trouble you saved yourself.

● When you're painting cabinets down low, do you crouch down to get the underside of the bottom shelves, or do you just dab at them in hopes of getting the job done? Next time, use a mirror. Lay it flat below the shelf, and you'll see that nothing is missed without standing on your head. This trick will work for any low situations. And if you'll wipe up splatters as soon as they occur, your mirror will still be useful later on.

● Painting back in the recesses of a cabinet will go a lot faster if you pour your paint into a small, flat aluminum dish from a frozen chicken pie. This way, you don't have to back the brush out and dip each time you need more paint on it. If you put the can inside the cabinet, you can't see down into it as well as you can the flat dish.

● For years, I've been painting the narrow edges of shelves with a small brush. The other day, I was painting in a closet and dripped paint on the shelf. To prevent more dripping, I used the roller in my hand to wipe the paint off the edge of the shelf. I suddenly realized that it painted the edge with ease. When it came time to do the shelves, I tried out my new discovery and find it's faster by far to use a roller.

● Where two paint colors are to meet on one wood surface, here's a trick that will eliminate masking. After the top color is dry, score a line with a pocket knife along a straightedge. With moderate care, you can paint up to the line without going over. The result will be as straight a line as if masked, but without the risk of the tape pulling up the paint as it's removed.

● If you have to paint a flight of stairs, two methods will still allow you to use the stairs while the paint is drying. One is to paint every other stair one day. Then when the paint's dry, go back in and do the remainder of the steps. The other is to paint each step, but go over only a little past the midpoint. This leaves you a strip of unpainted stair to walk on. When you get ready to paint the other part, let the paint overlap on the middle, because that's where you get the most wear anyway. Either way beats trapping yourself at either the top or the bottom of the stairs until the paint dries.

Any time you require a second coat, be sure to wait until the first is dry, and don't hurry the reinstallation of hardware or the use or newly painted areas.

● When painting an interior wall with a roller, the motion is up and down. If a second coat is required, you may have trouble seeing exactly where you left off each time you reload the roller. If you miss a strip, it'll show up later; and if you overlap too much, you're wasting paint. Take a

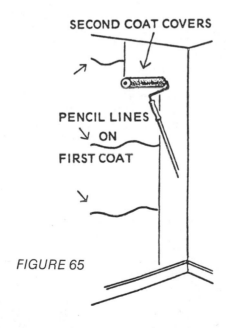

SECOND COAT COVERS

PENCIL LINES

ON

FIRST COAT

FIGURE 65

pencil before you start the second coat and draw a horizontal line all the way across the wall (Figure 65). Your roller strokes will cover the pencil mark, and you can tell exactly where you left off.

● How many times have you had to mix up just a dab of paint for a touch-up job? Most of us end up mixing much too much for the task. The best container for these tiny touch-ups is a bottle cap. Mix with a match stick. Try it and see how often you come up with just the right amount.

● When you have a small touch-up paint job, it's a pain to have to carry the bucket around for a few little dabs here and there. Hold the paint-can lid in your hand and transfer some paint with the brush from the can to the lid. Dip in several times, but don't get enough paint out to overflow. This will give you enough paint for the touch-up on a handy palette. When you're done, you can put the lid back on and if you're quick, any leftover paint will drip back into the can.

● After a paint job, there are sometimes a few spots that you missed, particularly when the color is about the same shade as the old paint. I have found that if you touch up with a rag dipped into the paint rather than a brush or roller, you're less likely to have a spot that will show up. I just dab at the spot, and it seems to work well for me.

CLEANUP

We'll talk about cleaning brushes and rollers later, but I do suggest that you do some other cleanup as soon as you're through painting. As soon as the paint is dry, remove all the masking tape. If you don't, it may not come off except by blasting. Any spilled paint or paint flecks that get on anything they shouldn't must be wiped up immediately. Latex may require a quick swipe with a damp cloth, and oil-based paints may need help from the appropriate thinner. After paint sets up, it may be difficult to remove without damaging the surface below.

● I'm what you call an enthusiastic painter—a kind way of saying I'm a little sloppy. While painting the bathroom ceiling, I splattered paint all over the bathtub. The man at the paint store gave me a formula for getting the paint off: a quarter pound of TSP (trisodium phosphate) in a quart of hot water. He did warn me that this solution was very caustic, and I should wear gloves and not let it get on me or the chrome. Next time, I'll know to cover the tubs and sinks.

● If you're a messy painter like me, you may have splatters all over your floor. I sure did. I have found that you can remove the paint drops by applying cooking oil from the kitchen on the spots. Leave the oil on for several hours, and it will soften up the paint so it can be wiped away. Cooking oil will not affect vinyl flooring.

● Latex paint splatters can be easily wiped up with a damp cloth if you catch them right away. After they set up, however, they are hard to remove. If they happen to be on a stained surface, almost anything you do to remove them will harm the surface underneath. My cure is to make a bandage to fit over the spots. I use several thicknesses of gauze, then saturate the bandage with any clear oil. After two days, enough of the oil has penetrated under the paint so it can be wiped away with a towel. The oil doesn't harm the finish underneath, since it won't penetrate the varnish or shellac.

● If you have some paint spots where they shouldn't be, and you've avoided trying to get them up, maybe you'll want to try a recipe I've used with success. Mix a tablespoon each of turpentine and household ammonia. Dip 0000 steel wool into the mix and rub gently over the spots. Of course, be sure that the mix won't harm the surface under the paint spots. I'll bet this will remove the spots before your eyes.

● For removing paint splatters from window panes, the razor blade has long been the accepted tool. If you aren't careful, it can also result in a few slices of your fingers. If you don't want any more scars, try a hard typewriter eraser on the paint spots. The abrasive surface of the eraser will cut right through the paint, and can't do very much harm to yourself.

● Most people feel a razor blade's the only way to scrape off paint splatters on windows. Among the several other ways that work well is to use a penny—a one-cent piece. This scraper will flick off the paint with never a possibility of a cut finger. Try it!

● With all the tricky masking methods, when painting windows I still get paint on the glass. I also still use a scraper to remove it. I haven't progressed much, but I have learned one smart trick. Before starting to scrape, I go all around the edge of the pane with a utility knife and cut through the paint. This outlines just how close to the frame the scraper should go, and I never take paint off too close to the frame or the putty.

● The next time you get paint splatters on your face or hands, remove them with oleo. Just rub it on the paint, and when all the paint is off, wash away the oleo with soap and water.

● The kitchen grease that wives pour from their frying pans is an excellent substance for helping to clean paint off hands. My wife keeps it in a container in the refrigerator, and I dig out a tablespoonful and rub it into my hands. After a few minutes of working it into the skin, I wipe it off with a paper towel, and then wash my hands with soap and water. It really helps get all the paint off, and is a lot kinder to hands and noses than turpentine.

● Even though the home handyman usually has special clothes for painting, there is always a time when it seems OK to tackle a small job with your good clothes on. Then a week later, you discover that you got paint on your favorite golf shirt. In most cases, a tablespoon of household ammonia mixed with a like amount of turp will remove the paint spot. Dip the spot in the mixture for a few moments. Then take a rag saturated in the mixture and rub the spot. If that doesn't do it, you'll now have another painting shirt.

● I read your book and was surprised you didn't include this old remedy for lingering paint odor. My grandfather used to add a tablespoon of vanilla extract to a gallon of paint. It doesn't affect the color of the paint at all; even white paint is not changed. Then after the painting is done, there's no paint odor. Try it!

● As you know, turpentine odors don't wash off your hands with plain old soap and water. I have found that a squeeze of toothpaste on the hands after using soap and water will wash away whatever is left—including the odor.

EXTERIOR PAINTING

Now that you have the technique, you can move outside without too much fear. You'll probably need ladders or scaffolding, so read up on ladders in Chapter 16 to be sure you use them safely. If you have lots of high painting to do, you might want to consider renting scaffolding.

● When you're painting the side of your house, a scaffold is lots more convenient than a ladder. If you don't want to rent scaffolding, maybe you can use a sturdy wooden picnic table instead. It's just the right height for getting the upper part of the house. Of course, it has to be a table that you were going to refinish before summer anyway.

As with interior painting, it's very important to clean the surfaces.

● The sprayer that fits on the end of a garden hose will do an excellent job of cleaning the outside of the house for painting.

Be sure you follow the detergent treatment with a rinsing, and then let the surface get *totally* dry before you paint. Any mildew should be killed with the following formula: ⅔ cup of TSP, ⅓ cup powdered laundry detergent without ammonia, 1 quart liquid laundry bleach, and 3 quarts of warm water. Scrub the mildewed surfaces with this, then rinse. You can avoid future mildew problems by trimming back bushes, trees, and hedges that hold moisture and prevent air circulation. There are also mildewcides that the paint dealer has to add to your paint, but these won't kill the mildew that's already there.
Other preparation steps may include caulking joints, removing all loose paint, replacing any damaged wood, and resetting any loose nails. Caulking is covered in Chapter 7. A wire brush and sanding remove loose paint. Then use additional sanding to feather the sharp edges so the surface feels smooth.

● A propane torch is a great paint remover if you do it carefully. One danger is using the torch to remove paint on split siding. You could get something smoldering inside the walls and not know about it until you have a fire going. If it is sound siding and is shiplapped, aim the flame down so it can't go up under one of the planks. If you're not going to be careful with the fire, you'd do better to hand sand off all the old paint.
● I made an addition to my paint scraper that makes it a much better tool. I installed a wooden drawer knob onto the back of the scraper near the blade. This converts it into a two-handed tool, which gives better control and greater power, and makes it less tiring.
● The best paint scraper is one I made (Figure 66). I took a block of scrap wood and tacked a long piece of wire screen to it. Then I wrapped the screen round and round the block, pulling it as tight as possible. The wire

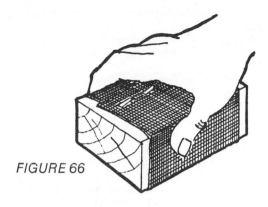

FIGURE 66

was wrapped so it didn't overlap itself, and so it covered most of the block except for about an eighth-inch space between each turn. The other end was tacked in place, and I had a paint scraper that was easy to handle and really took off the old paint.

Small gouges in wood can be replaced with a wood filler made for exterior use. Rotting wood should be removed and replaced. Be sure you remove well beyond the rotted area, as many types of rot will spread.

When all this is done, you must prime all the bare spots or any new wood. The best primer you can use is the one recommended on the label of the paint you'll be using. Be sure to let the primer dry before putting on the top coat.

● It's frustrating trying to paint over a white primer coat with a fairly dark color. You need only one coat for protection, but end up having to put a second coat on to totally hide the white. Now when I am going to put on a primer, I get tubes of color near the color of the finish coat and tint the primer. It doesn't have to match, just come close. This allows the finish coat to cover and does away with a second coat.

Before you start painting, be sure to cover drives, walks, and plants with a tarp. That's easier than removing the stuff later on, or replacing dead plants.

● Paint splatters on a brick wall or brick floor look bad. Usually you can remove the paint by rubbing over the spots with a brick bat of the same color. What paint isn't actually abraded away will be well disguised by the brick dust that comes off in the rubbing. It may not take it off, and you'll have to resort to chemical warfare, but give this a try first because it's the supereasy way out.

● When painting windows, cover the sill with aluminum foil, and you won't have to worry about drips. The foil can be formed around the sill and will stay in place. After the painting is finished, the shield can be moved to the next window.

● When painting outside, loop a piece of rope around the screen-door handle. Then you can go into the house without leaving paint fingerprints on the door.

● When doing exterior painting, I always make sure to have cleaner outside. Otherwise, I'll get paint on the doorknob getting in to the cleaner. This is something most people don't think about. If I'm using oil-base paint, I keep a container of solvent along with my paint. If I'm using latex, I keep a bucket of soapy water. Even though the water gets cold, the paint will wash off.

● When I spray painted our garage, I dropped large grocery sacks over the plants close to the building. One big plant needed a plastic cleaner bag. This was much easier than covering them with drop cloths, and a lot less messy since the bags were all thrown away when the painting was done.

Start at the top and do the main body of the exterior first. Then go back for the trim. Don't go back for a second coat until the first is fully dry.

Be sure you have the right weather conditions for painting. A mild temperature is best. Paint in low humidity, and be sure there aren't any rain clouds in the forecast. Plan your paint job so you can move around to avoid direct sunlight, which causes the outside coat of the paint to dry faster than the underneath part, which causes problems. Used properly, all these weather considerations can allow for some procrastination if you wish.

● After painting the eaves of the house, my wife looked over my handiwork and noticed a few skips. Rather than drag out my ladder and do my climbing act, I used a C clamp to attach the brush handle to a long strip

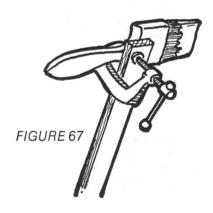

FIGURE 67

of wood. I angled the brush a little (Figure 67). This extension allowed me to do my touch-up from ground level.

● When painting an outside wall with a roller, a roller tray is hard to handle. Since this paint goes on real fast, a tray needs refilling too often. By taking the paint-tray grid screen and hooking it over the rim of a big mop bucket, I can pour in lots more paint, and still use the grid to remove excess paint from the roller. Naturally, the handle on the bucket makes it quite easy to move around.

● While I painted under the eaves of my house, the straight ladder was scratching up the siding I'd already painted. By gluing a pair of those wedge-shaped rubber doorstops to the ends of the ladder, I stopped the marring. The rubber pads instead of the ladder rested against the siding.

● When painting wooden frames on screens, be sure to run masking tape all around the screen next to the frame. For years I never thought of doing this; and when I did, I realized how stupid I'd been all this time. Then I began looking at other screens in the neighborhood and found there are a bunch of other people who never thought of this either.

● When I painted the exterior of our home, of course, I removed all the screens from the windows. In painting the windows, I had to have them partially open at times—a signal for every flying insect in the county to come in. To stop this invasion, I took the screens inside the house and taped them in place over the windows. Wide masking tape did the job, and we kept the bugs out.

● If you plan to paint screens, here's a good method: After painting one side, go over the other side with a dry brush or pad. Usually enough paint will have been forced through to allow for complete coverage of the other side without any clogging. Saves paint and unclogging time.

● When painting the frames of window screens, no matter how careful you are, some paint gets on the screen and fills in the openings. While the paint is still wet, blow it out of the mesh by using a small plastic container as a bellows. Use the kind that has a pointed spout with a small opening. Sure beats trying to wipe the paint out.

● In painting trim around our windows, I found the hedge underneath allowed me no space to set up my stepladder. The ladder was too short to lean against the house at a safe angle. I solved the problem with a pair of three-foot-long scrap boards and two C clamps. I clamped the boards to the outside rails of the ladder just above the second step, at such an angle that they were tight against the top step. The ends then could rest against the window ledge and allow me to use my stepladder as a straight ladder. The extra length allowed the ladder to be set at a workable angle.

● Unable to reach a span of trim I wanted to paint, I was faced with having to get a longer ladder. Instead, I decided to try a kookie idea my son suggested. I drilled two holes through the paintbrush just above the metal band (Figure 68). Then I used screws through the holes to mount the brush on the end of a long scrap of lumber. The bristles were at right angles to the length of the board. This gave me a long-arm brush that was fairly easy to handle. I finished my paint job without a new ladder, and when done, removed the brush.

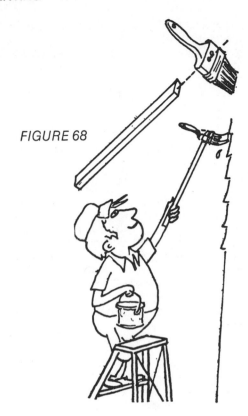

FIGURE 68

● Most basement windows have window wells, but most don't seem to let in enough light to brighten up the basement. One very simple way to get more available light is to paint the walls of the window wells with white or light-colored paint. You'll be pleasantly surprised at how much brighter the basement will be.

METAL PAINTING

Of all the paint failures around, painting of metal may lead the parade. Here again, preparation is important. If the metal is brand new, it usually has an oily film. Always give it a quick bath with paint thinner or another solvent. If it's a galvanized metal, like gutters and downspouts, you really should wait for six months to a year for the surface to weather. If you can't wait, bathe the surface with white vinegar, full strength. Then rinse away the vinegar and let dry before painting.

● If it's good to paint downspouts on the outside, it's gotta be good to coat them inside, too. That's where I use leftover dabs of paint. I tie a string with a weight to a large sponge. Insert the weight at the top of the downspout; it'll drop out the bottom so you can grab the string. Push in the sponge at the top and down a few inches into the spout. Then pour in paint on top of the sponge. Wait a few minutes for the sponge to drink up the paint. Pulling the string pulls the sponge through the spout, coating the inside as it goes down.

● How do you paint the back side of downspouts without getting paint on the house? I wanted to paint them so the metal would be protected, but the space between the metal and the wall was so slim I couldn't get a brush in there. I solved the problem by slipping a scrap of carpet in the narrow slit. I used a piece about a foot long so it stuck out on each side of the spout. By spreading paint on the center of the carpet and then rubbing it gently back and forth like a shoeshine rag as I pulled it upward, the downspout got painted, but no paint got on the bricks.

Shiny metal such as aluminum and stainless steel need to be given a scuff coat with steel wool to etch the surface.

Previously painted metal needs only to be cleaned, dried, and deglossed before repainting. If there are rust spots, however, they must be removed with a wire brush or chemical rust remover. Chipped places need to be sanded to feather sharp edges.

All bare spots must be primed, and for most metals, a rust-preventive primer is called for. Galvanized metals do better with a zinc-based primer. After priming, you can paint with almost any type top coat you wish. Be sure the top paint is compatible with the primer, that it's made for exterior use if need be, and that it's going to withstand heat if the metal is going to be subjected to such.

● There's no easy way to paint curly iron grillwork, right? Wrong. I use a large powder puff bought just for the purpose. Wearing rubber gloves, I pour the paint into a flat container and dip the powder puff in. It will hold a good supply of paint, reaches around the iron, and distributes the paint well. A job that used to take hours is done in a flash with this method.

● The black wrought-iron railings on our front porch were chipped and looked bad. I had planned to paint them, but broke my painting arm. I took a black wax crayon and rubbed over the chipped places. When they were filled, I took a rag and smoothed out the crayon. It worked great! This I could do with my left hand, but painting would have been impossible.

● Getting paint to stick on some metals is not too easy. If you'll first coat the metal with thinned shellac, let it dry completely, and then apply your paint, the paint will go on easily and will last longer and hold more completely to the surface.

PAINTING MASONRY

Many people decide to paint the patio to get away from the drab concrete gray. It may look super to begin with, but after a short while it may peel, bubble, or fade. All masonry is porous, and so presents more potential moisture problems than other surfaces. It's also usually outside, so there's also weather to attack the paint. In the case of a patio, you've also got a bunch of clods walking all over it. In this instance, selection of the proper paint goes hand in hand with preparation.

There are porch and deck paints made for masonry. The latex variety is very popular because of its ease of clean-up, and also because latex can be used under slightly damp conditions. There are also epoxy paints that last for a long time, however, and cement-based paints often used on a basement with moisture problems. Here's where talking with a paint salesman can pay off: He can tell you what paints are going to be compatible with your previous paint as well as with the particular surface.

Special paints require special steps in preparation, but here are some general steps. Repair all the cracks and surface damage, and then be sure to let the patching compound dry before you paint. (See Chapter 11 for concrete patching.) Remove any loose or flaking paint. Clean the surface completely. If the surface is very slick, you'll do better to etch it with a mild muriatic acid solution. If it's extremely porous, you may need a filler. Ask your dealer about this, and be sure the filler will be compatible with the paint you'll be using. Be sure the surface is dry before you paint; then just before you begin, vacuum to get all the dust up.

● If you have painted a porch, deck, or floor, foot traffic during the first week or so after it's dry leaves permanent marks. When I've waited as long as I can, I then use strips of waxed paper as runners. This prevents any scratches or marks until the paint has really set up hard.

● For painting concrete floors in the basement or garage, it's recommended that you use a paint roller with a handle. An even better tool for this is a sponge-type floor mop. One replaceable sponge pad will last for the entire job, whereas rollers seem to wear out on the big jobs. Pour the paint into a roller tray, then mop it on. You'll get a good coat that will result in the desired finish. Whether you use a roller or a mop, it sure beats bending over and using a brush.

● Even though the paint people recommend a long-nap roller for painting stucco, I experimented with a regular old scrub brush. It worked beautifully—got all the peaks and valleys with complete coverage. Also, a roller usually falls apart before too long, but the scrub brush lasted throughout the entire paint job.

● For painting, I use a child's wagon as a rolling roller tray. The regular wire-mesh grid from the roller tray fits over the side of the wagon. The wagon holds lots more paint than the tray, so I don't have to go back for a refill as often. The wagon is easily pulled around, so the paint is always right at hand. I used this when painting the concrete floor of my basement, and the work really went fast.

While I've seen excellent results on brick and masonry painting, I suggest you always think it over before you paint for the first time. Should you ever change your mind, a brick home that's painted cannot easily be restored to the old natural-brick color. Natural brick and masonry don't ever need touch-up and repainting. Before you do it, see if you don't sort of like it the way it is.

BRUSH AND ROLLER CARE

When you go into the paint store for brushes, the dealer will try to sell you the best brushes he's got. He'll tell you quality brushes give much better results and will last a lifetime. For most paint jobs, he's right. However, if you're not going to take care of the brushes, they may not last through the *first* paint job. Here are some tips to make brush and roller care a bit easier.

Clean your brushes and rollers as soon as you're through painting. Use soap and water for latex, and the proper thinner or solvent for other paints.

● For working latex paint out of brushes and rollers, a small old-time washboard is ideal. Stand it in a small tub of water, and you'll have worked all the paint out in no time at all.

● I use latex paints whenever possible. As you know, one big plus Is In the fact that brushes can be cleaned with water. For longer brush life, I use my wife's fabric softener in the last rinse water. It leaves the bristles as soft and easy to use as when the brush was brand-new.

● When you've finished cleaning a paint brush, you should sling most of the water out of it. But when you live in an apartment, it's a lot of trouble to go downstairs to find slinging room. I get around this by putting the brush inside a paper bag, leaving the handle out. Then I close the bag around the handle, and since the bag collects all the water, I can sling to my heart's content without spraying everything in the apartment.

● After you wash a paint roller, it's best if you can wring out most of the water. The best way is to slip the roller onto a shaft I've made from a twisted coat-hanger wire. I then chuck the shaft in my power drill, and when the drill Is turned on, it spin-dries the roller in short order. Of course, it slings water all over everything within a half mile, so I stick it in a grocery sack before turning on the drill. The bag catches all the water.

● Paint rollers come clean quicker if you have some sort of tool to press out the leftover paint. With latex, you can use your hand; but for other types of paint, I've made a tool from coat-hanger wire. I bent a long piece of the wire at the center to conform to the roller's curve. This bend goes a little less than halfway around the roller. I then bent back the rest of the wire and twisted it together to form a handle. When cleanup time comes, the Y-shaped tool can be pressed along the surface of the roller to squeeze out the paint—without getting it all over my hands (Figure 69).

● You recently ran a hint for making a paint-roller cleaning tool from a coat hanger that required cutting the hanger and bending. My method also uses a coat hanger, but requires only a simple bend, bringing the two ends of the hanger together so you have a handle. The curved hook fits around the paint roller, and you can easily remove latex paint as you run water over the roller.

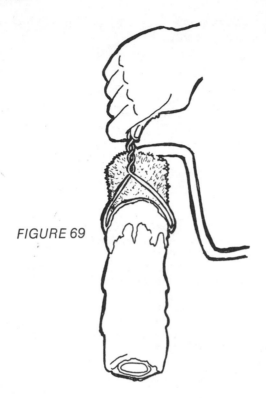

FIGURE 69

● The tall cans that tennis balls come in are ideal for soaking paint rollers in without having to use very much cleaning solvent. I just plop the roller in, and all but about an inch is in the solvent. When this part has had enough soaking, I take it out and put the other end in. When I'm through, the roller is clean.

● Many solvents can be used over and over again if you can get out the sediment. One good way to strain a solvent is to pour the dirty liquid into a clean plastic bleach bottle. Then stuff steel wool into the opening so that it stays in place. As you pour the solvent back out, the steel wool acts as a filter, straining out all of the sediment. Your solvent is clean and ready for use again.

● What with solvent evaporating faster than you can pour it and costing more than booze, my sealed brush soaker will certainly come in handy. It's made from a wide-mouthed half-gallon jar with a screw-on lid. Mount three cup hooks inside the lid. A small block of wood goes on top of the lid as a backing in which to screw the hooks. Hang brushes from the hooks with their bristles hanging down in the solvent. Screw on the top and the brushes soak without any evaporation.

● When soaking brushes in solvent, you'll find that the solvent evaporates rather rapidly. Not with my soaker, made from two bleach bottles. Remove the tops from the jugs so you have two tall containers. Notch one so a piece of coat-hanger wire can rest across the top. The wire goes through holes drilled in the brush handles so the brushes can be suspended in the solvent without bending the bristles. The other container goes over the top as a lid (Figure 70). It's tall enough to cover the handles that stick up. The lid rests on the wire. Then place tape around the join to seal the lid. No evaporation.

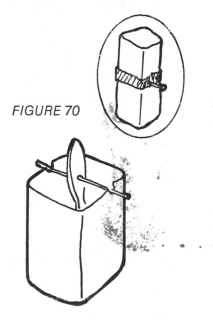

FIGURE 70

● Here's another plastic bleach bottle converted to a paintbrush soaker. I left the spout and handle intact and cut out a hole in the side, right under the spout. This gives an opening in which to pour cleaning solvent, and in which to insert the brush. Then insert the brush handle back up through the spout, and insert a nail into the hole in the brush handle. The nail rests against the lip of the spout, holding the bristles off the bottom of the bottle, but still suspended in the solvent. From time to time, I pull out the nail and work the bristles against the bottom to help remove all the paint.

● My paintbrush soaker seems to work well. From an old inner tube, I cut a square large enough to fit over the can in which the cleaning solvent will go for soaking. Cut a small X in the center of the rubber square, then force the brush handle through this hole. Push up the handle far enough so the brush will hang into the solvent without touching the container's bottom. Then lay the rubber square across the top of the can. Fold down the edges around the can, and hold them in place with a rubber band. The brush hangs in place, and no solvent is lost through evaporation.

● Finding a container wide enough to soak a wide paintbrush needn't hang you up. Use the paint-roller tray. Lay the brush flat with the bristles down in the deep part. Pour in just enough solvent to cover the bristles. You'll use less solvent, and you don't have to worry about rigging the brush to hang. And since you're using the tray for the big brush, why not put all the rest in too?

● For brush cleaning, I use a tin can just big enough for the brush to go into. This allows me to use much less solvent than with other—larger—containers. To position the brush so the bristles aren't touching the bottom, I select a large nail and drive it half-way through the brush at just the right point so the nail can rest across the top of the can while the brush soaks. When the soaking is done, I tap out the nail. The same hole can be used next time.

● To hang a brush in the cleaning solvent without having the bristles touch the bottom, use a coffee can. Pour in the solvent. Crimp the top of the can so the sides are against the brush handle when it's at the right level. Crimp it tight, and it'll hold.

● When I get ready to soak a brush in solvent, I insert an L-shaped screw-in hook into the handle. This is like a cup hook, but has a right angle instead of a curve. This allows the brush to hook over the edge of the container with the bristles down in the solvent. However, I position the hook so the bristles don't touch the bottom. When the brush is clean, I can remove the hook but still have the hole for reinstalling it next time I need to clean that brush.

● The hole in the end of a paintbrush handle is in the wrong place for hanging a long brush to soak in solvent. About the only way is to put the solvent in a bucket because ordinary coffee cans aren't deep enough. Rather than tie up a bucket or rig up some crazy holder, I drill another hole in the brush just above the metal band (ferrule). Then I can run a length of coat-hanger wire through the hole and let this rest on the rim of a small can. This lets the bristles hang down into the liquid. As a matter of fact, I now use this method even on small brushes, since it's easier to find a container of the right depth.

● To soak a brush in solvent without having to rig up one of those tricky brush holders, use a C clamp to attach the brush to the side of the container. Position the brush so the bristles don't touch the bottom of the container and get bent out of shape.

● The guy who put a glass flower frog in the solvent can so he'd have a surface over which to work brushes for cleaning has a good idea. But I use a flat tuna can punched full of holes with an icepick. The holes are punched from the inside and leave a rough exterior. With the can in the bottom of the solvent container, you have a bigger flat—but rough—surface that really helps clean the brush.

● When soaking a tiny striping or artist's brush for cleaning, use a blob of modeling clay to hold the brush suspended in the solvent. The clay sticks to the side of the container and can be positioned so the bristles of the brush are in the liquid, but not against the bottom. Embed the handle of the brush in the clay and it will stay there.

● After using a tiny artist's brush for striping or touch-up, I poke the handle into one of the corrugations of a scrap of corrugated board. Then adjust it so the bristles stick out enough so they will be in the solvent but not touch the bottom of the jar. Cut the cardboard wide enough so it can rest endwise on the lip of the jar. The weight of the brush keeps it balanced.

● A small striping or artist's brush can be soaked in cleaning solvent right in the solvent bottle. Be sure to clean the excess paint out of the brush before dipping it in the cleaner. Use a spring-type clothespin to hold the brush at the proper level in the liquid. After clipping the brush, the clothespin will rest across the mouth of the bottle.

● Sometimes an old, gummed-up paintbrush can be revived by just boiling it in household vinegar. When the vinegar starts to boil, work the brush against the bottom of the container. You'll be surprised at how this cleans and softens brushes that look like they could never be used again.

● When you want to recondition a paintbrush, after using a solvent to remove the paint, soak it in hot vinegar. The bristles will be soft and alive like new.

● If you have a nylon brush with bristles that look like a fright wig, you may be able to render first aid. Soak it for about five minutes in very hot water. Then place it on a flat surface and place the bottom of a flat pan on top. When it dries, usually it will be back in shape with all the bristles lying down as they should.

● My wife has become such a good painter that she does it all, but she does a lousy job of cleaning brushes afterward. To clean a good brush after she had painted, I tried a remedy that someone told me about, and it really came through. I added a couple of ounces of TSP (trisodium phosphate) to about a pint of boiling water. Then I put the brush into the mix and began working it against the bottom of the container. Next, I let it soak for a while and later worked it against the bottom again. When the water had cooled, I made another batch and did it again. When the brush was clean, I washed out all the TSP with warm water and detergent and have a good brush again.

● If you ever make the mistake of cleaning up paintbrushes in your kitchen sink, here's a mixture guaranteed to clean up the mess. Put a couple tablespoons of salt into a cup of turpentine and mix well. Scrub the sink with a rag dipped in this, then rinse away. It even takes away deep stains that your paint didn't leave.

● Latex paint in a roller tray is easily cleaned up with water. But before you send all that paint down your sink or hose it onto your driveway, put a handful of sawdust over the paint. Then take a crumpled newspaper and wipe out the tray. Nearly all the paint and sawdust mixture will come off. Now you can make the tray shine with soap and water in the sink without fear that you'll clog up the drain. If you hose outside, there is so little pigment left that it won't stain your concrete.

● Most people lay a paintbrush across the top of the can when pausing. This wastes paint down the side of the can and usually makes a mess. With a piece of coat hanger, you can easily fashion a wire shelf that fits on the paint can and lets you place the brush down so drips go back into the can. Bend the wire into a U shape that will hold the handle and be long enough to allow the bristles to be over the bucket. At the two ends, bend hooks that will fit inside the rim of the can and go in under the part of the rim that protrudes down in the can. This will keep it in place. A pair of kinks in the wire on either side of where the brush handle rests will insure the brush can't slide off.

● Between uses, I keep paintbrushes properly shaped by dipping them in water-soluble glue. I then brush off the excess and shape the brush. It hardens, and the brush stays as it was shaped until its time to use it again. Then I wash out the glue with water and have a perfect brush.

● An abused paintbrush can become so feathered at the ends that it no longer will do a good job. I had one like this and found that it could be repointed when wet. Then I put it in the freezer. It froze while pointed, and when thawed out, was again perfectly shaped.

● Did you know that moths sometimes get hungry enough to attack your natural-bristle paintbrushes? That's why when I store mine, I include some moth crystals in the wrapping. This extra precaution can save an expensive brush.

● When I finish cleaning a paintbrush, I slip a wide rubber band around the still-wet bristles. I select one that won't crimp the bristles into a bunch, but will be tight enough to keep them to a point and not allow any to flare out at the sides. When the brush is used the next time, it's in perfect shape.

● You have had several brush-holder ideas for regular paint-brushes, but nothing for the tiny artist-type brushes used for stripping. My quickie holder is made by clipping off several inches of wire solder from the roll. I form it into a coil by wrapping it around my finger, and leave a tab sticking straight out at each end of the coil to form a base. The wet brush fits between the coils and is held in place when not in use. The coils are lax enough that the brush can be easily picked up. When I'm through with the holder, the wire solder is still OK for soldering.

● While painting the other night, the old eyelids became heavy, and I knew I'd better wait until the next day to finish. I was too tired to clean the brush and roller, but knew they would be in bad shape if left out to dry. Since I was using water-based paint, I decided to try putting the whole mess in the freezer. The next morning, after letting the brush and roller thaw for a few minutes, they were just as good as the night before.

● Want an easy-to-make throwaway brush for touch-ups? A square of thin foam rubber doubled over and held in a spring-type clothespin will do a very nice job. When done, drop the foam rubber into the garbage.

Somehow you never figure exactly the right amount of paint to buy. Maybe this will help.

● The sanctuary of our church was due for painting. Our volunteer committee had to measure the height of several high spots in order to estimate the amount of paint we'd need, and also to be sure we rented scaffolding high enough. While we were trying to figure out how we'd get up there to measure, the preacher's wife went to the shopping center next door and returned with a helium-filled balloon. By premeasuring a long string, we were able to let the balloon reach up to the top for us.

Here are some helps with leftovers:

● If you don't have a container that can be sealed tightly to store leftover paint, put a plastic bag down into a large tin can. Push the bag against the bottom and sides of the can. Then fold down the open end of the bag around the outside of the can. Pour in the paint, then take a twist tie and close the bag. The paint is sealed against air in the bag and can be kept in the open can.

● A paint can reopened for the second time sometimes doesn't want to be resealed again. The dried paint in the rim has formed an irregular pattern, and if the lid and rim don't match up, the seal may not be there, and the paint inside will harden. When you put the lid back on a paint can, take a nail or the sharp point of your opener and scratch across the edge of the lid and the rim of the paint can. Then always line up these marks when resealing.

● You and your readers have come up with several ways to fight the paint that ends up in the rim of the can. However, I don't worry about it. When I get ready to put the lid back on, I place it in the groove. Then I slip a paper bag over the whole can. I use a hammer to tap the lid firmly into place. The paint in the groove of the rim will squirt out, but I don't care because it gets on the inside of the paper bag, not on me.

● When I have a little leftover paint that I want to keep, I drop a couple of clean pebbles into the can before sealing it. When I need to use the paint again, I just shake the can, and the pebbles do the mixing.

Paint isn't the only thing in the paint cabinet.

● Many times you need only a few drops of a solvent, but it's very difficult to pour a small amount. When this need arises, I punch a small hole in the metal cap, and this allows me to squirt or pour as few drops as I wish. Then I insert a self-tapping metal screw into the hole to cap it back up until I need to use it again.

Even the best effort can require some touch-up.

● That little dab of paint you saved for touch-ups will keep nicely in a shoe-polish bottle—the kind with a dauber will also provide you with an applicator. Be sure you remove all the shoe-polish traces from both dauber and bottle or you may end up with some odd-colored spots on the wall. Also, be sure you don't mistake the touch-up for shoe polish or you may be the only one in town with green shoes.

● When doing a touch-up, it's a waste of time and energy to have to strain out just a dab of paint. However, most leftover paint needs to be strained. By just dipping the bottom of an old tea strainer into the paint, you'll strain out any particles. Dip the brush in the paint inside the strainer. Do your touch-up. Then tap the strainer to knock out the excess paint. It's a real time and mess saver.

● If you have to touch up a ceiling or wall, and if you'd like the reach of a roller but don't want to mess up a paint tray, apply paint to the roller by painting it on with a brush. This would take too long if there is much painting, but is great for a touch-up.

Usually the easiest way to paint smaller objects is with a spray can. It's more expensive, but well worth it. Here's how to do it better:

● For spray painting drawer and cabinet knobs, use a cardboard egg carton as a holder. Turn the carton upside down, and poke the screws for the knobs through from the underside. Install the knobs so they are flush with the egg carton. Now they can be sprayed without your handling them, and the threads of the screws won't get painted. Everything is kept together, and when the paint dries, the holder can be tossed away.

● In the winter, anytime you bring a can of spray paint in from the garage or shop, you should warm it up before using it. The best safe way is to place the can in a container of warm water. Don't use water that's over a burner, as the can could get too hot and explode. Just warm tap water will do, and then you can spray away.

● Where do you go to spray paint if you live in an apartment? I found we have a spray booth right in our apartment—the fireplace. I open the damper, and all the odor is carried away. Any overspray that gets on the bricks is wiped off with a solvent rag, but really doesn't show up back there. Besides, next fall when we light a fire, it'll be covered over with soot or burned away.

● Aerosol spray paint is certainly easy to use, but you must take care to insure the vapor doesn't fall on the wrong things. The best way to prevent this is to use a spray booth, and the easiest way to rig one is to get a large corrugated box. An appliance or furniture store will usually have a great big box they'll be glad to part with. You may have to cut out a side, but other than that, there is no rigging to do—and it is free.

● I have salvaged an old lazy susan that my wife wanted to throw out. It is now the best paint-spray table for small items that I could find. I can spin the table around and spray all sides of the object. This means I can use a spray booth and contain the overspray without having to touch the object while the paint's wet.

13.
PLUMBING

Because most plumbing is out of sight (behind the walls, under the house, or even underground), many people haven't the foggiest notion how it works. Furthermore, they look upon plumbing problems as a big mystery, too complicated for the average person to know about. Actually, it's a fairly simple system—or two systems, since the incoming and the outgoing are entirely separate. The two systems are the water-supply and the drainage systems, and despite any Supreme Court decision, total segregation is a must.

The principles under which the two systems operate are basic laws of nature, in most cases, and both systems also depend on pipes for conveyance. So they are very similar—but separate.

Before we get into repairs, I think it would be well for you to understand the basics of each system so that you can see how simple the whole thing is. Then when there is an emergency or a need for repair, you won't be afraid to act.

The water-supply system brings cold water into the house— under pressure. In most cases, the pressure is caused by the city's having pumped water into a big supply tower—when you open a tap, gravity brings it out with the desired force. In some cases, a pump will supply the pressure, and sometimes a regulator will control it. But in most cases, it's just Mother Nature. The reason that water will come out of an upstairs faucet is because the original water supply is higher still. This also enables it to follow pipes that might go up over doors or around corners, or wherever it's needed.

You'll notice I said *cold* water. Your home also has a hot-water system, but it uses plain cold water that's been brought in and run through the water heater. Then the hot water is carried in separate pipes, usually right next to the ones for cold water.

After you have all that water in the house and have run it through washing machines, and over dirty dishes, and sprayed your bodies with pulsating showers, you have to get rid of it. That's where the drain system comes in. Drain pipes are all slanted down so gravity carries the wastewater away. (They have to be, because a pump would be too expensive.) Each drain has some sort of trap that holds water to prevent sewer gas from backing up into the house. There are also vents—usually exiting through your roof—that allow air into the drain pipes. The equalized air pressure helps the water flow out and prevents the water in the traps from being siphoned down the line.

There, in a nutshell, are the basics. There are lots of other things involved—like the fixtures, cutoff valves, clean-out plugs, and many more—but we'll talk about them as we run across them in projects or problems. It's easy to figure out that the biggest problem in the supply system is leakage. The big problem in the drain system is clogging. Either of these can be emergencies and call for quick action.

EMERGENCIES

Leaks in a supply system can do thousands of dollars worth of flooding damage—unless you know how to stop the water. *Right now,* before such an emergency crops up, is the time to learn what to do.

Locate all cutoffs. Each sink, tub, toilet, and lavatory should have its own cutoff. Appliances using water should also have cutoffs, but many don't. But even if they all do, the source of the leak could be in a pipe within your walls, so you should also know about the main cutoff—usually located somewhere near where the water supply enters your house. It can be outside the house or inside. Outside valves are usually connected to pipes that are buried down below where frost can reach them. This means the valve is in a box unit set into the ground or that there is a key, an L-shaped rod that comes up from the cutoff on the pipe (Figure 71). Inside cutoffs can usually be found just where the water supply comes through the wall, often in the basement. If there is a water meter, there is usually a cutoff right next to it. If you can't find it, call the water company and ask where they hid it.

Once you find the cutoff, make sure it works and that you know how to use it. A stuck valve is no help in an emergency. It's a good idea to turn all cutoff valves back and forth twice a year. This way, they won't have a chance to corrode or get stuck in the open position. It's best to find out now, rather than at two o'clock in the morning with your basement turning into a swimming pool.

It's also a good idea to tag the cutoffs as to what they control, and maybe even to note the direction to turn for cutoff. One reader suggested using the bottom of a plastic bleach bottle for the tag (Figure 71). Mark it with India ink. Cut a hole in the center so the tag can fit over the stem of the cutoff. Now you have a nondecaying tag with permanent markings.

After all this is done, take all other members of your household on a tour to explain what to do in an emergency. This should include children old enough to handle the situation.

Flooded basements caused by outside factors—like rain—are plumbing problems to the extent that the drain can't handle the excess water. For emergency purposes, remember that water and electricity don't mix, so don't go wading across the basement to plug in a pump or something. If there's any possibility that you'll come in contact with

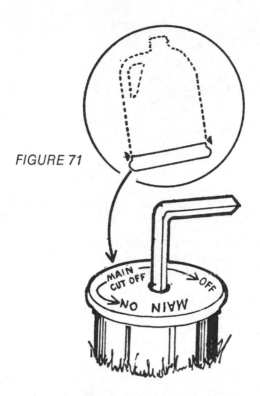

FIGURE 71

anything electrical, throw the main switch before you start mopping up. (This applies in any part of the house—not just the basement.)
These cutoff emergency steps haven't solved the problem, but they've stopped the flow to minimize damage.

PIPE LEAKS

Sometimes a pipe leak can be patched up, and most of the ways should be considered temporary. However, "temporary" can last for years ... or it may just be done to tide you over until the plumber comes, or until you have a spare weekend to replace the section of pipe.
Leaks in galvanized pipes are usually from corrosion, so patching in one place may work fine. But the corrosion is probably all along the section, and before long you'll have another leak. Before you do anything, cut off the supply to that pipe. Here are some patch-ups:

1. A pinpoint leak can be stopped by jamming a sharp pencil point into the hole. Break it off, then wrap waterproof tape around the pipe to keep the plug in place. Sometimes the tape by itself will hold the water in for a while.

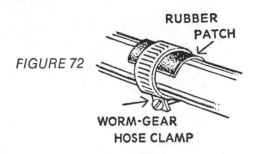

FIGURE 72

RUBBER
PATCH

WORM-GEAR
HOSE CLAMP

2. Place a rubber pad (a square from an old inner tube will do) over the hole, and then clamp it down tight with a worm-gear hose clamp (Figure 72).

3. Hardware stores carry clamp kits.

4. Metal epoxy will seal a hole on any metal if properly applied. This can be a permanent repair if done right.

Copper pipes rarely corrode and rarely develop leaks within the pipe except from a careless nail driven into them. Clamping doesn't seem to be as effective as with galvanized pipe, because copper, being soft, tends to bend. The leak usually wrinkles out from under the clamp. But if you can't replace the section right away, give it a try.

Leaks at joints are more common than holes in pipes. Threaded joints can sometimes be tightened. If that doesn't work, remove and apply pipe-joint compound to the threads and replace. This compound is inexpensive and comes in sticks, cans, or tubes. Teflon tape is

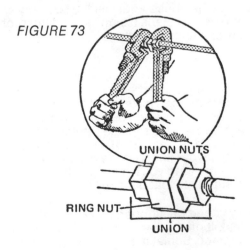

FIGURE 73

UNION NUTS

RING NUT

UNION

another plumber's product to use on threads. Leaky solder joints should be removed and resoldered (see page 193). Plastic pipe joints can often be taken care of with solvent weld compound for that type of plastic. With joint leaks, epoxy can also do the job.

Most often, the bad section of pipe is best repaired by replacing the whole thing. If you remove a pipe or piece of pipe in the center of a run of galvanized pipe, you must use *two* pieces of pipe to replace it. These two must be joined by a fitting called a union (Figure 73). The reason is that if you turned a piece of pipe into a threaded fitting at one end, it would loosen itself from the threads at the other end. The union is made to compensate for this.

Here's something to consider. If the leak is in some inaccessible area that might require ripping into a wall or floor, maybe you can reroute the pipe. It might be easier to box in a "dead" pipe than to replace a wall section. You'll find there are all sorts of fittings available, even those that adapt from one kind of pipe to another. If rerouting is your plan, be sure what you want to do complies with the local plumbing code.

CLOGGED DRAINS

Stopped-up drains are easier—but often messier—to handle. If the drain is clogged, the cardinal rule is easy—just don't run any more water. Sometimes, however, water will keep backing up in one drain, when the water source is in another, higher part of the house—perhaps from a washing machine or an upstairs bath. Don't panic—just figure out where the water's coming from. After you stop the overflow, you can go to work on the clog.

Most clogs are the result of the lousy diet we feed drains. When you pour grease down the sink, this stuff will keep flowing only until it cools and solidifies—on the walls of the pipes. Then all the vegetable peelings, coffee grounds, pumpkin pits, and leftovers get stuck in the grease, and before long this accumulation blocks the pipe. In bathtubs and lavatories, soap scum takes the place of grease, and hair is what gets stuck. Even though this is a messy problem, you can usually take care of it. A slow-running sink or bathtub can be due to hair caught on the pop-up plug. Lift out the plug and remove the hair. Most household clogs are close at hand, so the next thing to try is the plumber's friend or force cup. You don't have to have a PhD to operate this plunger, yet a lot of people fail. These steps will help:

1. Remove the pop-up plug, stopper, or strainer. Many folks wouldn't dare try to remove and clean, adjust or repair the lever up on the side of the tub that stops the flow of water through the drain. They figure they'd whip it out and never be able to get it all back in and working. But many times, removing a stopper is a must for proper treatment of a clogged drain.

While there are variations, most tub stoppers work like the following: The first type has no pop-up in the tub. The closing is done when the trip lever lowers a brass stopper plug into the path of the drain. To remove this, remove the two screws from the trim plate around the lever. Put a towel in the tub over the drain to catch the screws if the drain opening could devour them.

The other type has a pop-up. Sometimes this stopper is attached to a spring, and sometimes the end of the linkage fits into a loop in the end of the rod. With the pop-up pulled out at an angle, the connection of its linkage to the rod is separated. The lever can then be angled out after the screws are removed from the trim plate. Getting it back together requires some fishing and fiddling, but knowing what you're trying to do helps. Be patient!

Lavatory plugs are generally of two types. The first type has a slot that engages a pivot rod. Just grab the pop-up, twist it counterclockwise until it's disengaged, and then lift it out. The other type requires attack from underneath. Loosening the compression nut allows the rod to slip out of the eye so the plug can be lifted out.

2. Plug up other openings to the drain (such as the other side of a double sink or an overflow outlet). Otherwise, the force seeks the path of least resistance and squirts water out the other sink. Use stoppers, towels, the palm of your hand, or whatever will close the drain.

3. Make sure the rubber cup completely covers the drain opening.

● When using a plumber's friend in a sink that doesn't have standing water, there is often a problem of not having an airtight seal around the edges. This will result in poor suction. The seal can be made better by applying a light coat of cooking shortening all around the lip of the rubber suction cup. After the sink is unclogged, be sure to wipe the plunger clean and also remove any excess from the sink.

● When using a plumber's friend, smear petroleum jelly around the lip of the cup. You'll get a tighter seal and thus better suction and greater force.

● The sink at the weekend cabin got stopped up—and no plumber's friend. One of the kids had brought a hollow rubber ball, and while he went out to play, I sliced it in half. By placing it over the drain, I pushed it up and down and created enough suction to unstop the sink. It cost me the price of a new ball, but saved our weekend.

4. Now you're ready to go. Place the suction cup over the drain opening. If the water has seeped out of the sink, put some more in until there's an inch or so over the lip of the cup. The water helps form a vacuum.

Here's where most folks fall apart. They pump up and down a couple of times and step back. When the water doesn't go whooshing out, they give up. If the plumber's friend is going to work, you've got to work with it. Grab the handle with both hands and start a steady up-and-down motion. You'll begin to feel the force on both the upstroke and the downstroke. The upstroke is a vacuum and pulls back; and the downstroke pushes.

5. Keep pumping for about twenty strokes, and then step back

Usually the water will go whooshing out. If not, go through the routine two or three more times before going to the next attack. Even if the plumber's friend doesn't work, it's been a great exercise (good for the pectoral muscles), and also a great way to work off the frustration over the fact that the sink clogged up just before the company arrives.

The next best attack depends on the circumstances. It either involves removing the trap or using a plumber's snake—or both.

First, let's examine the trap. All sinks and basins will have such a U-shaped pipe underneath. This U shape often collects garbage, and may well be the problem area. To remove and clean:

1. First, place a bucket under the trap. Even if there's no standing water still in the sink, the trap will contain water. (And don't do as one reader confessed: He placed the bucket and caught all the water. Then to get rid of the water, without thinking, he poured it down the sink.)

2. If the trap has a clean-out plug, use a wrench and turn counterclockwise to remove. If the clog is here, poke in a piece of coat-hanger wire.

3. If there's no clean-out plug, or if the clog is bad, remove the entire trap. This is done by turning the two slip nuts. Use large pliers, a large adjustable wrench, or any of several special wrenches that will open wide enough. If the shiny chrome is going to be seen, protect it from the tool with a few rounds of tape.

4. Once removed, use a wire to gouge out the garbage. Then rinse out and replace.

Before replacing any plug, clean all residue from the lip of the plug and the drain opening. Wet-dry sandpaper or steel wool should do. Even tiny bits of residue can allow water to leak around the plug.

It's a good idea to smear pipe-joint compound on the threads. Also, be sure you include the rubber washers that go under the slip nuts.

● Through carelessness, the stub of drain pipe coming from a lavatory got bent out of shape and, therefore, the trap section would not fit on it. Rather than remove the pipe that was bent—one heck of a job—I super-rigged it. Using a rubber-hose section designed for a car radiator, I formed a trap piece and attached it using worm-gear hose clamps. The hose section extended far enough up on the bent pipe that it was clamped to a portion that wasn't bent. It works fine, and if I need to remove the trap, this is easily done by loosening the clamps.

● A good way to make sure there will never be leaks around a sink trap is to coat the regular washers with latex caulk. When this sets up, it becomes like rubber and gives a positive seal. However, if you should have to rescue a diamond ring from the trap, it will break loose.

● In putting a sink trap back on, petroleum jelly can be used on the threads to prevent leaks and corrosion that would make removal difficult later on.

The plumber's snake (auger) is so-called because it is as flexible as a snake. It can negotiate curves in the pipes to reach the blockage. Here's the way to use a snake:

1. If you're feeding in through the sink opening, remove the stopper, pop-up plug, and/or strainer. Poke the head of the snake down the hole and start feeding it in. If the stoppage is back in the wall, it's usually easier to remove the trap as described above and feed the auger directly into the wall—this means fewer curves to fight with.

2. When the snake hits a curve, slide the handle—if you have that type—up to within about six inches of the opening and tighten it in place. Now start rotating the handle, which causes the snake to twist, and sooner or later helps the flexible head make the turn. Since sometimes it takes a while, patience is the key word here.

3. Keep feeding the snake through the maze until you reach the blockage. Once again, set the handle.

4. Now work the snake back and forth against the clog at the same time you're rotating the handle.

5. Even after you've broken through, work the snake back and forth to break up the garbage.

6. Put the trap back in place if you removed it, and flush out the pipe with lots of hot water. The water will have more force if you stop up the sink, fill it, and then pull the plug. Don't pull it by hand if you have to reach into a sink full of hot water.

● Using a plumber's snake to unclog drains can be pretty messy. To keep the mess down, I keep a flat corrugated box outside the clogged pipe. When the snake is brought out, I coil it in the bottom of the box. This keeps the mess off the floor. The box also contains the snake and keeps it from springing out and hitting anything. I have also learned to put a container under the pipe to catch drippings that the snake brings out.

● After a plumber's snake has done its thing, and you bring it out, it's going to be messy. But if you have a large plastic bucket handy, you can curl the snake up inside the bucket as it comes out of the pipe. The mess goes in the bucket and can be carried outside. Then fill up the bucket with water, and the snake will soak clean.

● For clogged-up drains I have made a plumbing tool that works most of the time. I cut an eight-inch circle around the valve stem of an old inner tube. When I have a stopped-up sink, this circle is placed over the drain opening. Then I attach my tire pump to the valve stem and get my wife to hold the circle firmly in place over the drain. Now I give the tire pump a few brisk strokes, and this sends a blast of air down the drain. Usually this builds up enough pressure to blast through the clog. If you had an air compressor, you could really have an easy go of it. Keep in mind that if there is a double sink or any other route for the air pressure to take, it'll go there instead of toward the clog.

What if these measures fail? This can happen if the blockage is too deep in the labyrinth of pipes. Don't give up yet. Look for clean-out plugs. These may be on the side of the house, in the basement, or in a crawl space. The plug is threaded, and the square protrusion is for your wrench to grip onto. This often gives you a straighter shot into the pipe to reach the trouble spot. A flat sewer auger, called a plumber's ribbon, is used here in many cases. They come in longer lengths, resemble a giant clock spring, and have a snake head. They have the flexibility of a snake. In most cases, you'll do best to rent a long heavy-duty ribbon.

Sometimes another way to attack a clog that's hard to reach is with a ribbon down the vent stack. This is usually an open pipe sticking out the roof. It runs directly into the drain system, allowing air into the drain to prevent siphoning action that could suck all the water out of the traps.

A sucking noise made as water goes down the drain probably indicates a clogged vent. This should be taken care of with a plumber's ribbon worked into the vent from the rooftop. If not remedied, a siphoning action can develop that could suck the water out of the trap, making it possible for sewer gas to enter the house. If there is no vent pipe, install an antisiphon trap to silence the draining and protect the water seal provided by the trap. Ask your plumbing-supply dealer about this easy-to-install, inexpensive gadget.

Root growth in drains is a common problem in some areas. The clue is if you have a tree with water-seeking roots (maple, cottonwood, lombardy poplar, willow, or elm) within twenty feet of the outdoor pipe. This may be a job for a pro. However, you can rent an electric rooter that feeds into the pipe as it rotates. The head has cutter blades that clean away the roots as they go through. You might also want to try chemicals made especially for root removal.

I didn't suggest chemical warfare, because I believe the chemical drain openers are best used as a preventive measure. When a drain gets sluggish, these compounds—either liquid or crystal—may prevent complete blockage. They do sometimes work on a clogged drain, but if they don't, your next step may involve contact with water containing dangerous acids or caustics. There are solvent-type drain cleaners that are neither acid nor caustic, and they will often dissolve the grease and soap scum. Whatever chemical you use, in whatever stage of the problem, be sure to read and follow the caution notices on the container.

● Here's an old-time drain-cleaner formula passed on to me by my father. It is to be used regularly to keep drains fresh and free-running. It costs less than store-bought kinds and is not dangerous as they can be. In a large jar, put two cups of baking soda, two cups of table salt, and a half cup of cream of tartar. Cap the jar and shake it vigorously to mix. To use, I put about a quarter cup of the dry mix down the drain. Then I pour a cup of water down the drain. When the bubbling stops, I flush the drain with water from the tap. We never have drain problems.

●I never have a drain pain anymore since I started using an old, old preventive maintenance trick. My grandfather said if I'd put a half cup of kerosene down each drain, and then follow that with a pan of boiling water, the drains would stay clear. I do this about every month or so, and although we used to have problems regularly, we've had none since this was started.

Many communities don't permit any petroleum products including kerosene to be introduced into drains.

● The plumber used a rotating rooter gadget to get rid of the roots clogging my sewer line. However, he said they'd grow back unless I had a new sewer line put in. I said I'd have to think about it. Then a neighbor suggested that if I'd put rock salt down the drain and leave it overnight about once a month, the roots would be killed before they could grow. I tried this over a year ago and have never had any more problems.

● We use a liquid drain unclogger every month to keep the drains running freely. Rather than have to worry about getting the chemicals on the chrome drain opening, I purchased a plastic funnel with a hose attachment, used in automotive work. This gets the liquid right down the drain. Then when I flush the drain out, I also wash out the funnel so it's safe to put back under the sink.

TOILET TROUBLES

Too many World War II Navy movies have taught children about burial at sea. It's not uncommon for a teddy bear to get full military honors as he goes swirling down the commode. Of course, toys aren't the only cause for a clogged john. Mothers forget about diapers. Fathers place items on the tank lid to be knocked into the bowl. Excessive toilet paper or cleansing tissues can also cause a clog.

A clogged toilet rising toward the rim after a flush calls for quick work. Either turn the cutoff under the tank (Figure 74), or reach in and lift the float arm. Usually by the time you do this, the tank ball has already seated, and no more water is coming into the bowl anyway— and you almost made it before the overflow. After the water in the bowl goes down, by all means *don't* flush again to see if the toilet is OK. (See page 184).

Since the toilet is self-trapped, and since it goes right into a large drain pipe, the clog is usually very close at hand. You should be able to solve the problem with these steps:

1. First, try the plumber's friend. If you have lots of "burials at sea," there is a special toilet plunger you might want to get. Cover the outlet with the cup and have enough water in the bowl to cover the plunger. If there's so much water that you'll splash with the action, bail some of it out. When you think it's unclogged, pour water from a bucket to flush. This way you can control the amount that enters the bowl, whereas a flush from the tank could be enough to overflow.

2. Often a wire coat hanger can solve the problem. Straighten it

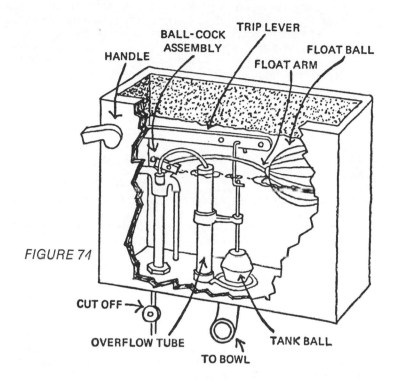

FIGURE 74

out except for the hook on the end. With this worked into the outflow opening, you can hook teddy bears, paper, or whatever.

3. A special tool, called a closet auger, can be used. It's a second cousin to the snake. A regular snake can also be used, but isn't as handy. Be careful with either kind not to break the porcelain or scratch the china finish. Work the snake back and forth to pull some of the blockage out to avoid compacting.

If you live near a babbling brook, the sound of running water is peaceful, but if the running water is in the toilet tank, the sound is somehow not peaceful at all. Plus the fact that it's just another water waster—and in some cases, a big one.

By knowing how a toilet works, you'll be better able to figure out what's causing it to run continuously.

The inside of a typical toilet tank (Figure 74) looks complicated, but it's really not. When you push down on the handle, the trip lever raises, pulls up the lift wire that raises the tank ball on the lower end of the lift wire, letting the water in the tank rush out and into the bowl below, flushing it clean. Meanwhile, the hollow float ball that was peacefully floating atop the water in the tank is no longer supported, so it drops. As it does, the float arm comes down and opens a valve in the ball cock so that new water flows into the tank. By now, that tank ball has fallen back in the hole so the tank starts filling up. This causes the float ball to rise. And when it gets up high enough, it closes the inlet valve in the ball cock so the flushing cycle is finished.

Here's what you do:

1. Very carefully lift off the tank lid and put it where it can't be dropped or stepped on. They are pure porcelain and too-often cracked.

2. If the water is not running over the overflow tube, it is probably seeping out around the tank ball. This can be due to any of several problems:

A. The guide could be out of place so the lift wires aren't over the center of the hole, and thus the tank ball falls to one side. Move it.

B. The lift wires themselves could be bent or burred. Cut off the water and straighten or file away the burrs. If need be, lift wires are easily and cheaply replaced.

C. The upper lift wire could be in the wrong hole in the trip-lever rod so it doesn't fall straight down. Move it.

D. The lift wires could be sticking in the guide. Cut off the water, smooth them with steel wool, and smear petroleum jelly on them.

E. The seat in the outlet valve could be corroded. Cut off the water; flush; and use a knife, wet-dry sandpaper, or steel wool to scrape away scale. Careful—don't break the porcelain.

F. The tank ball could be worn out. A replacement is only a buck or so and is easily installed. It's threaded and screws onto the lower lift wire.

3. If water is running over the overflow tube, lift up on the float arm. If that stops the water from running, that means the float ball is seated too high on the water. To correct this, bend down on the rod just slightly until the water shuts off at a level within about an inch below the top of the overflow tube.

4. If lifting the float arm doesn't stop the flow, the problem is in the ball-cock unit. Shut off the water. Remove the retaining pins, usually thumbscrews, and slip the lever out of the slot in the plunger. Lift it out. Replace the bad washers, and you've probably solved the problem.

An inadequate flush can result from an insufficient level of water in the tank. It should be up to within about an inch of the top of the overflow tube. If it's low, bend the float rod up a tad to raise the level. Or it might be that the tank ball comes down too soon because it doesn't raise high enough. Watch it through a flushing, and if the water level doesn't drop to about two inches or less, raise the guide.

Sometimes a toilet sings as it fills. Unless you can book it on the *Tonight Show,* you'll do well to fix it. The problem is one or more faulty washers in the ball-cock assembly.

Let's say, however, that you can't get the blasted thing fixed. Putting in a new one is a do-it-yourself endeavor. And there are some new types you may wish to look into that do away with the float arm and float ball. One uses a float cup that rises with the water. Another type is a low unit that shuts off from the weight of the water. Neither of these plastic units are expensive, and they come with easy-to-follow instructions. I have one of each and find they work well. You can also find conventional ball-cock assemblies in metal or plastic.

Lots of people ask about putting a brick at the bottom of the tank to save water. The idea is that the water the brick displaces is water that is saved. But look in the tank as it flushes. You'll see that not all the water runs out of the tank before the tank ball falls back in place, and the tank starts to refill. In fact, most of the water displaced by the brick is in the part that doesn't run out—so there isn't all that much savings. However, if you feel you have to put in a brick, be sure you don't drop it in or you'll crack the tank. Also, keep it clear of the tank's moving parts, or you'll foul up the workings.

● I have found a great use for leftover slivers of soap. I put them in the toilet tank. This retards the scale and corrosion that can build up around the opening from the tank to the bowl. But don't use any piece of soap big enough to get stuck if it should go down while flushing. Put the slivers over in the corner. Also, don't use the kind of soap that floats. It'll float right on out.

When there's a puddle of water on the floor under the tank, it's hard to tell whether it's from a leak or condensation, or both. Put one of those toilet-cleaner products in the tank—the kind that turns the water a bright blue. If the tank leaks, the puddle on the floor will turn blue, too. (If you don't want the blue water in the bowl for the next month or so, put laundry bluing in the tank for the test. (Since that blue "cleanser" inhibits bacteria, it will also slow the breakdown of solids in a septic tank or cesspool.)

Condensation or sweating of the tank happens when the tank is cold and the air in the room is warm and moist. Usually you'll see the tiny beads of "sweat" on the outside, especially in winter. If it's a big problem, there is a temperator valve that can be installed that brings in hot and cold water to the tank. A hint that retards condensation is to rub glycerin over the tank periodically. There are also kits with liners that are glued inside the tank, and trays that mount under the tank to catch the condensation as it drips off.

Now for tracking down a leak. It will either be from a crack in the tank, a threaded connection, or a worn gasket or washer. A cracked tank can sometimes be patched with epoxy, or a replacement tank can be put on. Threaded-connection leaks can be usually stopped by removing the nuts and putting Teflon tape on the threads. Before re-placing a gasket or washer, try tightening whatever is involved in holding the tank and bowl together. However, don't put much force into tightening, as this is an easy way to crack the porcelain. In fact, anytime you bring a wrench near a toilet, be careful.

FAUCET PROBLEMS

● Here's one for the husband whose wife is bugging him to use his weekend to fix the leaky faucet so she can sleep at night. Tie a string to the faucet. Be sure it's long enough to reach the sink. Then adjust it so the drip comes out along on the string. The water will follow the string silently down to the sink with no dripping noise. Both husband and wife will be able to sleep, and you can fix the drip after football season.

Unless the dripping faucet keeps them awake at night, most folks say, "What the heck. Why worry about a few drops of water?" But a drop per second adds up to about 1,200 gallons of water per year—and if it's a hot-water drip, you're also paying to heat the wasted water. The drain on your pocketbook is more than just a drop in the bucket.

Depending on where you live, the cost of having a plumber fix a drip will run from ten to thirty dollars—and it's worth it because in most cases, you'll save that much in less than a year. But the supplies needed to fix most drips cost a few cents. By doing it yourself, you pay for it the first day.

Even if water comes from a single spout, if you have separate hot and cold handles your faucet will probably work like the one in Figure 75. I know that looks like a backyard hydrant, but once you get the wings or whatever kind of handles off, you'll probably find the spindle and washer inside. Here are the steps to stop the drips that come from the spout—plus hints from readers at every step of the way.

1. Shut off the water supply. If there's not a cutoff at the fixture, use the main cutoff. Remember, you have to cut off both the hot and cold lines to make the repair.

● How do you go about fixing a leaking hydrant when the &*(%$ builder forgot to provide a cutoff for the hydrant? I packed dry ice around the pipe leading up to the faucet. This froze the water in the pipe and allowed me to remove the old washer and replace it without cutting off the entire water supply to the house.

2. Now, if your faucets have handles other than those in Figure 75, you'll probably have to remove them to get at the packing nut or locknut. A common type requires the decorative button to be flipped off, exposing a screw that's removed so the handle can be slipped out of the way. Others have a small set screw holding the handle on. Once the handle is off—or if you can get to the packing nut or

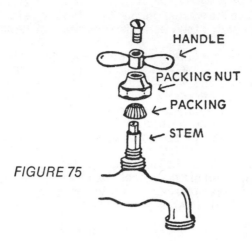

HANDLE

PACKING NUT

PACKING

STEM

FIGURE 75

locknut without removing the handles—use a wrench to remove it. If the wrench must grip an exposed piece of chrome or gold plate, wrap it with tape for protection.

Wrenches and chrome fixtures aren't compatible. One home plumbing expert has cut some half-inch rings from an old radiator hose. Each ring is slit. When he has to work on a faucet or anything with a shiny chrome piece that will be clamped by a wrench, he slips a rubber ring around the chrome and lets it act as a buffer to protect the finish. Even slit sections from an old garden hose will come in handy in these situations.

Since most parts are brass, don't let a tool chew up this semi-soft metal. Pad it with tape. Also, where possible, let penetrating oil soak loose stuck parts.

● We have a leaky hydrant in our unheated washroom. The faucet washer that needs replacing requires removing the entire head, and it's stuck. No doubt if I stayed down in that cold room for an hour or so, I could get it off. But I'll wait until it's warmer. All I did was screw another hydrant on the old one. The new one doesn't leak, so it catches the drips. Yet it can be turned on, and we can use the hydrant.

3. Next, turn the stem the same way as you would to turn on the water, and back it out.

● Any time I work on a faucet or other plumbing parts, I put all the metal pieces in a bowl of vinegar. This works to clean away all the scaling, corrosion, and sediment on the parts. By the time I'm ready to put them back in place, they are clean. Vinegar is cheap and safe, and I keep a jar of it and reuse it many times over.

4. Remove the washer and replace it with an exact duplicate. If the brass screw holding the washer isn't still perfect, replace it too.

● Replacing a faucet washer doesn't take much time . . . unless the tiny brass screw holding the washer to the spindle or some other small part happens to drop into the sink and down the drain. To prevent this, spread a towel out over the drain. This will catch everything that you drop, and maybe prevent your having to remove the trap.

● The urge to stop a dripping faucet came upon me when the stores were closed, and the assortment pack of washers had ninety-nine different kinds—none of which fit my faucet. I noticed that the washer was bad on one side, but that the side next to the spindle was smooth. I inverted the washer and put the faucet back together. When I turned the water back on, no drip. I realize this would only work when the washers are the flat kind, but it does work. (Hate to tell you, but this solution is only temporary.)

● My wife finally nagged me enough that I decided to fix the drip in our kitchen faucet. After getting the thing all apart, I discovered the washer I had was a tiny bit too big. Since it was Sunday, I couldn't get another. Rather than put the mess back in and go through another week of nagging, I chucked the shaft of the faucet into my drill with the oversized rubber washer in place on the end. I then put the drill in my vise to hold it steady. With the drill turned on, I brought a piece of sandpaper against the washer. This wore it down evenly and smoothly until it was the right size.

● Usually by the time most of us get around to changing a bad faucet washer, it's so badly chewed up that the numbers indicating the size aren't legible. This means the whole spindle has to go to the hardware store to get the right size. After you get the right size, write it down on a shipping tag and tie this to the pipe underneath. Then when the faucet starts to drip again—and it will—you can look under and know exactly the right size washer to use. (I would recommend getting extras to have on hand, but we both know you wouldn't be able to find them when the need arises.)

If you have doubts about what size washer or what you need for any type of faucet repair, take the spindle in with you to the hardware store.

5. Stick a finger down inside and feel the seat. If it's not clean and smooth, you need an inexpensive reseating tool that cleans and smooths the seat. Take the spindle to the hardware store to be sure you get the right size tool. Seats too shot to shave can usually be replaced. The seat is threaded and requires a hex wrench or seat-removal wrench; both seat and wrench are inexpensive.

● Not all faucet seats are removable. If, when you look down into the faucet, the seat has a hexagonal-shaped opening, it should be the removable kind. If it's round, it's probably not removable. There is a special tool that fits into the hexagonal opening so you can turn the seat out . . . or you can use an Allen wrench if you have one big enough.

6. Coat the threads of the spindle with petroleum jelly before putting it back in and putting the whole thing back together.

Single-handle faucets—those with one control knob or handle for both hot and cold—are very popular. There are several different types. All look complicated, but are supereasy to repair—all I've run across have repair kits available. The kits have all the tiny O rings, springs, diaphragms, and other parts that could go bad. They also have a very detailed, illustrated instruction sheet.

A few types of two-handled faucets are different. If you have an oddball, it's still a do-it-yourself repair. You'll just have to search out a dealer with the parts.

FAUCET DRIBBLES

A hot-water tap often flows freely when you first turn it on. However, as the water gets warm, the water slows to a trickle. This is a sign that the heat is causing the washer to expand, closing the opening—meaning you need a new washer.

Most indoor faucets have an aerator—a sort of filter that breaks up the stream from the faucet to prevent splashing. If it is clogged, the faucet will allow for only a dribble of water. To clean, remove the aerator and clean all the parts. The unit turns counterclockwise to come out. Keep track of the sequence in which the parts fit into the unit. Soak them in white vinegar and use a toothbrush and a wire to remove all the sediment. Don't use a toothpick—it'll break off, and you'll have a new challenge. (Shower heads that force you to stand over in one corner of the tub to get under the stream are probably just clogged. The vinegar, toothbrush, and wire trick works here too.)

What about faucets that ooze water around the handle when the water is on? That's easy. First, try tightening the packing nut. If that doesn't work, the packing is shot. You already know how to get to it— same steps as above. Packing can be a single blob of rubber or plastic, or some stuff that looks like burned spaghetti. There may also be extra washers or O rings at the top of the stem. Get the bad pieces replaced, and you've de-oozed the stem.

A faucet that chatters or whistles is telling you there isn't enough room for the water to get out. First, put in a new washer. Next, check for a buildup of deposits in the faucet that could be restricting the flow. Mineral deposits within older pipes will probably mean you'll eventually need new plumbing. One other possible cause is a sagging pipe in a long run that can be bent enough to restrict water flow. Use straps to lift and straighten. A kinky copper pipe would have to be replaced.

If the faucet stem binds, it will squeal as you turn it. Shut the water off, remove the stem, and coat the threads with petroleum jelly. A too-loose stem will vibrate and should be replaced.

INSTALLING NEW FIXTURES AND OTHER PLUMBING REPLACEMENTS

There are times when the old plumbing is so shot or so out of date that you want to change it. Or maybe what you have is inadequate, and you want to add to it. No doubt you can do some or all of it yourself, but before you start anything, be sure what you want to do is OK with the local plumbing code. You could probably replace a faucet without getting a permit, but adding a bathroom could require advance approval, inspection on completion, and—in some areas—the work would have to be done by a licensed plumber.

Putting in a new sink, lavatory, tub, shower, or toilet from scratch is not your ideal first project. Even if the code permits it, it's a big job. But replacing a fixture isn't. The water-supply pipes and drains are in, so in most cases it's a matter of taking out the old and putting in the new. That's oversimplification, but it's a whale of a lot easier than starting from scratch. I won't go into details, but offer these suggestions:

1. Go for as high quality as you can. Going to all the trouble to install a cheap fixture doesn't make sense.

2. Double-check the measurements of the existing drains and supply pipes with relation to each other. While adjustments can be made with extensions, being able to hook the new fixture right into the old pipes is a big plus.

3. Make sure you can get the new fixture into the room. No problem with a sink or lavatory, but a tub can be a problem. Many one-piece shower-tub units have to be installed while a home or room is being built or you'll have to rip a wall out—or install it in the entry hall.

4. Measure again to be sure the piece fits into the space available for it.

5. Be sure what you're doing conforms to the local plumbing code.

While I won't try to cover everything you could do to update your plumbing, the projects I'll cover are the most popular, and the procedures here will probably allow you to tackle the others.

New toilet seats are very decorative. You can get all different colors, even your old school colors with a picture of the mascot on the lid. Many lids have decorative touches, landscapes, still lifes, nudes, and snappy sayings. There are hand-carved lids of real and fake wood. Padded seats offer added comfort. There are even shapes that aren't the traditional oval, but will fit on conventional johns. After you locate the seat that suits your fancy, you're ready to begin.

1. Remove the old seat. Turn two nuts counterclockwise to remove, and then lift out the old seat.

That really sounds easy, and if it works out that way, fine. However, it probably won't because the nuts are subjected to years of extra moisture and may be rusted or corroded over. They may also be in a recess and thus hard to get at. If the nuts are stuck, use penetrating oil. Give it time to work. If they still won't budge, *don't* use force. If the wrench slips and hits the bowl, you could crack it, and then you'll need a new toilet to go with your new seat...and maybe some other new things to replace those you flooded.

2. If the wrench isn't going to get the nuts, you'll have to use a hacksaw to cut them away (Figure 76). As with the wrench, be careful that the hacksaw doesn't slip and break either tank or bowl. To protect from scratching and chipping, here are a couple of tricks: Run a strip of narrow tape along the side of the blade that will be next to the bowl. Then smear it with petroleum jelly. Another way is to tape a piece of shirt board or similar cardboard to the bowl where the blade will touch. Smear this with petroleum jelly.

FIGURE 76

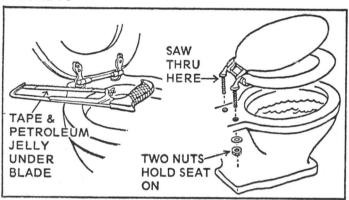

SAW THRU HERE→

TAPE & PETROLEUM JELLY UNDER BLADE

TWO NUTS HOLD SEAT ON

3. With the old seat out, the new is easily put in place and secured by tightening the two nuts. First smear the threads with petroleum jelly so there won't be a problem next time you want to remove it. Don't overtighten or you could crack the bowl.

Now the best seat in the house will also look great.

NEW FAUCETS

Nothing jazzes up an old sink or lavatory like putting in a new, modern faucet. It's usually easy. And while you're at it, why not consider the single-handed type? They're nifty once you get used to them and learn how not to scald your hands. Most faucet manufacturers who cater to the do-it-yourselfer publish pretty complete instructions with their faucets—check these before you buy. So you'll know what you're getting into, here's the basic routine.

1. Turn off the water, both hot and cold, under the sink.
2. Now look underneath to see how your old faucet is connected. If there is a flexible tailpiece, nicknamed a speedee, use a

basin wrench (Figure 77) to unhook it from the faucet. When it's undone, use the wrench to remove the locknuts, which will release the old unit. If there is rigid pipe, use the same procedure, but the rigid pipe won't come loose as easily.

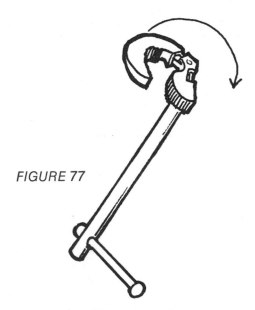

FIGURE 77

3. Clean the surface over which the new faucet fits. Measure the distance from the center of the two outside holes—most are eight inches. If yours isn't, get a new unit with adjustable mounting studs.

4. Put the new unit in place with the two tubes going down through the middle hole. Be sure to include the gasket that goes between the unit and the sink.

5. Install the washers and nuts to the mounting studs and secure the unit. Check from the top to be sure it's centered and squared and that the faucet spout is aimed outward.

6. The two copper tubes must be very gently bent into position. Some units require crossing the tubes to connect the hot tube to the hot-water supply line. If you crimp the tube, you can ruin the performance (see the copper-tubing tips later in this section).

7. Reconnect the supply lines. If the compression fittings from the old faucet don't fit the new, don't worry. There are adapters to suit all situations.

8. Turn on the water, remove the aerator, and check for leaks. With the aerator off, you'll also flush out the lines. (It's a good idea to do this anytime you work on a faucet unit.)

There may be variations: Some sinks have spray units. Lavatories may have stopper lifts. But these don't present any real installation problems.

Changing shower and tub fixtures may be as easy as the routine we just went through. Putting on a new shower head is no problem, and that includes the popular pulsating type. Putting new handles, trim plates, and a new spout is also a snap and can make a big difference in looks. But you may not be able to remove the old faucet for a complete new one because many aren't easily accessible. Also, you might not be able to use the exact model you like best because a new single-handle faucet handle won't cover the two openings for the old handles. This requires a tiling job, and some tile colors are hard or impossible to match.

PIPES AND CONNECTIONS

To install new or replacement fixtures, you have to work with pipe. Some homes may have oddball types like brass, lead, fiber, or clay. However, most local codes won't allow all those types of pipe, so unless you're adding on—using the same type that's already there—check the code. (For example, plastic pipe is often acceptable for a lawn sprinkler, but not for drinking water.)

The several types most used in home plumbing are the following:

Copper is the most common type pipe in use today. It can be rigid pipe or flexible tubing. It's long-lasting, lightweight, and easy to work with, and resists corrosion and scaling. Flexible tubing comes in long coils and can be bent to aid in making things meet up—it can curve around corners and be snaked behind walls. You do have to be careful in bending because a crimp or kink will restrict the flow of water. There are spring-type benders to aid in making gradual bends. Quoth a reader:

● If you ever have to replace a pulley for a V belt, hang onto the old one. It is ideal to use as a bending jig for copper tubing used in plumbing. It will allow you to bend the tube without kinking it.

Either type can be joined with the process of sweat soldering. The tubing can be joined with insert fittings.

Sweat soldering is easy—if you follow the rules. You need a propane torch, an inexpensive tool that is perfectly safe to use if you just take care. Be sure to protect anything combustible around the flame. For the actual soldering, make sure there is a good fit between the pipe and the fitting, and that the pipe is perfectly round. The pipe and fitting must be completely dry; otherwise, the heat will turn the moisture to steam, and this will turn your soldered joint into a leak.

A trick to take care of a pipe with moisture back in it is to wad up bread into a ball and poke it into the pipe. It'll hold the moisture back. Then when you turn on the water again, it dissolves the bread, which comes out at the faucet. (This may not apply to some sourdough bread I once baked—it was a new substitute for adobe bricks.)

Next, both the pipe and fitting must be cleaned where they join. I use emery cloth outside the pipe, and a special round wire brush for inside the fitting. Really make the copper shine. Even if it looks shiny before you start, clean again. As one reader puts it:

● The key to good sweat soldering is to completely clean the metal. Some of the copper connections are too small to insert a finger wrapped with emery cloth to clean. Stick an end of the abrasive strip into a cotter pin and wrap it around a couple of times. Cut off the abrasive. When inserted in the copper connection, twist the cotter pin in the direction the emery cloth is wrapped, and it won't come unwrapped. The end of the cotter pin can even be chucked in a drill for more rubbing power if you wound the abrasive in the direction that the drill turns. It sure beats getting your little finger stuck in a chunk of copper tubing.

Next, brush a thin film of paste-type flux on both surfaces to be joined and fit them together. Give a twist to evenly distribute the flux.

The heat from the torch is applied to the fitting—not the solder. Incidentally, use a solid-core wire solder. In fact, keep the solder back out of the way at first. Play the flame over the fitting evenly. Now touch the tip of the wire solder to the place where the pipe goes into the fitting. If it melts, it's hot enough. If not, take the solder away and heat some more. Once the metal is properly heated, an amazing thing happens. Capillary action sucks the molten solder into the joint like magic—even if the fitting is above the pipe. When a bead of solder appears around the rim, you're through. For a neater-looking joint, wipe away the excess with a scrap of terry cloth, but don't burn your hand. Let the joint cool before you run water through it.

The other ways to join copper tubing are flared fittings and compression fittings. They cost more than sweat soldering, but are quick, simple, and effective. They are self-sealing and also offer the advantage of easier removal if you ever need access to the joint.

With a flare fitting, the tube end is slightly flared out with a tool for that purpose. There are two things to watch out for: Be sure you slip the flare nut over the end of the tubing before you flare it, and make sure the end of the tube is cut off square. An inexpensive tube cutter is by far the best way to cut copper pipes and tubing. You should always check ends for burrs. If you have to clamp, do so far enough back from the end so that if the vise dents the soft metal, you still have a perfectly round end.

The compression fitting uses a compression ring that seals against the tube and the fitting to make the joint (Figure 78). It requires no tools except wrenches to tighten the fitting.

Galvanized pipe (steel) is the old-time threaded pipe that was once used for most home water-supply lines. It's cheap and sturdy, but is subject to corrosion, and lime and scale build up inside. Sometimes the corrosion eats right through the pipe, or the buildup completely

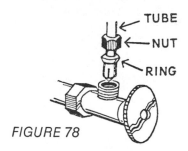

TUBE

NUT

RING

FIGURE 78

closes it. Cut galvanized pipe with your hacksaw. It must then be threaded with a die. Unless you're going to plumb an entire house, you probably wouldn't want to buy this tool, so have it done. Most hardware stores are equipped to do this. Before screwing a fitting in place, smear the threads with pipe-joint compound or pipe dope, as it's called. Then when you tighten, leave about three threads still showing.

Plastic pipe is super. It won't rust, corrode, clog, or rot. It's easy to work with because it's lightweight, cuts easily, and joins as easily as if you were gluing it together. It's also inexpensive. It does have one disadvantage, as mentioned earlier—many local plumbing codes won't accept it.

There are different types of plastic pipe, and some can't carry hot water. Just be sure you're using the proper pipe for each type line.

The stuff cuts easily with a fine-toothed hacksaw. I do suggest you cut in a miter box to get perfectly square ends. A light sanding will remove burrs.

Joining is called solvent welding, a tricky name, for you brush on the special solvent cement, fit the pieces together, give them a quick twist, and hold on for about fifteen seconds. It actually fuses the two pieces so they are one, and rarely do you end up with a bad joint.

Cast iron pipe is included in many drain systems. Most is joined and sealed at the joints with oakum (a sort of treated rope), which is then covered with molten lead. It's not your normal home-handyman chore. Another type is joined with a sleeve, and a screw-driver is used to turn a worm-gear clamp to tighten. This type you can tackle.

NOISES

When you run water, if it sounds like Buddy Rich and Johnny Carson are having a duel of the drums, you should do something about the noise.

The noises that occur every time you turn on water are the result of pipe movement. The pipe is moving because of the force of the water, and is hitting against something. The first step is to track down the movement. With the water on, check all the pipes that are accessible in basements and crawl spaces. If the movement is within the walls, you still may be able to silence it with stops of some sort at both ends where the pipe comes out of the wall.

The actual method for steadying the pipe depends on the situation. Here are some tested ways to do-it.

1. Often the only thing you need do is anchor the pipe with a U-shaped pipe clamp to stop vibration.

2. Sometimes, within such a device, the pipe can still move. If so, slip a slit section of old garden hose around the pipe and under the clamp.

3. Often a slit piece of garden hose by itself around a pipe will stop its knocking against a wall.

4. A pipe running along a masonry wall may need to be held away from the wall. Attach a scrap board to the wall between wall and pipe. Masonry nails will anchor it, and a pipe strap will clamp the pipe to the board.

5. When a long run of pipe is causing the noise, or if the pipe is inside the wall, rather than stop several places in the middle, see if wooden blocks at each end won't stop the movement.

6. Parallel pipes that are so close they hit can be soldered together, or else separated by something like pieces of old inner tube, sponge rubber, or garden hose. So that the pads won't fall out from vibration, run tape around the pipes where you've stuck in the wedges.

Another noise that happens only when you shut off the water is called water hammer. The force of the water running rapidly through the pipe suddenly has no outlet. The quick stop of all that force causes shock waves, which cause hammering. A proper plumbing installation has an air chamber (Figure 79) that prevents the hammering. When the

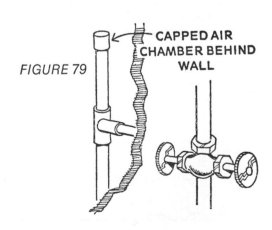

FIGURE 79

CAPPED AIR CHAMBER BEHIND WALL

shock wave hits, the air compresses and absorbs it. If this malady is recent, it means your air chambers have become filled with water. Try cutting off the water supply and draining the pipe. Open taps to allow air to enter the system. Then when you turn the water back on, the air chamber should be on duty again. (Yes, the faucets will gasp and wheeze until the air is all out of the main lines.)

Sometimes the air chamber gets corroded and must either be cleaned out or replaced. If you've always had water hammer, there are air-chamber gadgets at plumbing-supply houses that can be added. Another noise that affects only the hot-water lines is caused by steam or sediment in the tank.

If you're building a new home or an addition that includes plumbing, be sure to build quietness into the plumbing system. Anchor, pad, and situate pipes so they don't knock. Include air chambers. Use pipes of an adequate size. Often the size called for in the local plumbing code is the minimum and might cause some noise. Finally, wrap as many pipes as possible.

Condensation forms on pipes and can drip off, causing damage. Some people use buckets at just the right spots to catch the drips. But there is a better way: You can stop condensation by insulating the pipes. There are pipe wraps, self-sticking tapes that are easily applied, compounds that are brushed on, and jackets that fit around pipes. The insulation also dampens the noise.

CLOSING THE SUMMER HOME FOR THE WINTER

An unoccupied lake house or mountain retreat should really be buttoned down for the winter. In addition to taking precautions to prevent frozen pipes, there are other things to be done. Here's a good routine to follow:

1. Turn off main water supply.
2. Cut off the gas or electricity to the water heater and hook hose up to drain tank.
3. Use drain valve to drain pipes in water-supply lines.
4. Open all faucets.
5. Flush toilets, then use sponge to remove all water from tank.
6. Pour permanent-type antifreeze into all drains so that traps will not freeze. Never leave a drain trap dry, as sewer gas may enter the house.
7. Remove all foodstuffs that would attract rodents.
8. Patch up all entryways that might let rodents in.
9. Turn drawers upside down if they are empty so this doesn't represent a nesting place for rodents.
10. Remove any canned or bottled items containing liquids that might freeze.

There may be other things in your particular hideaway that will require attention. Getting started with these chores will get you to thinking about other possible trouble spots during your absence.

THAWING FROZEN PIPES

This is one problem that never has to happen. If you prepare for the sudden freeze, you can prevent frozen pipes in even the coldest areas. However, more problems along these lines seem to arise in areas where they don't have really cold weather. These folks are not that afraid of a frozen pipe because "It just doesn't happen in the land of sunshine." Anyplace, even Florida or California, can have unusual weather.

First, let's cover some steps of preparation, though some apply only to new construction.

1. Do as much as you can toward properly caulking and insulating your home. Pay particular attention to north and west sides where pipes may be close to the outside wall. The more cold air you keep out, the better your pipes will fare.

2. Make sure that where new plumbing runs underground, it is piped below the frost line. This varies in different parts of the country, so check with the local building code or the United States Weather Bureau.

3. Plan for pipes to run along inside walls wherever possible.

4. Wrap all pipes with insulating material. It's inexpensive, and there are several types that are easy to put in place.

5. In late fall, cut off the water supply to outside hydrants. Open the tap and drain the water from this pipe, if possible. Just in case there is any water left in the exposed pipe, leave the tap open. If you ever have to replace an outside faucet, there are frost-free types you might consider.

6. Heat tapes or heat cables should be used on pipes that are subject to freezing and that cannot be adequately protected otherwise.

7. If you don't have protection, turn on the tap to a trickle, and the pipe will be less likely to freeze. This isn't a surefire freeze stopper, but will often help because moving water doesn't freeze up as quickly.

8. If you have inadequate protection, an outside heat source directed at the pipe may prevent a freeze. Sometimes a large light bulb hanging next to the pipe is enough. There are also small space heaters that can be moved into place. Be sure that the heat source isn't hot enough to ignite anything around the pipe.

All this doesn't do a lick of good if you already have a frozen pipe, so here are some tips on thawing frozen pipes:

1. First, open the tap to the frozen pipe. This will relieve any pressure that builds up when you apply heat for thawing.

2. Now you're ready for heat. There are many heat sources that can be used to melt the ice. Whatever you decide is best in your case, start thawing at the frozen spot nearest the tap and work back. This lets

the water run out as it melts and doesn't let steam or water build up pressure that could burst the pipe. Now about heat sources:

A. Boiling water is fine, but if it will make a mess, you may be no better off than you would with a burst pipe. If the water will do, however, wrapping the pipe with a towel to retain the heat makes it go faster.

B. Heat lamp

C. A hand-held hair dryer

D. An electric iron

E. A propane torch can be dangerous if the flame will be too near anything combustible. Also, this much heat directed right on the faucet for any length of time could damage the washer inside. If copper pipes are involved, keep in mind that solder joints could be melted by this type heat if it is left on a joint too long. An asbestos or other fireproof sheet should be placed behind the pipe to help contain the flame.

Drains can also freeze. In most cases, however, the freeze-up is in the trap, since the rest of the pipe should be clear. Boiling water down the drain will usually solve this problem.

If you ever have to thaw out a pipe, the process will convince you that it's well worth taking precautions ahead of time. However, I'd suggest you take my word for the value of the precautions. If that pipe happens to freeze and burst, you'll have problems you wouldn't believe. You could ruin walls, floors, drapes, carpets—and that's enough to wreck your entire day.

14.

WALLS

Walls are pretty much background for all your furniture. However, they're an important background that gives privacy and protection, shuts out noise, and provides a place to hang Aunt Nellie's picture. Most homes built during the past thirty years are of hollow-wall construction. This means the wall is hollow with only framing inside. The framing has vertical studs, usually every sixteen inches, covered with some sort of wallboard—most often a gypsum board, with paneling coming in second. The wallboard (also called plasterboard or Sheetrock) is usually textured with joint compound. However, it can also be painted, papered, or paneled.

INSTALLING WALLBOARD

The plasterboard is usually nailed to the studs with coated wallboard nails. It's suggested you space the nails every seven inches. Drive the nails in carefully to avoid splitting the paper covering. However, you do have to drive the head below the surface: a technique called dimpling.

Dimples don't look cute on a wall, so they have to be hidden. The spaces between the sheets of plasterboard also have to be hidden. This is done with a process called taping and bedding. (It doesn't always go the way it's spozed to, so it's often called a lot of other things we can't repeat.) I wish I could tell you a simple way to do it, but it really takes a little practice and a lot of luck—or vice versa.

The joint compound is spread and worked into the recess created by the tapered edges with a wide-bladed knife. The tape is then pressed into the bed of compound. Whatever is squeezed out needs to be smoothed. Then comes one of the musts—*wait*! Let the compound dry fully, even if it takes twenty-four hours. The next coat is a very thin one and extends on either side of the first. Wait again. Then apply a third coat that goes out about six inches on either side of the previous coat. When it dries, you need to sand to feather the compound into the wall.

Of course, all those cute dimples also have to be hidden, and this is done with three coats of joint compound.

TEXTURING

With the taping and bedding done, you can now cover the wall. If texturing is your bag, it's easy to apply. Using a paint roller gives an interesting overall texture. However, there are other ways to create textures. Make a practice board of about two square feet, and play around. You can make a pattern, and if you don't like it, smooth it and try again. A notched trowel does an interesting job. You can crosshatch or make straight lines, wavy lines, or whatever. One reader sent a picture of a wall done by raking her fingers back and forth in the wet mud. If you want the high points in the texture to be more pointed, pull the mud out from the wall with a damp trowel. Another reader textured with a whisk broom. You get the idea—play around in the mud.

● Wind a length of rope around a paint roller and sew the ends of the rope in place. Leave spaces or not as you spiral the rope (Figure 80). You can try it horizontally or vertically. This will give you a sort of unique texture, and the process goes fast.

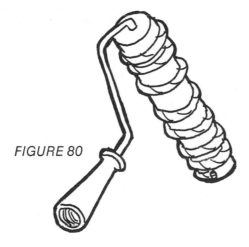

FIGURE 80

PATCHING HOLES

After the wallboard is up and put to use, somebody's always poking a hole in it. The hole may be from only a nail, or as big as the fist that made it. For the small ones, try this:

● Toothpaste is an instant patching compound for nail holes. If the walls are white, you won't even need to paint.
● When you get ready to move from one apartment to another, you always have holes in the wall from the pictures. This means the management comes in and tries to gyp you out of part of your security deposit. I

have found that all the holes can be patched with a paste made from equal parts of table salt and powdered laundry starch. If the walls are white, it's perfect as is. If not, I mix in water colors until I have matched the wall color—and eliminate that hassle.

● You have run several hints on how to patch up holes in apartment walls so that when you move out, you can avoid losing part of your deposit because you had the effrontery to hang pictures on the wall. My method is different and works well: I use white all-purpose glue. Pour some in a flat dish, and then mix in strips of toilet paper to form a sort of papier-mâché. If the walls are colored, you can use colored toilet paper, and then add water colors to match the wall coloring. When it reaches the right color and consistency, work it into the holes, and they'll be patched and hidden.

● To fill a nail hole in a plaster or textured wall, I mix a paste from kitchen cleansing powder and paint. Use the same color paint as is on the wall and mix it to a putty consistency. When dry, the hole will be hardly visible, and the patch will last a long, long time.

● Here is another way to patch up the holes in plaster or Sheetrock walls before you move out of the apartment. Pastel artist's chalk comes in many colors; get a stick that matches the wall. Shave the end into a point and stick the point into the hole. Break it off at the wall, and the hole is perfectly hidden.

● If you have a number of nail holes in a plaster or textured wall and want to fill them fast, here's how. Mix up spackling compound and make it a little thinner than normal. Now take an old medicine dropper and fill it with the patching liquid. You'll be able to fill up the holes very quickly and easily. (Just be sure the dropper doesn't get back into the medicine chest—talk about a stopped-up nose!)

Don't try to patch the larger holes all at once. A big blob will shrink. Do it in stages. You may also need some sort of backing. Use one of these ideas:

● Use a lid from a large tin can that's bigger than the hole. Cut a slit on either side of the hole so the lid can be slipped in sideways (Figure 81). But before you slip it in, punch a large nail through the lid; and when the lid's inside the wall, use the nail as a handle to pull the lid flat against the wall. Then apply the patching compound, holding the nail all the while. When the patch hardens, push the nail through, and patch over the nail hole.

● Window screen is flexible. Run a string or wire through a scrap of screen bigger than the hole. Force the screen through the hole and use the string to pull it against the wallboard as backing.

● For large to medium-sized holes, wad up pieces of newspaper and jam these into the hole. When you let go, the wad expands and wedges in the hollow space between the walls. Use enough wads to fill the space and provide a good backing.

● When a hole in a plaster or Sheetrock wall is too big to be patched with just spackling paste, but not bigh enough to use a solid

slit wide enough
to admit lid. . .

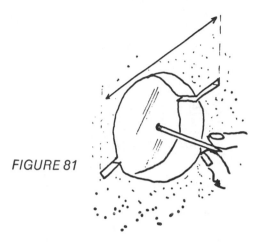

FIGURE 81

piece as backing, stick in a wad of steel wool big enough to hold against the sides. Keep pushing until it doesn't stick out anymore, and then apply the spackling.

● When patching a hole in a plaster wall, I build a base in the hole by stuffing in wet facial tissue. This also helps fill the hole and hold the plaster in place. You will use much less plaster patch and get just as good a result.

● As backing for a plaster patch, use a crumpled blob of aluminum foil. As long as it has a back and a side or two to rest against, it will stay in place and can be formed to fit. Just crumple it enough to give the rigidity needed.

● To weave a backing right in the hole, tap nails into the edge of the hole so they radiate like spokes. Good-sized nails are best. Put them all the way around, about a couple of inches apart (Figure 82). Then take inexpensive wire, tie it to a nail, and stretch the wire across to a nail on the opposite side. Twist it around the head and then bring it back across to another nail to end up with a wire spiderweb that forms a base for the patch.

● Patching a hole in a plaster wall is no big chore. I find a piece of corrugated board is stiff enough to back up almost any size patch. I cut it just a hair larger than the hole and bend it slightly if necessary to put it throught the hole endwise. Now comes the clever part: I use a balloon to hold it tight in place against the inside of the wall. Before putting in the backing, I punch a hole in it for the end of the balloon to fit through. When the corrugated board's in place, the balloon will be in back of it, but the end sticks out so I can blow it up. As the balloon inflates, it pushes against the outer wall and pushes the backing against the wall to be patched

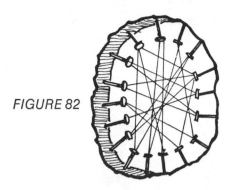

FIGURE 82

(Figure 83). When the balloon is inflated enough to hold tight, I slip a rubber band around it to keep the air in. Patch over the balloon end, and leave the balloon and backing inside.

● See if you can find a cork to fit the hole. A tapered cork can be pushed into the hole and will wedge in tightly. The part that's sticking out

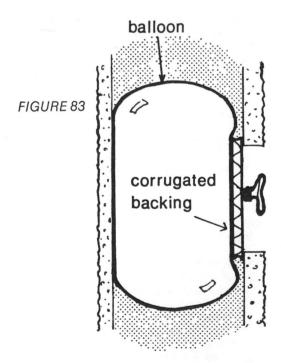

balloon

FIGURE 83

corrugated backing

can easily be shaved off. Now you can spackle over the cork to hide it, and no one will ever know what a corking easy way you did the job.

● For a hole too big to plaster, the first step is to cut out around the hole and make it into a rectangle. That way, you can cut another piece of Sheetrock to fit. Now for the backing. Just cut a slat of wood that will span the hole, and put it inside. Then pull it firmly against the back of the hole and insert countersunk wood screws through the wallboard and into the slat. A screw on each side of the hole will hold. A bigger hole might require two or more slats. Smear the slat with adhesive; butter the edges of the patch piece with spackling compound, and put it in place. When you are hiding the cracks and texturing the patch, you can also cover over the screwheads.

● If solid fill isn't important, simply tear off strips of the tape used to cover the space between sheets of gypsum board. Wet them with mud, the dry-wall joint compound. Place them across the hole, overlapping each previous strip about halfway. Be sure the edges are well set to the surface. When the tape dries, it becomes a taut, hard patch over which you can texture to match the rest of the wall for an invisible mend.

Plaster walls patch a lot like dry walls.

● Want that plaster-wall patch to hold better? I always take a brush and apply a coat of varnish to all the surfaces in the hole in the plaster wall. Then when the varnish starts to get tacky, I patch as usual. The varnish acts as a sort of glue, and the patch will really stay in place.

● Shoot a few staples into the lath behind the hole. Rig the staple gun so the staples don't go in all the way. Now when the patching compound is applied, it will wrap around the staples and hold the patch in place a lot better than if it were against bare lathing.

● Here's a better way to patch a hole in a plaster wall. After cleaning away all the loose plaster, I use a tack hammer and drive several tacks partway into the wooden lath slats behind the wall. When the patching compound is put in the hole, it locks around the tack heads for a much stronger bond. Sometimes patches don't want to hold otherwise.

● I have discovered a patching compound I can make myself, and it works well for plaster patching as well as wood crack filler. Pour a small amount of white all-purpose glue into a dish, then place several cleansing tissues in the dish. Work them around until they're completely covered with glue, wad them up, and keep kneading the wad until it becomes puttylike. You may have to add more glue. When it gets to be thin putty, press it into the place to be patched. It will dry hard and can even be sanded.

Cracks are also a problem.

● The punch-type beer-can opener that we used before pop tops came into being is still a useful tool to me. When I have to patch cracks in Sheetrock walls, I use it to scrape out and undercut.

● When you want to patch a narrow crack and don't want to have to chisel it out and undercut so the patch will lock itself in, mix wall sizing (that sort of glue that you use before applying wallpaper) with plaster of Paris. Then add the necessary water. The sizing will make the plaster patch stay in place.

● My magic formula can permanently patch hairline cracks in Sheetrock or plaster. I mix up a few drops of the paint originally used for the wall with an equal number of drops of clear varnish. Then I use a tiny artist's brush to paint this along the crack. It fills and, in most cases, blends in so I don't have to repaint to hide the filler afterward.

● I have discovered a better way to patch hairline cracks in plaster walls. Instead of spreading the compound on with a knife, I apply it with a tiny artist's brush. I make the patch paste a little runnier than is called for, and then just paint the cracks. It's easier and gives a much less obvious repair.

● When patching masonry cracks on a wall, you sometimes have trouble getting the mixture all the way down into the bottom of the crack. An old paintbrush can do this for you. After the hard part is brushed in place, finish putting the mortar on with your trowel. Don't plan on using the brush for any painting; wash it out and use it on your next patch job.

● Besides bringing us your column, the daily newspaper can help the home handyman another way. Place strips of newspaper in boiling water. After a while, the paper reduces to a pulpy substance. When the water's drained off, this pulp is a great crack filler for walls. It dries hard, can be sanded smooth and painted, and lasts an amazingly long time.

● If you're a slow worker, spackling compound starts to dry before you can get it all in place over cracks and holes. Use about a fourth less water, and replace it with white vinegar, which slows down the drying process quite a bit.

● Another slow-down trick is to add some sugar to the mix. Just sprinkle a little over the top and mix it in. Too much could attract all the ants in the neighborhood for the next several years.

● Mix in a spoonful of dry starch for each batch to slow it down.

● If you'd like to speed up the drying time of plaster of Paris, add a teaspoon of table salt to each quart of water used in mixing.

● Patching cracks in interior walls usually requires mixing up only a small batch of spackling compound. Use the aluminum pans from frozen pot pies.

● . . . Or use half of a hollow rubber ball. It's the perfect size to fit into my hand, which makes it easy to mix and use the compound. Cleanup is also easy.

● Use the lid to a saucepan. When the mixing's done, you have a container with a handle underneath that's easy to hold. The raised edge keeps the mixture from spilling out, as it would with the flat palette some people use. After the patching is done, the shiny surface makes it easy to wash the lid clean.

● I decided that squirting spackling compound into cracks would be a lot easier than troweling it. I sneaked into the kitchen and borrowed a gadget my wife uses for decorating cakes. I filled it with the patching plaster, and it worked beautifully. I cleaned it afterward, and no one was the wiser.

And here are a couple of other plaster pleasers:

● Instead of renailing popped-out nails in Sheetrock, here's a more permanent repair (I've found that adding more nails results in more pop-outs). Pull out the offending popper and replace it with a flat-headed wood screw about the same length. Turn it until it goes a little below the surface, then cover it over with spackle. I renovated an old house with this method, and it worked great.

● When cutting a hole in a plaster wall, outline the desired hole with masking tape. This allows you to cut or chop a smoother hole with less chance of chipping or cracking. If you're sawing the opening, saw right through the tape.

● If the texturing compound used on a newly repaired wall is water soluble, there's no need to sand it when you find it needs smoothing. A wet towel will do the smoothing without creating any dust. I find that warm water does a better job than cold. Just rub over the spot for a few moments, and you'll get it just the way you want.

● Most plaster-patching compounds require you to wet down the area around the crack to be patched. While rubbing the moisture on with a rag, you usually run the risk of loosening more plaster. The best way is to spray the water on. An empty window-cleaner bottle with sprayer does the job nicely.

● Taking down Sheetrock or any kind of wallboard usually results in a bunch of busted-up Sheetrock, because most people use a claw hammer to remove the nails. Sometimes you can just drive the nails on through. Use a rod the same size as the nail head and sink the nails on down. This leaves a nice neat hole that can then be patched with spackling compound. When this sets up, you've got Sheetrock that can be used over again.

● For those who have hollow-wall construction, there is an easy way to add decorative niches in the wall. Locate the studs and cut out a section of the Sheetrock between two studs. Nail crosspieces at the top and bottom of the hole connecting the studs. Now plaster over the exposed wood and the back of the Sheetrock on the other side. Paint to match the wall. It's a very striking place for a small statue or other decorative piece. I made enough niches hold all my golf trophies.

WALLPAPERING

Even though most of it isn't paper, that's what it's called. It can make a big difference in the looks of the wall and room. You can get washable wall covering, which is a big advantage. You can also get strippable wall covering, which will be great when it's time to repaper in a few years.

After you've picked out a pattern, figure out how much paper you need—it's a matter of square footage. Here are some facts: Every standard roll of wallpaper has approximately thirty-six square feet, no matter what the width of the roll. But you have to leave room for some waste. Use a figure of thirty square feet as a yield. Then get your dealer to double-check your figures. It's important to get enough to begin with because wallpaper manufacturers have a way of discontinuing patterns. Also, sometimes a different lot number won't match. Get enough to start with.

Before you start hanging the paper (why do they call it "hanging"?), be sure the surface is properly prepared. That means a smooth—but not glossy—clean surface, and it means patching any cracks.

● Even though cleaned as completely as possible, stubborn spots of dirt, grease, or bright colors can bleed through new wallpaper. I seal in any spot I'm not sure of by brushing clear shellac across it. When it dries, the spot is sealed.

Then, for any surface that would absorb moisture from the paste, you should apply a coat of sizing—a sort of glue. I really recommend using sizing on any surface to be papered.

● A paint roller does a quick job of sizing a wall.

The place to start papering is usually the most inconspicuous corner of the room. But wherever you start, the first panel of paper you hang must be straight, or else the entire room will seem to lean. The way to get it straight is with a plumb bob and chalk line (Figure 84). Measure out from your starting corner a distance equal to the width of the roll of paper, minus one inch. Strike your vertical chalk line along the wall at that point.

When you cut your first strip, make it about four inches longer than the height of the room.

● To cut heavy vinyl wallpaper, try electric sewing scissors. They cut quickly, easily, and straight. As far as I can tell, this didn't hurt the scissors.

After applying the paste or immersing the prepasted type according to directions, you should fold the strip so the top half is brought down—paste to paste—and the bottom half the same way. This makes the pasted strip easier to handle.

● After you have put the paste on a strip of wall covering, wait from three to five minutes before applying it to the wall. This allows the natural shrinkage to take place before you do all your smoothing. Not all coverings are bothered by the shrinkage, but with those that are, you'll end up with gaposis in spots.

● An old bathinette is a good water tray for the prepasted-type paper.

CHALK
LINE →

- PLUMB
BOB

FOLD PANELS

PASTE TO
PASTE

SMOOTHING
BRUSH
POUNDS CORNERS

FIGURE 84

● If you mix wallpaper paste in a bucket, you'll find there's no place to put down the paste brush after you've applied the paste. Solve the problem by putting a straight piece of coat-hanger wire through the holes in which the bucket handle fits. The wire doesn't get in the way when you dip in the brush, but will be there for you to use when you need to rest the brush for a moment. Place the bristles over the wire and the handle on the rim of the bucket, and all the drips will go back into the bucket.

● After mixing wallpaper paste, mix in a drop of blue food coloring into the paste. This light tint makes it easy to see that the paste is spread completely over the entire surface of the wallpaper. The white paste wouldn't show up that well.

● A long-napped paint roller spreads the paste on the paper faster and maybe a bit smoother. After you're done, be sure to wash the roller.

When you take the strip over to the wall, unfold the top half and place it next to the chalk line with the excess inch going around the corner. Leave a couple of inches sticking up beyond the ceiling line. I like to use my hand to smooth out the strip, working from the edge back toward the corner. When you have the top half smooth, unfold the bottom and smooth it. Next use either the smoothing brush or a sponge to move out the excess paste, always working toward the edges.

In the corners, and along the top and bottom, use the smoothing brush in a light pounding stroke, jabbing the end of the bristles into the corner. Don't trim off the excess at the top and bottom just yet.

● A paint roller can be used to smooth wallpaper up at the top so you don't have to climb up.

Now you're ready to cut out the second panel. Before you trim, if there's a pattern to match, be sure it does. After it's pasted, folded, and ready to hang, put it against the wall just a hair away from the edge of the previous strip. Then just slide it over to butt up against the edge. After you smooth each new panel, use your seam roller.

● A kitchen spoon will do a fine job of pressing down the seams. It's smooth and will glide right over the wall covering. Put your thumb in the spoon's bowl and grip the handle.

● An old furniture caster can be made into a very serviceable seam roller. Drill a hole in the end of a section of broomstick to accept the caster's stem.

Now you're ready to trim the excess off the top and bottom of the previous strip. Use a very sharp razor blade. As soon as it starts to get dullish, change for a new one.

● To make an old putty knife into a wallpaper-trimming knife, sharpen one side of the blade to a razor edge. The handle is much handier for trimming than other utility knives. Keep a whetstone handy and sharpen the blade when it starts to dull.

Now you're on your way. There's a temptation to skip over cutouts like windows and doors, but don't. It's best if you continue all the way around. When you come to a cutout, hold or tape the unpasted strip in place and crease it against the opening. You can then rough-cut it and apply it to the wall to be trimmed later.

● When people wallpaper, they often also cover the electric switch plates on the wall with the same wall covering. (There are those who do this accidentally and wonder what that lump is under the paper.) The better way is to plan on covering it. First you need to match the pattern. This can best be done by cutting a piece that will roughly match up. Then put the plate in place against the wall, but with the screws just barely in place, so there's room for the paper to fold over between the plate and wall. Move the piece of wallpaper around until it matches, then crease it along the top. Do the same thing for the most conspicuous side. Next fold the paper around the plate and snip off the corners in back with diagonal cuts. Cut an X for the switch slot. Coat the paper with paste and press it in place. Run tape along the edges on the back of the plate to make sure it stays in place, since the surface is slick and adhesion may not be the best. Now all you have to do is remember where the switch is.

● When repapering a room, you often will want to put pictures, mirrors, and other hanging things back in the same place. If you have used Molly bolts, you certainly want to reuse the same ones, but if you paper over them, you'll never find them. My trick is to wedge a toothpick in the hole in the Molly. Leave a point sticking out. When applying wallpaper, the point can be poked through the paper, and then you can find the same place.

● Did you ever put up a strip of wallpaper and find that you had it upside down? Usually, of course, you can peel it off and take care of the goof, but if you'll mark each strip on the back to indicate the top, it'll never happen. Also, if you have cut several strips before applying them to the wall, number them so you get them in the right sequence.

● Ever try to smooth wallpaper behind a radiator? Here's how: Take a board a little longer than the width of the radiator and wrap a bed sheet around it several times. Then with a helper on the other side of the radiator, push the padded board firmly against the wall and pull it down to the baseboard, keeping the pressure against the wall. This smooths the wallpaper firmly in place.

● To trim wallpaper behind a radiator, drill a hole in the end of a metal yardstick and bolt a double-edge razor blade tightly in place.

● Here's a hint for the apartment dweller who'd like to paper the walls, but the landlord won't permit it. I have put wall coverings on with that two-sided carpet tape. It's an easy, nonmessy way to paper walls. When you get ready to move, the wallpaper and tape come off, and the landlord will never know you improved his walls while you were there. Just cut the paper to fit and put the tape around all four edges.

WALLPAPER CLEANING

Even though you can now get washable paper, maybe you didn't. Here are some cleanup tips:

● On handprints and other soiled wallpaper spots, try an art-gum eraser.

● Grease spots on wallpaper can sometimes be lifted if you cover them with a blotter, then press with a moderately hot iron.

● Rub dry borax powder over soiled spots.

● A piece of rye bread can be rubbed over soiled wallpaper with good results.

● Dust grease spots with talcum powder applied with a powder puff. The talc absorbs the spot.

● Here's an idea for those with small children. I found that several of those pressure-sensitive shelf papers will receive the marks from both pencils and felt markers. By putting some of this over the walls in our son's room, he has a place on the walls where he can write and draw. When he runs out of room, it washes off. When we moved recently to another apartment, I peeled off the covering, and there were no signs that we had a budding Michelangelo. Needless to say, I've done the same thing in our new apartment.

● Painting over wallpaper is done quite often, and under the right conditions, it can work out. Many times, however, the paint acts as a solvent for dyes in the wallpaper pattern, which bleeds through the paint job. If you decide to go ahead and paint over the paper, do a small test patch first. After it has dried, check it under strong lights to see if there's any bleed-through. It may delay the paint job a day or so, but it sure beats getting it all done and finding that old familiar pattern coming back to haunt you.

● In the kitchen where there are greasy spots on wallpaper, use a paste made of cornstarch and water. It lifts the grease without doing any damage to the color of the paper.

REPAIRING WALLPAPER

Be sure to save some scraps of wallpaper. They may come in handy. However, you should put the scraps someplace where they'll get some light and air. That way, the scraps will weather and look like the stuff that's on the wall. If you have to patch, tear the replacement from the scrap, leaving an irregular edge. Then sand the back edges to feather it. The closely matched pattern will be barely visible.

● Also save some of the paste in a tightly sealed plastic bottle. If you don't have any paste, you can use white glue.

A bubble indicates an excess of paste that didn't get smoothed out. If the paste isn't yet dry, make a pinhole into the middle of the bubble and smooth toward the hole to force the paste out. If this doesn't work, use a sharp razor blade and slit an X across the bubble. Peel back the tips of the slit, remove the old paste, then squirt new paste in and smooth down the flaps. Even if they overlap a little, no one will know but me and you—and I won't tell.

REMOVING WALLPAPER

If you don't have strippable wall covering, and if you're going to repaper or texture the wall, you should remove the old covering. Some people just paper over layer after layer. However, sometimes the paste from the new softens up the old paste underneath. I think it's best to remove the old paper, though doing it isn't always easy. You need to penetrate the paper with water to soften up the old paste. You can rent steamers that do the job. One of the best ways is to apply very hot water to the wall with a paint roller. It helps if you add some detergent, which acts as a wetting agent to help the water penetrate a little better.

● I find that by adding vinegar to the water I use, the hot water soaks in better. I put a half a cupful in before filling up the bucket with hot water.

● Add some laundry starch to the hot water you're using to soak wallpaper for removal. This thicker mixture will stay on the surface longer and, therefore, give the water more time to soak through and attack the paste underneath.

● Make a mixture of two tablespoons of powdered alum to a gallon of warm water. Brush this on the wallpaper. When it dries, it will cause the paste underneath the wallpaper to shrink. This causes the paper to crack, and it then becomes real easy to peel off.

● With the paper very wet, I took a plumber's friend and put the suction cup in the center of a patch of wallpaper. Often this will take off the entire piece. It does have to be very wet, though.

● Some wall coverings are so heavy that steam or hot water won't penetrate. A quick way to scratch the surface is to rake the teeth of a handsaw across the wall surface. This process leaves lots of scratches with each pass.

● Our wallpaper had been painted, so when I tried to use steam to remove it, the moisture wouldn't penetrate the paint. I wondered if paint remover would do its job on the paper and allow the steam in. By the time the paint had softened enough, the paint remover had also gone through the paper, and the paste had also dissolved. The wallpaper came off almost by itself.

PANELING

Paneling has certainly become a do-it-yourself undertaking. You can get real wood in either solid or plywood, or you can get plastic-coated hardboard that comes in hundreds of patterns.

Panels are now applied mostly with adhesives. It's easier, faster, and often yields better results than nailing. Those manufacturers that cater to the do-it-yourselfer have excellent, easy-to-follow instructions.

While you can apply paneling directly to base studs, most paneling does better with backing because it's far from soundproof; and besides, if you lean against it between studs, it usually has some give to it. Therefore, if you have exposed studs, you should at least consider applying a plasterboard backing. Whatever the wall, you should make it fairly level. Check for highs and lows by getting a long straight board and a flashlight. Move the board over the surface and have a helper aim the light along the edge of your board. This will help you to pick out the gaps. Mark them. Sand down the high spots and build up the lows with dry-wall compound.

For the very uneven wall, you may do better to come in with furring strips. Masonry walls are nearly always better furred. In most cases, they also should be sealed and covered with a vapor barrier. With masonry, be sure to guard against moisture. Shims behind furring strips will provide an even surface for the paneling.

Although paneling isn't all that thick, remember that you have to allow for its extra thickness at the electrical outlets and switches. With the current off, remove the screws holding the boxes for these units to the studs and reset them out to compensate.

One very important trick people don't know is to bring paneling into its new home at least a couple of days before you install it. This gives it a chance to stabilize to the humidity of the room. Stack the panels with spacers between each so air can circulate around all surfaces.

With some panels, you may want to match wood grain or pattern. For this step, lean them against the walls all around the room. When you have them in the proper arrangement, number them and mark the top of the panel.

Remove all the baseboard and ceiling molding and any trim that will be in the way. Measure the floor-to-ceiling distance at several points on each wall. If you're going to use molding at the ceiling and baseboard, there can be a gap at each end that will be covered. But if you don't want a ceiling molding, you'll want to check to see how irregular the ceiling surface is. If it's too much so, you will want to cut the paneling to fit. Do this in the same way as you cut the side of the first panel—as we'll describe in the next paragraph.

Welcome to the next paragraph that you've been hearing about! The walls of a house are rarely plumb. If you just butt the panel against the corner, you may end up with it not being square, and so all the other panels will be out of kilter. The way to mark it is to place the edge of the panel right next to—but not touching—the corner. Then check it with a plumb line to be sure it's plumb. If not, use shims under the bottom to make it so. Then take a compass like you used in school to draw circles. Spread it so the point is against the corner and the pencil is on the panel. By pulling this down the wall, you'll transfer the contour to the panel so it can be cut. If you're going to use corner molding, you won't have to worry about this step unless the corner is way out of plumb.

Make this and all other cuts with a fine-toothed saw blade. When you use a handsaw or a table saw, cut with the panel facing up. If you use a hand power saw, you'll get a better cut with the panel facing down.

● On dark paneling, put a strip of masking tape along the line to be cut. The pencil mark will show up better, and you can cut right through both tape and panel at the same time. The tape also prevents splintering of plywood panels, whether they are dark or light.

Installing the panel with the special adhesive is easy. You distribute the mastic from a caulking gun in a wavy ribbon. If there are exposed studs or furring strips, run the mastic all along each. If these aren't present, use about the same pattern as if they were there.

● Make a V notch in the end of the nozzle of the cartridge that holds the adhesive. This makes the adhesive come out in a bead that sticks up in the middle and is the same thickness all along (Figure 85). This allows for a more even contact with the paneling.

The panel should be held in place at the top with a pair of nails. Be sure to check the edges for plumb before attaching the panel.

● If you don't have a helper, use a flat-bladed garden spade as a foot lever to raise the panel and leave both hands free.

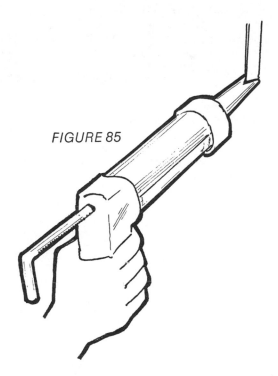

FIGURE 85

Don't drive the nails all the way in. Now press the panel firmly against the wall for an instant to let the adhesive get on the panel. Then pull it away from the wall at the bottom and place a block between the panel and the wall to hold it out. This allows the mastic to cure slightly. When it gets tacky to the touch, you're ready to again press it back against the wall. Now go over the entire area with a padded block and a hammer to tap the panel firmly in place.

If you'll be nailing the paneling up, there are finishing nails made to match the paneling so they hardly show. Be sure to get the right length, because you have to nail into something solid. If there are furring strips, or if you're going directly into the studs, you won't need as long a nail as if you are going through Sheetrock and into the studs. The nails should be spaced about every six inches along the edges and about every foot through the center. If you're going for studs behind the wall, locate these beforehand with a stud finder and put masking tape on the floor to let you know where they are. After you're through, countersink the nails, using a small nail set. There are putty sticks available to match almost every color or shade of paneling, so you can hide the nail holes.

When you come to a window, door, or other cutout, use the paper separator sheet between panels as a pattern. It's already the exact size of a panel and is totally squared up. Tape it in place and mark it, then transfer the shape to the panel.

As you go around the room, don't butt the panels tightly against each other, or you might get some buckling. Leave a little space for expansion. The tiny space can be hidden by running a felt marker of the same color as the paneling on the wall underneath before the next panel is installed.

Cutouts for electrical outlets are best made by drilling pilot holes and cutting out with a keyhole saw.

Remember that all the cutouts can be less than perfect if you use matched molding to cover corners and edges. Switch plates will also cover these cutouts. Matching nails and patch sticks also hide flaws well. You'll probably be amazed at how professional your first paneling job will look.

HANG-UPS

Walls can become more than background with a few well-placed hangings. The saying, "What goes up must come down" probably began when the first caveman hung a brontosaurus head on the cave wall, and a week later it fell down. It doesn't have to happen if you'll use the right hanger. A nail in the wall won't do in most cases.

Finding studs—If you can drive the nail into something solid like a stud in the wall, then it will hold quite a bit. Here are some tips on locating studs.

● Tap gently with a hammer, and the hollow spaces between studs will sound different from the solid places where the studs are.

● Place the side of an electric razor against the wall, turn it on, and move it along. Where the studs are, the tone difference will be dramatic.

My ears aren't keen enough to pick up these differences, so I rely on a tool called a stud finder. It's actually like a Boy Scout compass in that its magnetic needle points to the nails holding the wallboard to the studs. It also points to electric wires and plumbing pipes, so to be sure you've found nails, run tool up and down. Most studs never seem to be just where you want to hang your brontosaurus head.

Anchors—For very lightweight pictures, a number of picture hangers work fine. The only tip to installing is to put a piece of tape on a plaster or textured wall where the nail goes. This prevents chipping and crumbling.

● A popular decorating ploy is the picture wall, where a grouping of wall hangings covers a large section of wall. The exact arrangement is important. To get that, put brown paper on the floor and arrange the various pieces there. When you have 'em just right, outline the frames with a pencil. (Don't use ink or a felt marker, as it could bleed through.) Tape the pattern to the wall, and you'll know exactly where to install the picture hooks.

● We were ready to repaint, and this meant removing a grouping of some thirty wall hangings over the couch. Since our arrangement was perfect, we wanted to get all the pictures back just the way they were. Rather than trust to luck or memory, we took a Polaroid shot of the wall.

● If you want a picture to always hang straight, put two small tabs of that sticky carpet tape on both sides on the back. Position them at the two lower corners of the frame. [A loop of any tape, sticky side out, will do the same.]

● Two hooks are better than one to keep a picture hanging straight. Line them up about an inch apart and run the picture wire over both.

● As far back as I can remember, I have been told that warm nails will go into plaster with less cracking and chipping. I was having a particularly bad time of this chore, and even though I didn't believe this, I put some nails out on a cookie sheet and warmed them up. From then on, they went in the wall with no more cracks or chips. I still don't believe this, but it worked.

● In trying to get a picture to hang at just the right angle so there's no glare from the glass, I finally came up with a wedge cut of rigid plastic foam. I discovered that this also stops the picture from ever hanging crooked. I've put these wedges behind all pictures, and now they never need straightening.

● My method of taming a wobbly picture frame and setting it at a perfect angle may not be the best, but it works. I cut right-angle triangles from a piece of Peg-Board and attached them with small wood screws to each corner of a frame. The holes in the Peg-Board were used for the screws. The frames are now true and strong, and the braces are light enough so that there's no problem with their being too heavy for the hooks.

For slightly heavier objects, tap a plastic wall anchor into a predrilled hole, and then install a screw in the anchor. This causes the anchor to expand out and push against the sides of the hole. This is good for curtains, lightweight drapes, and things of that ilk.

● When hanging curtain rods in a Sheetrock wall, the screws never stay very long. Wall anchors are the answer, of course. But I couldn't find the wall anchors when we moved in, and we wanted to get the drapes up for a surprise housewarming party that we accidentally found out about. Rather than use wood screws, I decided to try self-tapping screws for use in metal. That was months ago, and they're still in place. I know they'll come loose eventually—when they do, I'll then add wall anchors. Meanwhile, I have a semipermanent temporary installation.

● If you are caught without a wall anchor, cut a short length of pencil stub from a round pencil. Poke out the lead. Drill a hole in the wall a tiny bit smaller than the pencil. Tap the pencil in place. When you insert the screw into the hole in the pencil, it'll expand the wood against the wall and will hold tight.

The next step up for dry wall is the Molly. This is a trade name, but if you ask for a Molly, whatever brand the store has will be similar to the one shown in Figure 86. These hold considerable weight. They're often used for tracks holding bookshelves. Mollies come in different sizes for different wall thicknesses and different weights.

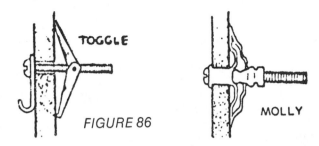

FIGURE 86

● Did you ever start to put in a wall anchor only to find that the hole you drilled had hit a stud? Or maybe when you started to turn the anchor to flare it behind the wallboard, the part that spreads immediately hit the stud and bent the anchor, and it never did work out right. The simple way to avoid this is to drill a tiny hole. If it hits the stud, then just use a wood screw instead of having to use an anchor. If it goes through and misses the stud, then use a paper clip as a probe. Straighten the clip out, and then bend an L on one end that sticks out as far as the anchor will flare out. Work this into the tiny hole and then rotate it. If it's close enough to hit a stud, you can decide whether to move the hole over and go into the stud, or over far enough the other way for the anchor to do its thing.

Toggle bolts are even heavier-duty hangers. They will hold the maximum that the wallboard can stand.

● Because the springy flange on a toggle bolt is so big, you have to drill a hole much larger than the bolt part. If you want the bolt to fit snugly, you can add a sort of bushing to take up the slack. Get a piece of dowel the same diameter as the drill bit used for the hole, and cut off a section the depth of the wallboard. Then drill a hole through the center of the dowel the same size as the diameter of the bolt. Slip this in place before inserting the flange into the wall, and the bolt won't have any play.

There are special anchors for masonry and other types of walls. A trip to the hardware store will give you an idea of what's available. The right anchor will keep your things hanging in there.

● A cotter key will serve as an excellent self-anchoring eye to be installed into a masonry wall for all sorts of hanging chores. Just clip off one flange of the cotter key about a fourth of an inch. Bend the other flange down slightly and if it does not already have much of a point, point it. Then drill a hole that will be a tight fit for the cotter key and drive it into the wall. When the end hits the end of the hole, the point is bent into the masonry and anchors the eye in place.

OTHER WALL WONDERS AND WOES

Baseboards

● Here's how I took care of a warped baseboard. I drilled a couple of pilot holes where the bulge was. Then I inserted wood screws. When these were screwed in tight, they pulled the baseboard back in line so it's flat again. I used countersunk screws filled over with putty, and put a dab of paint over them so they aren't noticeable.

● There are all sorts of methods to remove baseboard molding—most of them result in broken baseboard. Mine doesn't. First I pry the top loose with a claw hammer just enough to slip in a pair of thin sheets of metal with the tops of the metal sticking above the baseboard. Then I insert a long, tapered wooden wedge. After inserting several such wedges along the length of baseboard, I start tapping the wedges to drive them in behind the molding. By hitting each one along the way a few taps, the prying is spread, and you don't split the wood as with a hammer or pry bar. I removed all the baseboards in my house for remodeling without losing a single one.

● Rather than trying to remove the finishing nails from baseboards, I've found it's often better to just snip off the points with wire cutters.

Wall washing

● On dirty walls, use the Horatio Alger approach—just start washing from the bottom up. Otherwise, you'll get streaks from the water that trickles over the dirty, unwashed surfaces.

● Ever have water trickle down your arm while washing the upper part of a wall? Not if you'll fasten a bracelet of an old towel scrap around your wrist.

● When washing walls, you'll have less runoff if you use thicker suds. I keep my hand-held food mixer handy to whip up a frothy mix.

Kids' walls

● Our child had made a number of crayon marks on the walls in his room. I tried several remedies and would like to pass along the best—toothpaste. I squirted some on a damp cloth and spread a thin coat over each mark. After about ten minutes, the toothpaste and the crayon marks wipe right off, and with none of the odor some solvents have.

● Lighter fluid or mineral spirits paint thinner will get crayon marks off a painted wall.

● My husband came up with a clever idea I think is worth passing along. He installed Peg-Board panels on the walls of our toddler's room and put hooks and shelves on the panels. As the boy grew, all these wall fixtures were moved up. When our son started school, we added a desk, also held to the wall by Peg-Board attachments. It has grown with him too. It has been an easy way to acknowledge his growth without new furniture and fixtures.

● Kids have a way of using a bed as a trampoline, making the bed scoot away from the wall. In pushing the bed back into place regularly, we found it was scratching up the wall. By simply adding a pair of doorstops on the back of the headboard, the bed can no longer be pushed against the wall. The stops are the kind with rubber bumpers, designed to be screwed into the wall.

Unusual wall treatments

● I decided we needed some designs on our den wall, but I'm not an artist. Finally I found a design I liked in a magazine. Then I took a picture of it with my 35mm camera. When the slide came back, I projected it on the wall and traced the design. It looks great!

● Most apartment leases won't allow for any decorating that's going to be permanent. There are some things that you can do that *look* permanent, but can be undone when you're ready to move on. The new strippable wallpaper comes right off and never leaves a trace. A colorful toilet seat and lid can be taken off, and the old original put back. Wall-to-wall carpet can be put down using the tape that's sticky on both sides.

Brick walls

● Brick walls and fireplace brick inside a home can give an exciting effect. However, it isn't too exciting when your wife discovers what a dust catcher such a surface can be. You can treat bricks to make them less attractive to dust and make it easier to dust off what they do attract. First clean them completely. Then mix two parts boiled linseed oil to one part turpentine. Brush this over the entire surface and remove any excess with a rag. This helps the dust problem and also gives the bricks a glossy finish. If you have doubts about whether your wife will like the glossy finish, treat one brick in an out-of-the-way corner to see how it grabs her. Boiled linseed alone could be used, but I like the mix.

Remember, boiled linseed oil is a term for factory-treated linseed oil, and doesn't mean you have to boil it.

● To remove traces of mortar that are left on a brick wall, use a power sander.

15.
WINDOWS

CLEANING

Hopefully, the only contact you'll have with your windows will be opening, closing, and occasional cleaning. Before you say, "I don't do windows," let me tell you it isn't all that big a chore. Here are some tips from readers to make this job even easier.

● When washing windows, I have a special waterproof pocket in which to put my sponge and rags. This means when I get through, I'm not quite so wet. The pocket is made from an old rubber hot-water bottle. I just snipped off the spout and neck and made slits in which my belt goes. This gives me a quite handy waterproof side pocket.

● If you need a squeegee for cleaning large windows or glass doors, you can make one easily from an old automobile windshield-wiper blade and your locking-grip pliers. The pliers will lock securely in place to the blade and form an easy to grip handle for your squeegee. (You can even borrow a good wiper blade from your car if, in clamping the pliers on, you're careful not to bend or crimp the metal on the blade.)

● If you want to clean windows without possible water spots, use a large dry cork. Just place the cork flat against the window pane and rub. It will make the glass really sparkle, and you don't have to worry about water dripping down on your wife's carpet.

● Window washing is an ideal togetherness chore. While you clean the outside, your wife can clean the inside, and you can smile at each other while you work. Here's a system that will make for cleaner windows: Use only up-and-down strokes on the outside, and crosswise strokes on the inside. That way, you can tell at a glance which side has the streaks. If you can't get your wife to help, do the inside first. It may save a second climb on the ladder outside. If you really want to do it the easy way, get your wife to do both sides.

Use this one anytime you need two liquids at once.

● When cleaning windows on a ladder, having a bucket for the cleaning solution and one for the rinse water makes for a very crowded ladder. I place a two-pound coffee can in the middle of the bucket and fill it with water. Then I mix my cleaning solution in the bucket around the can, making sure its level is no higher than the level in the coffee can. This keeps them segregated, and yet allows me to carry the whole bit up in one bucket.

● Here's my magic formula for cleaner panes: To a gallon of warm water, add ½ cup household ammonia and 1 cup of white vinegar. Then stir in 2 tablespoons of cornstarch.

● The best glass polisher I've found is a dry blackboard eraser. Be sure the windows are completely dry, and then be prepared for gleaming panes.

● If Jack Frost has been leaving his calling card on your windows, there is a way to keep frost from forming. Clean your windows with a solution of saltwater instead of your regular cleaner. Don't rinse them off, just wipe them to a shine with crumpled newspaper. True, they won't polish out quite as bright, but you'll cut down on the frost problems. The other way to do away with frost on the windows is to move to Acapulco.

● Rather than do my famous balancing act on the ladder to clean outside windows on the second floor, I spray them from ground level. I use the sprayer attachment that fits on the garden hose. Regular detergent would leave spots, of course, so I've experimented with automatic dishwasher detergent that's advertised as leaving glasses spotless. It really works. Even if it's not as good as doing it by hand, it sure beats climbing.

● If you live in a glass house like we do, you know that window-cleaning liquid costs a bit. I have discovered a cheaper way to make my own. To a quart of water, I add two tablespoons of vinegar and a half cup of ammonia. Then fill up a spray bottle and go to it. This formula is enough to do windows for a long time and leaves them just as clean and shining as the expensive stuff.

● You once told about using wadded-up newspaper to clean windows, but you failed to mention that you end up with a mountain of wads of paper to police up afterward. I hate bending over to pick up paper, so I use a clothespin to attach a large grocery sack to my belt. It's my litterbag for the wads of paper, and I don't have to do any picking up.

It's best to avoid doing windows when the hot sun will hit your work. Otherwise, the cleaning solution may be dried by the heat rather than being squeegeed away. Drying on the glass will probably leave a film.

WINDOWS THAT WON'T RAISE

There are many hernia-causing windows around that just refuse to budge—for several reasons. First, check to be sure the window is unlocked. Don't laugh; it has happened. However, the most common cause is that the window, not being of sound mind and body, mistook a paint job for a glue job. Look all around the seam where the window sash and the frame meet, and you may be able to spot the places where

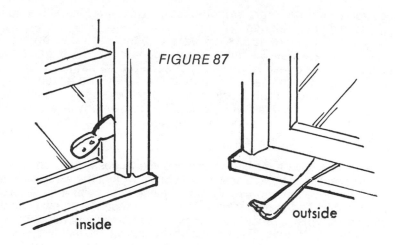

FIGURE 87

inside

outside

the paint has sealed. If paint's the culprit, take a razor blade or utility knife and slit the paint seal all the way around (Figure 87). If you painted inside and out, slit inside and out.

Now you should be able to raise the window. If not, inspect the track to see if paint's too thick there. If so, sand away the excess; in extreme cases, use paint stripper to remove the layers in the track.

If it still stays, try a lubricant in the track. Rub a bar of soap or the stub of a candle on the surface. Better still, spray with a silicone lubricant. Then take a flat pry bar and insert it between the bottom of the sash and the sill, using a small block as a fulcrum. It's best to do this from the outside if possible, because you're liable to dig into the wood slightly.

Sometimes the problem is caused by shifting or settling, or by moisture that causes the wood to expand. Place a scrap two-by-four against the frame and start tapping the block with a hammer. Go all the way around the frame. Often this will move the frame a slight bit away from the sash to relieve the pressure. After doing this, you may also wish to employ the pry bar. And remember the old slogan, "If at first you don't succeed, pry, pry again."

Incidentally, the next time you paint, there is a trick to prevent this kind of sticking. Paint with each moveable sash in an open position. Then after you have painted—but before the paint sets up— move the sashes up and down to prevent the seal.

See also hint on painting wooden frames of screens in Chapter 12.

UPS AND DOWNS OF SASH CORDS

You can raise a properly operating window to any height, and it will stay there. This is because the window has a balance system. In the case of most wood windows, there are ropes attached to weights with a pulley in between to give balance.

If the wood windows are very old, the rope can break; the weight within the wall will fall, and the window will no longer stay in place. Fixing this doesn't require any specialized training. You buy new rope, reattach it to the sash, run it over the pulley and attach it to the weight. One minor problem—how do you retrieve the weight? There should be an access plate. It may be covered by many layers of paint, and you may even have to resort to stripping all the paint off the area to find it.

● If you have ever had to remove the access plate on a wood window to replace a broken sash cord, you know that the screws holding the plate are hidden and usually set in place with paint. I finally found them, and then had to use paint remover to expose the screw slots and unseat them. When I repainted, I backed the screws out about halfway and painted the heads. Then when the paint on the screws and the window frame was fully dry, I turned the screws down tight. Now if I ever have to remove them, they'll come out. This idea is a must for any screws that are to be painted and that might need to be removed later.

Once you remove the plate, usually held by countersunk wood screws, you can fish the weight out. Then you will need to remove the stop strip so you can get to the hole in the sash where the knot goes. From there on, it's a snap.

Since you know the new rope will break in another thirty years, you might want to replace ropes with sash chain. It's handled the same way except instead of knots, springs are used to attach the ends to the sash and the weight.

If you can't get in to get at the weight, there is an alternative—a unit called a sash balance. The balance is built into a unit that fits into the same place where the pulley now is. Remove the pulley and attach this unit there and to the sash, and you have it made.

Aluminum windows often have a spiral rod encased in a tube that gives the balance. These spirals come loose, and you may have to cut a one-by-two so the window can be propped open. If you're patient, however, you can rewind the spiral so it again has tension. The tool to use is a piece of coat-hanger wire cut to about eight inches. Use pliers to make a very small L bend in the end, an eighth inch or less. Before inserting this in the small hole in the spiral's end, raise the rod by pushing on the bottom with a finger. It'll spiral back up. When there's just an inch still sticking out, insert your tool and wind clockwise. (Another L bend in the bottom will make it easier to crank.)

As you turn, the spiral wants to go up inside. Keep pulling it down. When it begins to get hard to crank, let it go on up. The pin sticking out above the hole has to engage in a slot. It will—eventually. Then slip the wire out of the hole, and the job is done. Try it a few times to be sure the pin is engaged.

MINOR BREAKS

Sometimes a window may not need replacement. For example, the kid down the block gets a new BB gun, and he puts a hole in your window. You can seal out bugs and air by using clear fingernail polish. Just dab a tiny bit into the hole, and as soon as it dries, dab again until the hole is closed. This even works on stained glass windows, because fingernail polish comes in almost every color imaginable.

If you spot a crack that has started across a pane of glass, you can sometimes stop it from spreading all the way. Use a glass cutter to score an arc-shaped line just beyond the crack. Often the crack will spread only as far as the arc.

Cracks can also be sealed with fingernail polish, shellac, or silicone sealant.

A pane with only a corner out of it can be temporarily patched with a triangular piece of glass or plastic. Use a piece bigger than the missing corner and fix it in place over the missing corner using clear silicone sealant. Another adhesive used for this type of patch is clear shellac. This will hardly show and will give you an excuse to procrastinate for a long while.

● I don't know how it happened, but we discovered scratches on our picture window. I remembered you had once mentioned the use of jeweler's rouge for chipped places on crystal stemware, so I thought that ought to work on the window. It did! I removed all the scratches, and the window is still just as clear there as elsewhere. I was able to get the jeweler's rouge from a jewelry store when I explained I wasn't going into competition with them.

● One of our windows cracked, and I sent for your free glazing guide. When it finally got here, it was too cold to get out and replace the glass. My wife insisted I do something because the cardboard I had taped over the glass to keep the wind out was fairly ugly. I tried something that really worked: I painted over the crack with clear shellac. I even raised the window and coated the outside too. (After all, I can stand cold for a few seconds.) The crack is sealed. The shellac dried clear, so it's hardly noticeable. When spring rolls around, I'll think about following your directions for replacing—maybe.

REPLACING A BROKEN WINDOW PANE

The first step toward replacing a broken window pane is to remove the old glass—very carefully! In fact, it's best to wear gloves while removing the slivers. Wiggle each piece back and forth until it lets go. If it's stubborn, don't force it. Get out your trusty hammer and tap toward the outside. It's also a good idea to place a large box under the window to catch the shards.

● If gloves aren't handy when removing sharp shards of window pane, I use three-quarter–inch masking tape to protect my hands. The

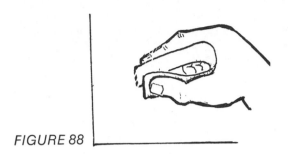

FIGURE 88

tape goes sticky side down against my thumb and follows the contour of my hand around and along my index finger (Figure 88). I use enough tape to wrap around the end of the thumb and finger. Then I can grasp pieces of glass with the thumb and finger and wiggle them out of the frame without the glass coming in contact with my skin.

● When a window pane gets broken, it can be very hazardous getting the rest of the slivers of glass out of the frame. My method is to tap them out with a hammer. To be sure no flying splinters come back at me, I hold a square of window screen against the frame and hit the glass through it. The screen doesn't block my visibility, just the shrapnel.

● When I replaced some window panes, I ended up with pieces of glass down in the carpet. Not wanting to slice up my fingers getting the glass out, I found that a chunk of modeling clay picked up all the slivers. Why didn't I use the vacuum cleaner? It was broken and was my next project, which I didn't want to tackle that day.

After the glass is removed, scrape away all the putty that's left. If the putty is all dried out, it will be difficult to remove. Heat will soften it. Play the flame from a propane torch over the putty, but be sure not to leave it on any one spot long enough to burn down your house. Another heat source is a hot soldering iron held against the putty.

● Although I work with some pretty sophisticated gadgets here at NASA, I'm fairly inept at doing the handyman chores around the house. However, I discovered a way to soften dried putty around window panes. Apply rubbing alcohol with a cotton ball over the putty and then ignite it. The heat softens up the putty, and it's then easy to scrape out. There's not enough alcohol on the cotton ball to become a fire hazard, and the alcohol burns away fairly fast anyway.

If you can't use heat, brushing linseed oil over the surface helps soften it.

● Thanks for your piece on replacing window panes. I have another way to remove the old dried putty: Brush on muriatic acid and let it dry. Usually the putty is softened and can be scraped out. For real stubborn cases, a repeat may be necessary.

● Our postman watched me chipping away at old hardened putty around a broken window. He told me that I could brush the putty with lacquer thinner and wait for about a half hour, and the putty would be soft. I did, and it was. Try it!

Remember, lacquer thinner is highly volatile—so no flame around it.

If it's a wooden frame, hidden in the putty will be some small metal triangles called glazier's points. Save them. If the window frame is metal, there will be some spring clips for you to save.

● If you're all ready to put in a new pane of window glass and find you forgot to get any glazier's points, look to see if you have a corrugated fastener or wiggle nail, as it's often called. Snip small sections of these, and they will work every bit as well as points. In fact, since the corrugations stick up, they are easier to tap in than regular flat glazier's points. A section with more than two or three of the points of the wiggle nail will do fine. When covered up with putty, no one will ever know.

Remove the last traces of the old putty with coarse sandpaper or a wire brush. If the frame is wood, paint over the newly exposed wood with linseed oil. This seals the wood and prevents it from drinking the oil out of the fresh putty.

Now comes a very crucial step—measuring the opening for the new pane. Measure the inside of the frame both vertically and horizontally. Next, subtract about one-eighth inch from each measurement. (With a very narrow frame, subtract a little less.) The reason for the subtraction is so the pane will be a bit smaller than the frame in which it is to be set. This takes care of any expansion—which could crack the glass—due to temperature changes. It also compensates for the fact that many frames aren't perfect rectangles. Just before you leave to go buy the new pane, measure the opening one more time—just to be sure.

While the hardware dealer is cutting the pane to size, go pick up a can of glazier's putty or glazier's compound. You'll find the compound a little easier to work with.

To set the pane, dig out a blob of putty and roll it between your hands so it becomes a long string about as big around as a pencil. Press this against the frame all the way around where the glass is to fit. Now you're ready to put the pane in place.

● Sometimes when putting in a window pane, the putty doesn't want to stay in place when you start to smooth and spread it with your putty knife. Here's an old glazier's trick that will help: Coat the area to be puttied, both the frame and pane, with white all-purpose glue. When the glue gets tacky, apply the putty, and you'll have no more problems.

● Handling putty isn't the kindest job on a lady's hands, but since I am the "handy ma'am" around here, I recently had to put putty around a new pane of glass. The old gooey putty really was messing up my hands until my neighbor (another handy ma'am) brought over a can of talcum powder. By sprinkling talc on my hands, no more putty stuck to my fingers. It was not only neater, but also smelled better.

● I have a backyard greenhouse and have to replace panes of glass from time to time. A rubber suction cup added to the end of the handle of my putty knife lets me easily pick up panes of glass without having to run my fingers along a sharp edge. This also helps hold the pane in place while I'm setting it into the frame. I'm surprised some toolmaker hasn't brought out such a putty knife.

● When installing a new pane of glass, most of us will come back in a week or so and scrape off the little paper stickers on the new pane. Actually, it's just a whale of a lot easier to remove the stickers *before* installing the glass. Just place the pane on a flat surface and scrape them off. Then put the pane in.

It's best if you place the front side of the pane toward the outside. I can almost hear you now: "What did he say? I thought glass was the same on both sides?" But if you sight along the edge, you'll see that the pane has an ever-so-slight curve. The side that bows out should face the outside. If it is a small piece of glass, you may not be able to detect the curve. But if you can spot it, put it in right.

Now you can press the pane into place. Push it firmly against the bed of putty you applied to the frame. Don't worry about the putty that squeezes out of the frame. Make sure the glass is solidly against the putty all the way around. You'll be able to spot air pockets. At these points, push a little harder.

Speaking of points, you didn't lose those glazier's points, did you? Now's the time to install them, or the spring clips that hold the glass in the frame. The clips will have slots, but the points have to be pushed into the frame. They should go in every four to six inches all the way around the frame. They don't need to go in very far, so use your putty knife to push them in place. (I've known a few handypersons who have used a hammer to drive the points in and have ended up breaking the new pane.)

● As a substitute for glazier's points, I have used broken-up pieces of an old single-edge razor blade. Using two pairs of pliers, the blades will snap easily and can be broken so there are tapered sections for easier driving into the window frames.

● I recently needed to use piece of a razor blade as glazier's points. If you try to break these blades, you can cause sharp splinters to fly out, and this could be dangerous. If you'll hold the blade under water while snapping it to pieces, there are no flying shards.

● I use a magnetic screwdriver to push glazier's points into the window frame. I can't drop them before they are into the wood. This leaves my other hand free to hold the pane in place.

● Your marvelous *Super Handyman's Encyclopedia* suggests if you should be putting in window panes and not have glazier's points to use old phonograph needles. I feel that most people wouldn't have these on hand either, since most record players now use a cartridge. However, everyone has paper clips. If you use wire cutters and clip off about a half-inch, U-shaped section, it can be pushed into a window frame and will hold the pane in place until the putty is applied. I clip them at an angle so the piece of paper clip has a sort of sharp point and goes in easier.

● When removing glazier's points around a pane of glass or pieces of a shattered pane, the first thing to do is to bend them outward. Usually a small screwdriver or putty-knife blade will do this. Then grab the point with a pair of pliers and pull it out. Never try to tap it out while the point is still flat against the glass. If the pane isn't broken, it will be.

● Those small glazier's points are hard to hold in place while trying to tap them into the window frame around a pane of glass. A small blob of putty will anchor the little devil in place and let you get your fingers out of the way. Since you're going to putty over the whole thing anyway, you can just leave the blob there.

To finish off the outside, apply small blobs of putty all around against the glass and the frame. Press them in place, and then use your putty knife to smooth. Work toward getting a triangular seal that comes up flush with the outer edge of the molding and down to cover the inner frame that you can see through the glass.

Take a look at the other panes around you and try to make your putty seal match the others in the window. Rake away the excess as you go, putting it back in the can. Also, now you can rake away the putty you squeezed out on the inside.

● A putty knife will sometimes pull the putty away from the frame because the putty sticks to the blade. This problem will never happen if you'll keep the blade wiped with linseed oil. Keep an oil-soaked rag handy and rub lightly so just a very thin coat stays on the blade. The oil doesn't harm the putty.

● To keep a putty knife clean so that no putty sticks to it, I carry a small container of soapy water. By dipping the knife in the soapy water regularly, the putty just doesn't stick to it. The wet blade also does a better job of smoothing the putty in place.

After the putty has set for several days, paint over it. Make sure your paint goes all the way up to the frame and down to completely cover the putty with just a hair of paint over on the glass. This will seal the putty against drying out.

● Before putting the putty in place, if you'll mix it with paint to match the window frame, you may never have to paint.

Now that wasn't too painful, was it?

GLASS CUTTING

If you have a number of panes to replace, or if you make your own picture frames, you can save money by doing your own glass cutting, rather than having the glass cut to size at the hardware store. The glass cutter is a very inexpensive tool. Keep it well lubricated and free of dust. If the wheel doesn't turn freely, your best bet is usually to buy a new one.

● A glass cutter should be stored in oil or kerosene to keep the small roller blade in tip-top shape for cutting. I have a wall holder in my shop made from an empty shotgun shell and a metal pipe strap. The strap holds the shell in an upright position. In the bottom of the shell is a small circle of sponge. I pour oil into the shell so the sponge is well soaked. The cutter wheel is kept oiled, and the sponge also cushions it against being dulled when dropped in place. Also, I always know where the glass cutter is—with other storage ideas, you can never find the holder or the cutter.

● When I am going to be using my glass cutter away from the workbench, I take a blob of modeling clay and stick it over the cutter wheel. The clay has enough oil so it doesn't dry out, and it protects the wheel from other tools while I'm carrying it around. The clay doesn't stick to the glass cutter—when you want to use the tool, the clay peels right off.

If you like this idea, don't get the clay in between the wheel and the inset it's housed in or you're in trouble. I had to use a brush to get all the clay out.

I wasn't the only one who didn't really dig this idea:

● One of your readers suggested putting a blob of clay or putty over a glass cutter wheel to protect it. That's a dumb idea because that stuff is going to stick, and you can't cut glass with a dirty wheel. My idea is much better: I cover the tip of the glass cutter with a slip-on rubber pencil eraser (Figure 89). It protects the cutter even in a tool box, and yet when you need to use the tool, the cutter wheel is clean. I have also found

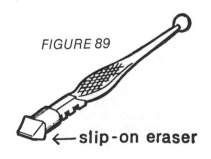

FIGURE 89

←slip-on eraser

several uses for the eraser, such as using it to clean some residue off metal. The glass cutter is a good handle for the eraser.

To cut, you need a flat, clean surface for the glass. I prefer a solid surface, but here's another school of thought:

● I've kept a scrap of carpet around for a long time and have discovered a great use for it. Recently I had to replace a bunch of window panes and found that the glass cutting went easier using the carpet as a pad under the glass as I cut it. No danger of scratching or breaking the glass as I moved it around.

Next, you want to start with a clean piece of glass. It's wise to always lubricate the wheel with machine oil or kerosene just before you start, and it's also a good idea to brush some of the lubricant all along the line to be cut. Place your straightedge along the line to be cut, and be sure it's firmly in place.

Always start at the edge away from you and pull toward you. Don't start at the very edge, but about one-sixteenth of an inch from there. The stroke is important: It must be constant pressure with no stops all the way to the edge nearest you. The wheel does *not* actually cut; it just scores the glass. This is where practice comes in, because there's no way I can tell you how much pressure to exert. Experiment with scraps until you get the feel. Don't ever go back over the line—one pass all the way along and off the edge is the best way.

Now comes the moment of truth: snapping the glass along the scored line. The method I like to suggest as best of all for the new glazier is to place finishing nails under the glass with one at each end of the scored line. Line them up with the score. Now you can push down firmly on either side of the line with your hands, and with any luck at all, the glass will snap with a perfect line. After you gain confidence, you may try other methods, such as placing the line along the edge of a table and tapping it until the scored line snaps. Or if you get really fancy, you may just use a karate chop. For skinny slivers that need to be cut off, the teeth on the side of the cutter will snap away the pieces.

One thing to keep in mind—do the snapping as soon as possible after scoring. Believe it or not, glass sort of "heals"; if you wait too long, the line won't snap. Also, if the edges are to be handled, you can take away the sharpness with wet-dry sandpaper. In fact, fitting the sandpaper into the groove on a scrap of tongue-and-groove wood flooring makes for an ideal sanding block, since it will fit around the edge and keep your hand away from danger.

SCREEN PLOYS

Window screens are designed to let light and air in, but keep bugs out. If a screen develops one small hole that you can hardly see, every bug within three blocks will find its way through. There are several types of holes, and each can be repaired.

Quite often a hole is made by the wires stretching, without any actually being broken. An ice pick can be used to push between the wires and guide them back into place.

If there are a few broken wires, move everything back in place with the ice pick, and then dab around the broken wires with clear fingernail polish or thinned shellac. Brush on a thin coat and let dry. Keep adding coats until the area is closed.

With a long rip, you'll need to sew it back together. Use the ice pick to get everything in place. Then either use nylon thread or some of the wire peeled from a screen scrap. A treatment of shellac or nail polish will prevent raveling.

When there is a bigger hole, you'll need to patch. Cut a square from a screen scrap at least two inches bigger than the hole and pick away at the strands on all four sides to leave about a half inch of unwoven strands sticking out. Bend these wires as shown in Figure 90 and fit this patch over the hole. The wires can then be folded flat on the other side and will lock the patch piece in place. Some folks sew around the patch to be sure it stays. The hardware store will have kits with patches made like we just described.

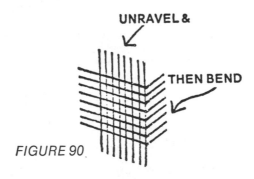

FIGURE 90

With fiberglass screens, you can heat a patch, and it will fuse to the screen. However, don't use too hot an iron and don't let it actually touch the material.

If the screen is too shot to patch, replacing the entire thing is really easy. With a wooden frame, you remove the molding that hides the edges of screen. (Take care with the molding, as it breaks easily.) Once you start prying and get one part up, the rest usually comes out easily. If possible, leave the brads in place in the molding. Now rip out the old screen and be sure to remove all the tacks or staples.

The key to a good screen job is tautness. You need to bow the frame slightly so you can attach the screen first to each end. Here are a couple of tricks to help you accomplish this:

● I place the frame of a screen door or window between two sawhorses. Then I tie a weight in the center. I use just enough weight to cause the frame to bow down about an inch. This lets me tack the new screen at each end; then when the weight is removed, the screen is pulled very taut for tacking along both sides.

● By placing a screen on a long tabletop with a two-by-four under each end, you can then use C clamps to bow the frame in the center (Figure 91).

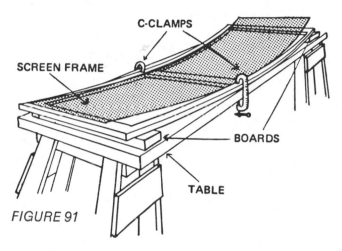

FIGURE 91

And if you don't have a table long enough, place long boards on each side under the two-by-four's so you have something to clamp to.

And instead of using tacks, it will be worth the investment to buy a staple gun to secure the screen. It's superfast and easy.

● Stapling new screen to a wooden window or door frame becomes easier with a slight alteration to the staple gun. Since only the front part of the staple gun rests against the solid frame, I always build a platform for the rear part. I merely tape a block of wood that will be the same height as the frame of the window (Figure 92). This means the staples always go straight into the wood. The job goes much faster.

With aluminum framed screens, the mesh is held in place by tubing called splines. The splines are pushed into tracks around the edge, and this causes the screening to be pulled taut. An inexpensive splining tool makes the job easier, although it can be done with a screwdriver or other tool to poke with.

● Cutting wire screen into odd shapes is an easy task, except that screen is not exactly the best surface on which to draw your design. Put masking tape on the screen and draw on this. No problem following your lines, and less chance of getting stabbed by a fresh-cut edge.

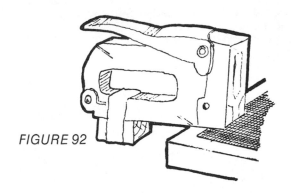

FIGURE 92

● My wife uses some hair rollers that are bristled like a round brush. By inserting a wire handle into the ends of one such roller, I made a super window-screen cleaner. It's handy and really gets into the openings as it rolls to remove the dust and dirt. I used it when I removed the screens and have hung the roller with the screens so I can clean them before re-hanging them in the spring.

● Wanting to clean my screens before putting them away for the winter, I went looking for the vacuum cleaner. The old tank-type had worn out, and my wife had replaced it with an upright that had no attachments. I still vacuumed the screens. I turned the unit upside down and moved the screens back and forth over the vacuum.

WINDOW ACCESSORIES

You put windows in so you can see out and let light in, and almost immediately you cover them with blinds or drapes or shades. These extras create new problems.

Shades

Remember the old joke about the guy who starts to raise the shade and goes up with it? There are shades with so much tension that they can pick up Harvey Martin and Too-Tall Jones. Others are so loose that they won't even make it back up alone. But adjusting the tension is easy.

First, take a look at the tips at each end that are resting in the brackets. One will be round, the other flat (Figure 93). The flat end is where the mechanism is, which includes a spring plus ratchets and pawls. Don't worry about these—I just wanted you to know they were there. To tame a too-tense shade, take the end with the flat pin out of the bracket while the shade is up. Using your hands, unroll the shade about two revolutions. Rebracket it, and see if it's tame. If not, keep doing this until it's right.

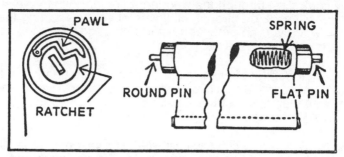

FIGURE 93

The shade that's lost its pizzazz needs more tension. Pull the shade down about two revolutions, and then lift out the flat-pin end and roll it up by hand. If this doesn't give it the desired pep, do it again.

Some shades fail to stay in the position you want them in. This usually means that the pawl inside isn't catching on the notch. If you carefully pry off the end cap at the flat pin end, you may be able to clean the mechanism and solve the problem. The shade makers suggest you never lubricate this mechanism, but before junking a shade, I've used graphite as a last resort. This solved the problem of the slipping catch. Do that at your own risk, as the shade makers may come out and picket your home if they find out.

If your shade does a wobbly when it goes up, it may have a bent pin. Gentle pressure with pliers may solve this.

If the shade falls out on your head every time you touch it, the brackets are too far apart. Either reposition them or try bending them inward a tiny bit. For those mounted inside the casing, a shim of cardboard moves them closer. By the same token, a shade that binds has brackets too close together; either bend the brackets out or move them.

● When a window shade has to be shortened in width, here is a tricky way to mark the shade for cutting. With the shade rolled up, mark up the place where it needs to be cut. Then insert a thumbtack into the shade at several points along the line around the shade. Now unroll the shade. The thumbtacks will have left a perforated line all up and down the shade. It will be easy for you to use a large pair of scissors to cut along the dotted line and end up with a smooth edge and a straight line.

● Cleaning window shades can often do more damage than good. I've found a soft eraser does the job without damage.

● A flannel rag dipped in white flour will clean many dirt spots off shades without hurting the material.

If you're a regular reader of my column, you know that I'm a great believer in oiling almost everything that moves. One definite exception is the roller mechanism on a window shade. The oil will quickly soak right through the wooden roller, and when the shade is rolled up, will soak on through all layers of shade—ruining the entire affair. So when you go on a lubricating binge, don't even think about those fancy shades in the living room.

An added bit of privacy can be had by painting the outside of window screens with a coat of white paint. I don't know why it works, but it does. With the paint on, from a distance of about six feet or more, you just don't see through.

● You can easily cut down the width of a window shade. Cut from the end with the round tip (the end with the flat pin is the end with the spring cavity). Remove the cloth shade from the roller and saw the roller to size. Then slip the barrel and pin off the discarded section and place them on the roller. Cut the shade with scissors to fit the roller.

But enough of this shady business.

Drapes
The two main drapery problems are that draw drapes don't draw properly, or that the whole thing falls down on you. For the latter problem, check our tips on hanging things in Chapter 14. Now for the draw drapes: Look at the two slides that are supposed to move the drapes back and forth. Note that one carrier has the draw cord knotted in the two holes, while the other has the cord looped over a lug. If the drapes aren't drawing properly, first check to see that the two ends are knotted and properly positioned in the holes. Then unhook the loop from the lug and pull the cord to open them completely. Then, while holding the cord tight, manually push the unhooked side over completely. If there's no slack in the cord, you can now hook the loop over the lug, and the drapes should open and close with both drapery panels moving at the same time.

● Before installing a new draw-drape cord, run it through a pan of melted paraffin. This'll make the cord last longer. It will also make the drawing process a lot smoother and keep the entire mechanism lubricated.

Venetian blinds
Probably the biggest problem with blinds is adjusting them—and that's something that takes practice. No matter how you angle the slats, you always have to lift up a slat to be able to see what you want to see. Repairs, however, are usually a bit easier. The two things that cause problems are the cords and the ladder tapes or webbing.
As you can see from Figure 94, there are two separate cord systems: the tilt-cord system and the lift-cord system. When a cord breaks, you can get replacement cords. Before you remove the old cords, however, it's best to make a simple sketch to be sure you get the

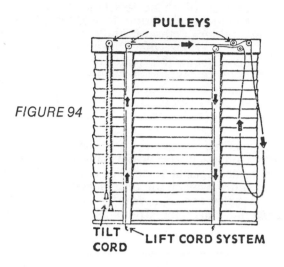

PULLEYS

FIGURE 94

TILT CORD   **LIFT CORD SYSTEM**

cord back in the right path. The tilt system is a snap because it just runs over a pulley, but the lift cord runs around several pulleys. When replacing a lift cord, start at the side opposite the actual cord you pull. Then run the cord all the way through as shown, and adjust the size of the loop before you cut off and knot the other end.

The little metal or plastic clip is called the equalizer. It regulates the pull on each side so they stay the same. The same thing can be accomplished with a knot, but it doesn't look as good.

● When we put up new venetian blinds, the man who brought them out suggested something that makes sense. By rubbing the cords with clear paraffin, the cord will be less likely to fray, the blinds work easier, and the cord won't discolor with age.

● A sneaky way to install a new cord in a venetian blind is to sew the replacement to the end of the old cord. Then pull out the other end of the old one. As it comes out, it pulls the new cord into place. When the replacement has been pulled all the way through the maze, clip the stitches, and you're in business. This clever trick won't work if the old cord is broken somewhere in the middle of the mechanism—you'll have to read the instructions.

Replacing the ladder tapes is also an easy task. I've found the best way is to place the blinds out flat on the floor. Then you need to remove the cords that run through the slots in the slats. To do this, you have to untie the knots at the bottom rail. Some blinds have a clamp over each tape, while others have staples holding the tape over the knot. With the knots untied, you can pull the cord through all the slots, and then the slats will come out of the ladders. Now look at the tube at the top of the unit. You'll note that the ladder is held there by a clip or hook. With this out, the ladder comes off and the new one can be engaged. Then you put the slats back, weave the cord back through the slots, and before long you've got the thing back like it was.

Sometimes the ladder crosspieces come loose from the tapes. Now you could sew this back, but it's not all that easy to get to. Maybe you'll like the trick of gluing the pieces back. There are special transparent, flexible, and waterproof glues that are made for fabrics.

● Our venetian blinds had no way to be secured at the bottom. This doesn't in any way affect the way they look, but each time we opened the door or windows, they rattled against something. I stopped the rattle by simply adding a pair of screw eyes on the underside of each bottom rail and a cup hook on the sill below each eye. With the eye over the hook, the blinds are held straight and can't rattle. The hooks and eyes don't look bad, either.

● We tried to get our landlord to spring for new venetian blinds because the once-white tapes were so dingy. No luck. We tried to clean them, but found that we had to do them one at a time in the bathtub. Then we came up with our super idea. We painted the tape with liquid white shoe polish. The dauber made the process go fast. This was a quick and easy chore and left the tape white and bright. The blinds look like new.

● Our apartment is blessed with venetian blinds that my wife hates. However, I have come up with a slat-cleaning brush she thinks is great. I took a vegetable brush and used wire cutters to snip through the center of the brush loop. Then I flattened out the two arms of the brush, pressing them tightly together. This means the brush will now fit on both sides of the slats. She can quickly clean the slats with this invention.

● The very best thing to clean venetian blinds and louvered shutters is an old-fashioned feather duster. However, try to find one on the market. When I gave up on finding one, I got a brainstorm and borrowed a sable paintbrush from my husband's shop. It's a big brush, and I find it does just about as good a job as the feather duster. After I'm through, I clean the dust out of the brush and sneak it back out, and King Kong has never known.

16
WORKSHOPS

TOOLS

One of the keys to doing it is to have the right tool for the job. This doesn't mean you have to have an elaborate workshop or even an extensive collection of tools. For the person who wants just the basics to cope with problems that arise, here's what I'd suggest—whether you live in a house or apartment.

Claw hammer: Don't get one too lightweight. I'd suggest a sixteen-ounce size.

Screwdrivers: A set containing both regular (slotted) and Phillips.

Slip-joint pliers: Medium size is most useful.

Adjustable wrench: A ten-inch size is probably most versatile. Some of the cheap jobs look great, but will not last.

Measuring device: A yardstick, at the very least. However, a retractable steel tape is better.

Utility knife: Retractable blade is a must.

Stapler: Get one that handles several sizes of staples.

Level: Lightweight aluminum torpedo is my choice for a one-level family.

Plumber's friend: Be sure the suction cup will cover the biggest drain.

Assorted nails and screws: The hardware store will have assortment packs of each that should tide you over.

Lubricants: A spray lube is my first choice.

Tape: Electrician's and masking types.

Power drill: An inexpensive addition that will have dozens of uses. Many experts wouldn't include it on a basic list.

Saw: A crosscut saw will also cut with the grain.

Flashlight: Check it regularly to be sure it works.

It's best to keep all this inventory in one place. If you don't want to buy a toolbox, a large plastic bucket will do. (When you graduate to something better, you'll always be able to use the bucket.)

Don't bother to buy a lot of painting equipment until it's needed. The same would be true for other specialized tools and materials.

Whatever you buy, usually you'll be much better off buying good quality tools. Stick with the brands you know, or buy from stores that stock only quality merchandise. There's usually only a small difference in price between good tools and shoddy ones. Sometimes there is a way to get quality tools at bargain prices. After you get to know a little about tools, you can often pick up items at garage sales. One bargain-hunter suggested:

● To be sure I'm getting a good price on a garage sale tool, I carry a mail-order catalog in the trunk of my car. I can easily check the price of a new item and know whether the garage sale item is priced right.

I've also found that most garage sale items are priced with a little haggling room. Many people who hold the sales are actually disappointed if you don't haggle a bit. At least give it a try.

● There is a place for the cheapos from the bargain bin. I found that my wife and kids were abusing my good tools—for example, using screwdriers for chipping, prying, and digging. First I went into orbit, but then I went down to the bargain bin and bought a whole bunch of tools. I painted the handles on all with a special lime green. The rest of the family knows to reach for the green tools to avoid my turning green.

Planning your actual workshop must be done by you. Space varies with every case. Sometimes all you have is a corner in the garage, while others have a full basement that can handle more tools than Daddy Warbucks could afford. Also, what you put in your shop depends on what type do-it chores you'll get involved in. For all shops, there are a few factors to keep in mind. Can you get the tools and materials you'll be using into the shop without ripping out a wall? Is there adequate electricity? Will there be sufficient light? Is there any structural problem with heavy equipment? Will the tools and equipment be safe from theft and from the elements? Of course, if you do any construction or wiring to get your workshop under way, you may need a building permit, and certainly you must be sure what you're doing complies with the local code. Keep safety in mind.

Now let's look at some of the wild and wonderful ideas for specific tools and materials around the shop.

WORKBENCH

Not every home will be able to have one. I've seen 'em almost as big as a tennis court, and others the size of a TV tray. Maybe these hints will help you.

● Being renters, we avoid heavy furniture, but I know the value of a workbench. Mine is a pair of metal two-drawer file cabinets with a wooden door laid across them for a top. When we have to move, my sturdy bench comes apart instantly.

● There's no space in my apartment for a workbench so I converted the breakfast table. I made a particle-board cover with edges so the tabletop is completely covered. It fits snugly. When I'm through working, my bench top leans against the wall behind a door.

● I keep most of my hand tools in two drawers in my workbench. When I need tools away from the bench, however, the drawers become easy-to-carry tool totes, as I added handles to them. The handles are sections of broom handles cut to fit exactly inside the drawers from front to back (Figure 95). Nails hold the handles in place near the top of the drawer. Since the broom handles don't stick up over the top, the drawers still go in and out easily; and they don't get in the way when I look for something in the drawers.

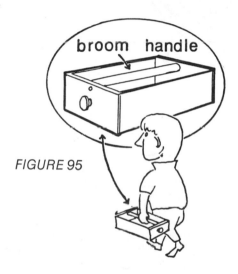

broom handle

FIGURE 95

● Shop drawers collect sawdust and all sorts of dirt and should be cleaned out every year or so. The cleaning is one heck of a lot easier if the drawers have rounded corners. Wood putty or caulk can be put into each corner and curved nicely with a finger. When this sets up, you have rounded corners and a drawer that's much easier to clean. This idea even has merit for some drawers in the house.

● I suddenly realized that my weighty shop drawers were too heavy for the front frames on which they rested; and when I pulled the drawers in and out, they were eating away at the frames and wearing them down. Rather than replace the crosspieces, I mortised out places for small angle-iron lips that cover the area where the drawer rubs. The drawers work much easier, and it should be a while before the weight wears out the metal.

● Putting compartments in a shop drawer would be an easy task if you have the tools to cut slots in the sides for dividers to slip into. I don't have such tools, so I had to resort to my brainpower instead. By cutting lengths of old curtain rods to fit, I solved the problem. I mounted pairs of the sections of curtain rod opposite each other on the inside of the drawer (Figure 96). They are positioned so the troughlike side of the rod sections face each other. The dividers are quarter-inch hardboard and slip right into the slots.

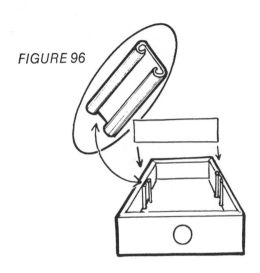

FIGURE 96

● Every home handyman has at least one junk drawer where you put odds and ends of small parts that you hope will come in handy someday. However, when you need a particular gadget out of this hodge-podge, it can take a half day of digging and looking. I make it a little easier—I lined the bottom of the drawer with aluminum foil. This reflects light and adds to the visibility; also, the light background makes it easier to spot different pieces. Now it only takes an hour or so to find something I could have picked up at the hardware store in fifteen minutes.

● A good shop-drawer divider can be made from sections of dis-carded garden hose. Cut these sections about a half inch longer than the drawer is wide. Tape them together, one on top of the other. Wedge this divider in the drawer where you want the separation; because it's a tiny bit longer than the drawer width, it will stay in place. When you need to move or remove it, however, it comes right out. For a deeper drawer, use more sections.

● When I built my workbench, I made the drawers dustproof by using wire mesh hardware cloth as drawer bottoms. I keep all small parts in containers, so there is no problem with them falling through. The chips and sawdust go on through to the floor.

● Many home handymen would rather keep bottles of shop liquids in drawers instead of on shelves. There is less likelihood of dropping them. However, nothing's gained if every time you open a drawer the bottles turn over and spill. I strap them in place. I stapled discarded antenna wire to the sides of the drawers in such a way as to leave loops for the bottles. The loops, tailor-made for each bottle, keep them firmly against the side of the drawer. It only takes a few minutes to secure every bottle in your shop.

● Many eggs are now packaged in plastic cartons instead of the old cardboard jobs. These containers make excellent divided trays for workbench drawers. They'll hold all sorts of nails, screws, tacks, and small parts; and these trays can easily be taken out of the drawer for on-the-job use.

● If you have leftover scraps of corrugated fiberglass roofing, here is a great use for them. Cut a strip about three inches wide that is the width of your workbench. Attach the strip along the backboard of the bench. The corrugations provide slots for holding many small and medium-sized hand tools. Small tools that might go through are stopped by the bench top. It's also a very colorful addition to the shop. If you don't have a single piece long enough, several short strips will do. I predrilled the strip and used screws to mount it.

● Scraps of leftover copper tubing can be made into shop drawer pulls. All you have to do is flatten each end of the tubing and drill a hole in each flat spot for bolts. Then bend the center part out to form the handle and mount this on the drawer. The material is soft enough to be shaped by hand, but when attached to the drawer, is sturdy enough to do the job.

● One of the things I stuck in my junk box was the old toilet-tissue holder we had replaced with a fancy one. Installed on the end of my workbench, it holds side-by-side rolls of masking tape, cellophane tape, and friction tape (Figure 97).

FIGURE 97

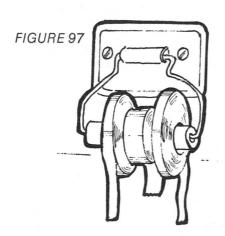

● One of the best small tool holders for your bench top is a brick with holes in it (Figure 98). Some bricks have as many as ten holes. These will allow you to put quite a number of tools—such as screwdrivers, pliers, nail sets, and other small items—in a holder that's right at your fingertips. I also have used a brick on the top step of my stepladder to corral my tools.

FIGURE 98

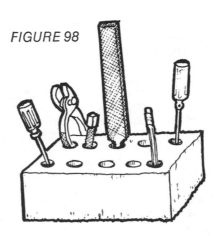

WALLS

Shop walls are very important since many tools are suspended there for storage.

● I didn't have any spacers to hang Peg-Board with, so I devised a method of using bottle caps. Two bottle caps, one on top of the other, have about the same thickness as the spacers you buy. The caps are punched, and a screw, nail, or bolt goes through to attach to the wall. The smooth side of the cap goes against the Peg-Board.

● After installing my Peg-Board shop wall, I needed to drill some larger holes in it. The first hole was a disaster because the Peg-Board was out from the wall as it should be. I solved the problem by inserting a scrap of plywood between the wall and the Peg-Board behind the spot to be drilled, and the new holes were neat and clean.

● With a Peg-Board shop wall, the hooks sometimes move around enough that they enlarge the holes, making the hooks loose. If this happens, a strip of masking tape over the hook shank (Figure 99) will hold it tight against the wall.

● If you have Peg-Board shop walls and want some quick light-duty hangers, insert some wooden golf tees in the holes. Push them in until they're snug, and you're all set.

● To provide extra wall space for hanging tools, install Peg-Board between the legs of your bench on each side for the tools you use most often. My bench has metal legs, and I just drilled four holes to attach the Peg-Board with bolts.

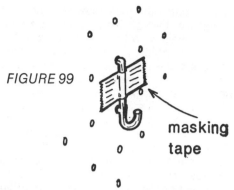

FIGURE 99

masking tape

● Here's an addition to your workshop wall that'll hold all sorts of shop items. I use plastic bottles with the tops cut off. I use flat shampoo bottles, round detergent bottles, and gallon jugs depending on what tools and other items go in them. To attach them to the wall, I poke holes with a hot ice pick and then hang them from regular Peg-Board hooks. This way, I can remove the holders if I need to. If labels are needed, a strip of tape does the job.

● The next time you see a sale on those gun racks that go in the rear window of a pickup truck, get a few. They make dandy racks for all sorts of things other than rifles. By putting them on shop or garage walls, you'll be able to find dozens of uses for them. The plastic covering over the metal allows you to use them for almost anything without scratching. Used in pairs, they'll handle garden tools horizontally.

● I store lots of things in plastic bleach bottles and hang these containers from my garage wall. I have inserted large screw hooks in the studs. The handles on the plastic jugs will hang over these hooks, and the container is handy and yet doesn't take up shelf space. Also, things that should be kept out of the reach of children can be hung high above their reach.

● To hang small baby-food jars containing small parts from a shop wall, use discarded children's wooden blocks. Drill a hole through one side of the block and out the opposite side. Now mount jar lids on the four sides of the block that don't have a hole in them. Fill the jars with screws, bolts, and other small items. Drive a large nail through the hole and into the shop wall, and you have a whirligig holder. Remove the jar you need with just a twist.

● In nailing coffee cans to a shop wall for storage, driving a nail at the top is no problem, but how do you put the second nail in the lower half of the can? I finally decided how: Take a punch-type can opener and use it to make a V-shaped hole in the side of the can, using the bottom rim as the edge to hook the opener onto. Then I drive a nail into the wall, leaving the head protruding just a fraction. The V opening is slipped over the head of the nail, and when pushed down, the point of the V will rest against the shank of the nail. The head will not allow it to come off unless it's lifted up. Then I drive a nail in at the top, and the can is fastened securely.

● Little sections of plastic pipe make ideal tool holders for the shop wall. This material is easily drilled so that the holders can be mounted either with screws on the wall or with hooks on Peg-Board. Different diameters and the ease with which it can be sawed make possible a holder for almost every tool. I use these on my Peg-Board wall with just a plain hook instead of buying a lot of special hooks for each tool.

● An empty shotgun shell and a pipe clamp will provide a useful wall holder for all sorts of small items. Select the size clamp that'll hold the shell securely. The shell is ideal for drill bits, small screwdrivers, a glass cutter, and other little things in the shop. The shell will also act as a reservoir for a little oil so that the tools will be protected from rust.

● Like many home handymen, I keep many small shop items in baby-food jars. Unlike most, however, I hang mine from my Peg-Board shop wall by attaching small angle braces to the lids (Figure 100). The brace is mounted with one leg bolted to the lid and the other sticking up flush with the edge of the lid rim. The hole in this leg fits over a Peg-Board hook. Even larger-sized jars can be hung this way and can be taken to the job site with the lids still on.

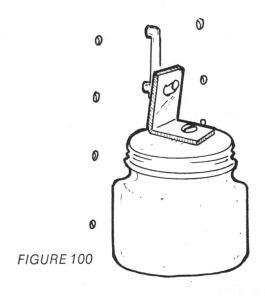

FIGURE 100

● I made a series of small wall cabinets for my shop wall from empty wooden cigar boxes, which I spray painted before mounting them to the wall with nails. They are mounted so that gravity keeps the lid shut and I don't need any kind of catch. These cabinets house all sorts of small cans, tubes, and cartons of shop items. Plastic lettering tape tells me what's in each one.

● Those plastic litterbags that service stations give to hang in your car are also good additions to the home workshop. I have several hanging from hooks on my wall to hold small tools and parts. A felt marker can be used to label the bags. Since the bags have a hanger hole, they're also easy to carry to a work site.

LIGHTING

All do-it projects require proper light. Here are some bright ideas:

● A white ceiling in the shop reflects light for better visibility.
● For the auto tinkerer, paint the garage floor white. When you're working under the car, you'll have light reflected up to your work.
● For working underneath a car, a trouble light doesn't quite cut it. I use my high-intensity reading lamp. It has a swivel so it can be aimed in all directions, a shade so light doesn't get in my eyes, and it's small enough so there's no problem moving it around to position it.
● I made a foldaway hook above my workbench that's come in handy for hanging dozens of things, like holding my trouble light out from the wall when I need extra light on the bench. It is a large strap hinge with a notch cut in the end to serve as a hook. One leaf is mounted to the wall, leaving the leaf with the notch free to swing out when needed. When not in use, it's flat against the wall.
● If you're going to have any trouble with the electric cord on a trouble light, it's usually because of flexing or pulling where the cord enters the base. This problem can be eliminated by simply doubling the cord up against the handle and taping it there. (Don't put the tape so far up on the handle that it gets in your way.) Now any tugging and twisting won't put such a strain on the cord.
● I have added a handy miniature trouble light to my toolbox. It is an ordinary pen light along the side of a spring-type clothespin. Now it can be clipped to any number of things and provide light where needed without my having to hold it.
● When you're working where there's need for a trouble light, but no place to hang it from—like under the house—here's a trick: Drag out a concrete building block (Figure 101). The openings provide a good place in which to stick the handle of the trouble light so it can be held upright to shine on the work.
● The hook on a trouble light is great if there is something to hook it onto. For those times when there isn't, I'm all set, as I tied a rubber suction cup to the light hook. The suction cup hangs out of the way when not needed, but when there's nothing to hook my light to, it will stick to almost every kind of surface.
● The hook on a trouble light allows the light to hang facing only one way. Many times there is nothing to hang it from that will direct the light where it's needed. For help at these times, I keep a harness snap with a swivel eye. The swivel eye goes through the hook on the light, and the snap at the other end hooks onto whatever's handy. The swivel allows

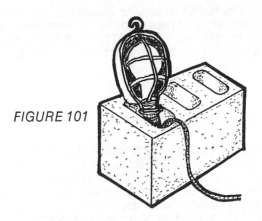

FIGURE 101

me to turn the light in any direction to make it shine where I want it. When not in use, the snap attaches to the wire grill over the globe so it won't get lost.

● Working in the crawl space under the house required positioning my flashlight so I could use both hands and still have the light where needed. The combination jack handle-tire iron from the trunk of my car came to the rescue (Figure 102). Its sharp point allowed me to stick it into the ground. Then I looped a large rubber band around the iron, over the barrel of the flashlight, and back over the tire tool. It was held in place yet could be adjusted to suit.

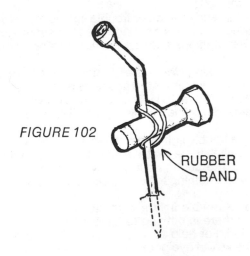

FIGURE 102

RUBBER
BAND

● If you've ever had a flashlight roll off a work surface and break, you'll like my holder. I cut a circle out of the center of a plastic coffee can lid so the flashlight barrel can be slipped through. Then I sliced off one section of the lid to form a flat edge. It can be positioned to shine on the work by just adjusting the lid along the barrel.

● My funnel light is a little different from the one suggested in your recent column. I ran wire through the funnel and installed a socket inside the funnel and a plug on the other end. An S-hook is taped to the cord, and the light hangs in place, with the funnel directing the beam of light down on the work. It's particularly good for working in an auto engine. The hook can be taped at different points to adjust how far the lamp hangs down. I like it better than a trouble light since the funnel keeps the light from shining in my eyes.

● We replaced one of those pull-down lights in our dining room with a new chandelier. Rather than give the pull-down to my brother-in-law, as my wife suggested, I installed it over my workbench. I can pull it down for concentrated light when working on something that needs it, or raise it for broader coverage.

HAMMERS, HAMMERING, AND NAILS

Newer metal- and fiberglass-handled hammers all have rubber grips. I wrapped my old wooden hammer with a foam peel-and-stick stripping tape. The new grip really gives it a great feel.

● I wrapped the handle with electrician's tape.

● After I had to replace a handle, I stuck the hammer in a warm oven for about thirty minutes. This dried all the moisture out of the wood. Then I took the hammer out and drove the handle in some more. A second visit to the oven resulted in more drying, and when the handle was driven in a third time, it was really on tight. After you saw off the excess and install the wedges, the wood will absorb moisture from the air and swell even tighter in place.

● To improve my hammer, I drove a short, big-headed nail I had magnetized into the end of the hammer handle. Now I can stick the handle into my carpenter's-apron pocket, and the magnetized nail will pick up the nails or tacks I need. Sure beats ramming my fingers into those sharp points.

● My method for taking care of a loose hammer handle is easy. I take the head off and wrap the end of the handle with a strip of fine-grit emery cloth. The grit side is facing in against the wood. Reinserting the handle takes patience, but it will go back in. When the wedges are driven into the end of the handle, the hammerhead is on to stay.

● Removing a wooden handle from a hammer, hatchet, or pick is much easier if you drill a hole through the eye and into the wood. If there's a metal wedge in the handle, you may have to drill two or more smaller holes.

● Maybe it only happens every twenty years, but my wooden

hammer handle broke off. Ever try to remove the stub that's still in the hammer? Burning the handle out could have a bad effect on the metal. I put it in my vise and drilled several holes through the wood, avoiding the metal wedges. This made the stub easy to tap out, as the holes relieved the pressure of the wood against the hammer.

● When I broke off the handle of my ball peen hammer, instead of putting in a new handle, I just bought a new hammer. I converted the old hammerhead into a new tool I needed (Figure 103). By welding the head to a length of pipe, I have a hammer that can drive nails with a straight up-and-down stroke. It comes in handy in narrow situations where it's impossible to swing.

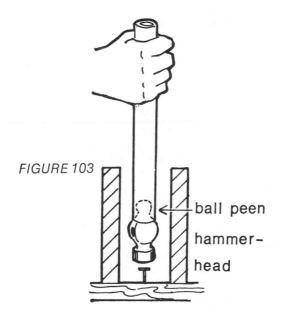

FIGURE 103

ball peen hammer-head

One of the perils of hammering is the smashed thumb. Here are some ways to hold a small nail and yet keep your thumbnail away from the whocking. Hold it in a bobby pin (Figure 104) or wire paper clip until the nail is started. Then pull, and the holder will let go. Or in the teeth of a comb, or in the slit end of a soda straw, or in a slit in a plastic credit card. (American Express—don't bang around without it.)

● To start a tiny nail without banging a finger, use a small paint-brush as a nail holder. Just poke the nail through the bristles, and they will hold it upright. Place the nail point where it belongs and tap it into the wood. As soon as the nail is started, pull the brush back out of the way.

● Driving nails up high usually requires a ladder. Not for me. I have a long metal rod with a magnetized tip. I place the nail on the magnetized tip

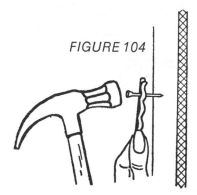

FIGURE 104

and hammer the other end. With a little practice, I have become very proficient at my long-distance nail driving. It's a lot easier than dragging out a ladder for driving a few nails.

● Ever have to drive in a nail up higher than you can reach? If you can reach the spot with your hammer, you can install the nail without climbing. Take a scrap of aluminum foil and punch the nail through the center of it. Now place the head of the nail against the middle of the hammer face and wrap the foil back around the hammerhead. The foil will hold the nail solidly against the hammer and keep it sticking straight out. A medium hammer blow will get the nail started, and a slight tug will pull the nail out of the foil.

● When nailing up high where your holding hand can't reach but the hammer can, here's an old carpenter's trick: Wedge the nail into the V of the claw with the head of the nail back firmly against the hammerhead (Figure 105). The nail will stay in place there. Now reach up, and with a firm stroke drive the nail in. The force will put the nail far enough in to stay, but will jar it loose from the hammer. Turn the hammer around the right way and drive the nail on in.

● If you're not careful, driving nails near the edge of a board can result in splits. One method I have used on soft woods is to chuck the nail in a hand drill and drill it into the wood. Once it's gone through, then it can be tapped on down without danger of splitting.

● To prevent splitting the wood, your tip of blunting the head of a nail before driving it in is good, but I like mine better. I push each nail through a bar of soap before driving. Not only does this keep the board from splitting, it makes the nails go in easier.

● One of those opener keys that come on cans of sardines or peanuts can be converted into a handy tack holder. Unwind and remove the metal strip. Use heavy-duty tin snips to clip off the end of the key, leaving a slot on the end. Crimp this in just a little bit so it will hold the size tacks you will be using. Now you can hold the tacks, but not have your fingers down close enough to get smashed by a bad hammer blow. Soon as the tack is started, a tug releases the hold the key has on it.

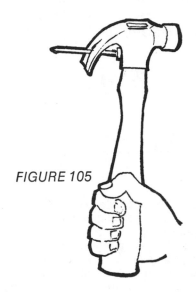

FIGURE 105

● When clinching a nail, hammer the point so the clinch is across the grain. This will give it a much firmer grip than if it were with the grain.
● Here's a use for the plastic piece that holds the cans of a six-pack together. Split it into three rings, loop it over your belt (Figure 106), and you have a hammer holder. Loop the other half over a ladder rung.

FIGURE 106

● You can make a regular hammer into a mallet that won't mar the work by slipping a rubber crutch tip over the face.

● If you ever run across a rubber roller like they used to have on washing machine wringers, latch onto it. This will be the best rubber mallet you ever owned.

● We have given up croquet, but I hung onto one of the mallets and have put it to work in my shop. I faced one head with leather, cut off the handle to a more convenient length, and have found all sorts of uses for it.

● A soft mallet that's worn down to the hard part can be refaced with an old rubber shoe heel. Glue the heel in place, and after the cement has set, trim the rubber to match the face. Since I have five kids, they're constantly outgrowing shoes, which leaves me with lots of heels.

● If you have a friend in a shipping department, ask him to save the wooden plugs that go in each end of a roll of brown wrapping paper. Once you have one of these, taper a wooden broom handle and wedge it into the hole. Cut if off to a handy size, and you have a free mallet that will be very useful.

Hammers can also remove the nails they've driven in.

● When using a claw hammer to extract nails from wood that you want to protect, try this trick to save the finish of the wood: Slit a three-inch length of old garden hose and slip it over the head of the hammer, leaving the claw exposed. Now, when you're pulling nails, the hose and not the hammer will be against the work.

● A claw hammer can gain extra leverage if you tape one of those wedge-shaped rubber doorstops to the top of the hammerhead, with the point of the wedge back toward the claw. This makes pulling nails out a lot easier and faster, and won't scratch up the work.

● To protect the finish of wood when pulling nails with a claw hammer, I loop a heavy rubber band around the hammerhead. Then I twist it and hook it around the hook, leaving the crisscross over the end of the hammer. Only the rubber band comes in contact with the wood.

● I keep a square of foam-rubber padding in my tool box. When I have to use my claw hammer to remove a nail in finished wood, the pad goes under the claw to protect the finish.

● I place a plastic fly swatter under the hammer, and the metal and wood never touch.

● When pulling out nails with a claw hammer, I find the best, easiest, and thinnest thing to use to protect the wood is my putty knife. It even has a handle for easier holding.

● When molding is removed, many home handymen ruin it trying to extract the finishing nails with a claw hammer. I once suggested snipping off the protruding points and leaving the heads in the wood, but I now just grasp the points with pliers and pull the nail right out through the back. When the molding is reinstalled, you can fill up the old holes at the same time as you cover the countersunk heads of the new nails.

● When I had to remove and then replace a piece of molding, I found that the finishing nails needed to be re-covered to be hidden. Putty or wood filler would have stood out unless repainted. I couldn't see re-painting the entire strip of molding, so I searched our son's crayon box until I came up with a color that matched the stain on the molding. This hid the nails and blended in perfectly.

● When there are lots of nails to pull, you can spend lots of time getting the nails out of the claw. Often they get wedged in there and require some knocking to get them loose. I find that by putting a rubber band in the V of the claw, nails cannot become wedged in. I knot the rubber band twice, making the knots as close together as possible. Then I stretch the band as I slip it into the V so that there is a knot on either side. Then the knots hold the band in place and don't allow the nail to get all the way in to lodge itself.

● If you have ever pulled the head off a nail while trying to extract it with your claw hammer, you probably have uttered a few of what we call handyman terms. Grab the shank of the nail with the chuck of your hand drill. Tighten it down and start to twist. It usually gets the nail out.

● After you've ripped the head off the nail while trying to remove it, what's your next step? Grip the end of the nail with a pair of pliers. Then use the claw hammer under the pliers, with pressure against the pliers. The nail will come out. If you have locking-grip pliers, the job is even surer.

● We had decided to throw away a drawer full of nonmatching old nonsilver silverware. I saved a few pieces for possible shop use and found a way to convert a tablespoon into a useful shop tool. I cut a V notch into the tip of the spoon, then sharpened the end. About halfway back on the spoon part, I wrapped tape so it formed a sort of roof over the bowl. This weird-looking gadget is now the world's greatest tack puller. The sharp V slips under the heads, and the spoon's shape makes it a natural lever. When the tack comes up, it rolls back into the covered part; I can pull quite a few tacks before the spoon fills up.

What about storing and carrying nails?

● When I buy nails, I transfer them from the sack into coffee cans. I have found the can will hold half again as many nails if you pound the bottom of the can against a hard surface after it's filled. This causes the nails to filter down toward the bottom, and you can keep adding and pounding for more nails per can. I keep the plastic lids on to keep moisture out.

● Empty coffee cans with plastic lids are great shop bins for nails—until you accidentally drop the can. Most times the lid pops off, and you've got 467 nails to pick up. A wide rubber band cut from old inner tubes will keep the lid from coming off.

● To protect nails stored in coffee cans from rusting, put a tea-spoon of baking soda in with them.

● When I needed to use a small supply of nails or screws, rather than put them in my pocket, I put them in a small coin purse—the kind you squeeze, where a slit opens across the top. This way, I don't have to fish in my pocket or get stabbed.

● When I'm using tiny brads or nails away from my bench, I carry them in an empty matchbook. I stick the points in behind the striker part, and then fold the cover over. It will hold quite a few nails, and they aren't loose in my pocket.

● Acoustical-ceiling scraps come in handy as a shirt-pocket tack or brad holder. Cut it into a rectangle that will fit into your pocket with about a half inch sticking out. Load it up with tacks by pushing the points into the top of the holder. They are easily extracted for use. Sure beats carrying them in your mouth or having to fish them out of your pocket.

SCREWDRIVERS AND FASTENERS

Almost all of us have ruined a screwdriver at one time or another. Probably the best way to screw up a screwdriver is to use the wrong type or wrong size, which will always botch up the screw head and often ruin the screwdriver. The screwdriver should fit the slot, and that means you need a set of these tools with both regular and Phillips-head tips. If you're going to have to buy new ones to complete your inventory, spend a few extra pennies and get good ones. Those from the bargain bin won't last and won't get the job done as easily.

Remember that the screwdriver is meant to drive screws. It's not a pry bar, chisel, or ice pick, so don't try to convert it. Be sure the handle is clean and dry so that you get a sure grip. The best way to hold this tool is in a straight line with your forearm. This allows you better pressure and better control by keeping the blade lined up with the screw. If there's not room for this, and if you need good pressure, apply it with the palm of your other hand pressed against the top of the handle.

If lots of force is needed on a stuck screw, let penetrating oil do its thing before you have to strong-arm it. New types have a ball instead of the conventional handle for an even better grip. If you're going to work on electrical gadgets, be sure to use a screwdriver with an insulated handle. There are also new cordless electric screwdrivers that save lots of work, and there are screwdriver bits that fit hand and power drills for more power with less muscle. About half the things in your home are held together by screws, so you really should know how to use your screwdrivers best.

● Rubber bike-handle grips will fit over the handles of some screwdrivers. Cement them in place, and they provide a much better and more comfortable grip.

● Get extra holding power with a screwdriver by putting a little kitchen cleaning powder on the tip. The grit makes the blade stay in the slot.

● When a Phillips-head screwdriver starts to lose its bite, you can usually give the tool new life by running a triangular file along the grooves. Just a few strokes with a small file will usually put it back into shape.

● When you have a screwdriver too narrow for the screw slot, use a little tab of masking tape on the screwdriver tip. This will give the tip extra bulk without taking away the solidity of the blade. If the slot will accommodate the tape on both sides of the screwdriver blade, wrap it around the end. Otherwise, just cover one side.

● When you are using a screwdriver in a spot where you're not able to see the blade, you sometimes waste time trying to get the blade lined up with the slot. I have marked the handles of my screwdrivers so I can tell at a glance which way the blade's pointing. A straight line on the top of the handle and another at the side of the handle does it. I burned the lines with a hot ice pick, but any number of methods could be used. This also lets me know without taking the tool out of the holder whether it's a regular or Phillips screwdriver because the Phillips heads don't have the lineup mark.

● Lots of us have trouble remembering which way to turn screws, bolts, and valves to remove or open them. When in doubt, I use the old rule of thumb my grandfather used, 'Right is tight.' It won't always be true, but in 99 and 44/100 percent of the time, It will save you from straining like crazy to unscrew something when really you were tightening it all along.

Another memory trick is, "Left off? Right on!"

● To remove a really stubborn nut, hold your propane torch flame on the nut long enough for the heat to start turning it red. Then pour cold water on it. The quick expansion and contraction will loosen even the worst ones. Be sure you don't use this one if the extreme heat will do any damage to the surroundings.

● Sometimes a hard-to-remove bolt or screw will break loose if you first *tighten* it a tiny bit.

When wood screws no longer hold, it's usually because the hole has become enlarged. One way to solve that problem is to remove the screw and poke toothpicks into the hole. Keep poking the sharp points in until no more will go. Now saw or cut off what's sticking out, and it's almost like a solid piece of wood to insert the screw back into. Even better, dip the toothpicks in glue as you insert 'em. One reader puts wood putty in the hole before filling it with toothpicks. Others just fill the hole with wood putty.

Sometimes just wrapping the screw threads with steel wool, a pipe cleaner, or a blob of cotton will do.

Just dipping the threads in shellac, glue, or even fingernail polish can hold the screw in when these materials set up. These methods are also used when screws in metal tend to work loose from vibration. If you know you'll never want to remove a screw, coat the threads with epoxy.

● If the slot of a screw has been stripped so the screwdriver can no longer do its thing, often you can take a hacksaw and cut another slot at right angles to the old. Of course, this won't work on a countersunk screw.

● Cutting off a bolt is certainly an easy chore. However, after shortening the bolt, many times the nut won't go on because of burrs or a jagged edge. If you put the bolt on before making the cut, you avoid the problem. Put it above the cut, and after the cut is made, turn the nut off. As it comes off, it will restore the threads. If there's a problem getting it off, use a wrench. But once you get it off, you'll never again have any trouble getting it off or on.

● Sometimes installing a nut and bolt is next to impossible because the nut needs to be over a hole that's out of reach. Cut a strip of tape no wider than the nut is thick and use this to hold the nut on the end of a pencil. Tape it so the edge is against the pencil, leaving the hole exposed. Once you get the bolt started in the threads, a tug on the pencil will pull the tape loose. If a pencil isn't long enough, a dowel will be.

● How many times have you had to install a nut in a tight place, and while holding it against the hole, accidentally dropped it? Put a little rubber cement on your finger, and the cement will hold the nut until you get the bolt started.

● A nut driver is such a good little tool because it gets into small spaces. But if the nut, bolt, or screw falls out before you can get it started, you've got a problem. Keep a blob of rope caulk wrapped in foil in with the nut-driver set. When you need it, put a small quantity into the recess, and then insert the nut or bolt. It'll be held by the caulk long enough to get started. Then remove the caulk and finish the job.

● To install a nut where your hands can't reach, use a dowel scrap the same size as the opening in the nut. Turn it into the hole so the threads bite into the wood just enough to hold. The dowel will reach in and let you get the nut started on the threads. Then you can back the wood out to get a tool to finish.

● When the head of the bolt is hidden, trying to tighten a nut usually turns both nut and bolt, and so no tightening is done. Saw a slot in the end of the bolt, and you can insert a screwdriver blade into the slot and hold the bolt still while you turn the nut down tight.

● Often a bolt will stick out beyond the nut, and can be a hazard if you bump against it. If you try to saw if off, you often botch it up so that the nut can't be easily removed. Make plastic caps for the bolt ends from the barrel of a ball-point pen. You can usually find a size to fit even if you have to use the tapered part for smaller bolts. I cut the plastic barrel piece slightly longer than the protruding bolt. Then I turn the barrel so it threads itself over the bolt. If you hit this, it won't leave a scar.

● Probably the easiest way to turn in screw eyes is to insert the shank of a screwdriver into the eye and turn the driver like a crank. If there's no room for the screwdriver to turn, cut a slit in the end of an old broom handle that's just the right size to accept a screw eye. This provides a handle to turn screw eyes down easily and quickly (Figure 107).

The end of a good-sized pocket knife will have slots that allow most screw-eye heads to fit in.

SLIT IN
PIECE OF
BROOM
HANDLE

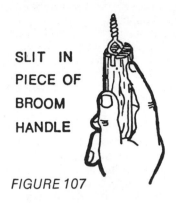

FIGURE 107

PLIERS

● Make self-opening pliers with an old hacksaw blade. Remove the teeth of the blade on a grinding wheel. Then bend the blade into a U shape to fit inside the U formed by the pliers handles (Figure 108). The blade is then cut off to fit and taped in place inside the handles. It gives good springing action, and yet doesn't interfere with the gripping.

● If you've ended up with a leftover left-hand leather work glove, snip off the fingers and use them the next time your pliers are to grip something that the pliers might bite. Slip a glove tip over each jaw. The leather will still give you a solid grip, but will keep the serrated jaws from chewing up the work.

FIGURE 108

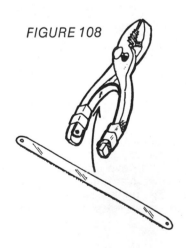

● When you need both hands for working and a third one for holding, maybe this trick will help. If it's something that can be gripped with a large pair of pliers, do so. Then place the pliers between your knees and hold them together. This holds the pliers in your "leg vise" and leaves both hands for working.

WRENCHES

While using a wrench, skinned knuckles usually don't have to happen. *Gotcha*s can be caused by a cheap wrench that has lost its bite, a dirty wrench that makes you lose your grip, or an ill-fitting wrench. If you pull on the wrench, you'll avoid injury if there is a slip. Push, and when the thing breaks loose, you could knock your knuckles. If you have to push, do so with the palm of your hand and without closing your fingers around the handle.

When you need a little extra leverage, don't go for the old trick of slipping a length of pipe around the handle. You may get enough extra leverage to break the handle. The better way is to go for a larger wrench.

● A rubber bike-handle grip can supply a better grip when fit tightly on an adjustable wrench handle.

● When your open-end wrench won't grip a worn nut, slip the tip of a small screwdriver in between the nut and the jaw of the wrench. This will take up the gap and still provide a flat surface for the wrench. If there's not quite enough room, step up to the next-size wrench and push the screwdriver blade against the nut so its tip pushes against the wrench. Usually a little jockeying around will result in a grip that lets you remove the nut.

● When I was younger, it seems they used to make the size numbers on wrenches a lot larger. I could see them then; now they are so small that I can't tell what size I've got. I compensated by painting the sizes on with bright fingernail polish. The brush that comes with the bottle is just the right size. This stuff doesn't come off with wear as regular paint would.

SAWS

● Protect the teeth of a handsaw by slipping a slit length of garden hose over the teeth for storage.

● Rub a candle stub over a saw blade as both a lubricant and to protect the metal from corrosion. The wax won't stain the work as oil can.

● With an electric engraver, I etched marks on the straight back of my handsaw so I can use it as a ruler. I taped both the saw and a yardstick together on a flat surface so I could mark accurately.

● For those who sharpen their own saws, wipe liquid shoe polish along the teeth of the blade. As you sharpen each tooth, the shoe polish comes off. That way, you can tell at a glance if you have missed any teeth as you go along.

● Light a candle and let it leave soot on the teeth, then sharpen.

● When I got ready to sharpen my Teflon-coated saw, the jaws of my vise were scratching away the Teflon. Warn others that they should sandwich the saw between two pieces of a soft wood so the bare vise jaws won't touch the blade.

● When you have to cut through gummy, sappy wood, your saw blade will end up being gummy from the pitch. My quick-clean method is to crumple up a piece of aluminum foil and dip it into kerosene. After a little rubbing with the foil, the blade will again be smooth, clean, and shiny.

● Cut through a bar of soap before sawing, and gummy deposits won't stick.

● Put paint thinner in a spray bottle and spritz the blade as you saw.

● Clean a badly gummed saw blade with spray-on oven cleaner.

● If the frame of a hacksaw sticks up too high for cutting in cramped quarters, remember that you can install the blade upside down so it faces into the frame. If there happens to be more room on the other side of what you're sawing, this may solve your problem.

● When you need to cut a number of duplicate pieces, use the same piece all the way through as your model. You'll end up with more uniformity in the pieces. If you change pieces, even the slightest error can be duplicated several times over. If you allow this difference to appear on several pieces, sometimes the width of the saw kerf makes you end up with a wobbly chair.

● I keep spare hacksaw and saber saw blades hanging from my shop wall. I put a metal shower-curtain ring through the hole in the end of the blades; it can hold quite a few. I then close the ring and hang it from a hook on the wall. When I might need extra blades away from the workbench, the ring with spares is easy to tote along.

● In an emergency, you can make a pretty good keyhole saw from just a piece of a hacksaw blade and a C clamp (Figure 109). Tighten the clamp down on an end of the blade as a side handle.

FIGURE 109

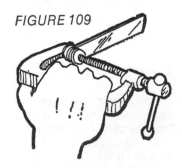

● If you cut off a board and it's just a hair too long, you know it's not easy to saw off another fraction. Push the two pieces back together and clamp them to a scrap underneath. Then run the saw blade back through the cut. You'll take a little off each side—maybe just enough off the work. If not, repeat. If you have to take off more than the width of your saw blade, then clamp a scrap to the work so the scrap sticks out beyond the work. Cut so you are sawing through both the sizeable scrap and small tab of the work. You'll get a smooth cut.

Power saws do most of the work for you. But it's not all automatic.

● If your fingers come anywhere near the blade, use some sort of a push stick to feed work through a table saw. If the push stick isn't handy, you may be tempted to get this job done without it. Put a string through a hole in the handle of the stick and hang it from the adjusting knob of the fence. That way, it will always be handy; and even more important, will remind you to use it.
● A pencil eraser on a dowel is a good push stick. It grips the work and is small enough for very small cuts.
● Make a right-angle notch in a plastic food scraper from the kitchen (Figure 110), and you have an excellent thin push stick.

FIGURE 110

● When running long stock through a saw or other shop machine, there is usually a problem of handling. If the outer ends of the stock aren't held level with the saw table, the weight can make it difficult and dangerous to work through the machine. Rig up support stands with a roller skate attached to each. A skate mounted with the wheels up not only supports the stock, but makes it easy to run through with the help of the wheels.
● Or, mount a paint roller in a vise or clamp it to a stand as a support when ripping long stock.
● I don't leave my power saw plugged in, as a child could accidentally turn it on. However, the plug can get smashed if left on the floor. Glue a small magnet to the side of the plug, and the plug'll attach itself to the side of the metal table and stay off the floor.
● Sprinkle talcum powder over a saw table and spread it out by hand. The work glides across the tabletop because the talc is a good lubricant, but it won't stain the wood.
● Use carpet sample scraps as protective covers for circular saw

blades. First squirt the carpet with old crankcase oil. Then sandwich the blade between the scraps with the pile side in. A wide rubber band holds the sandwich together for storage, or to carry in for sharpening.

● Or, cut a wide rubber band from an inner tube and stretch it around the teeth.

● Store blades in old record album covers.

● A small-sized frozen pizza's aluminum foil tray can be used as a soaker pan for circular saw blades. It's only slightly bigger than a blade, so you can get by with using the minimum amount of solvent.

● When jigsawing an intricate design that requires much turning, slip a piece of waxed paper between the work and the saw table, and the work will turn much easier. Position the paper so it won't get into the path of the blade—though it won't hurt anything if it does.

● Since you don't always use a saber saw where there's good light, put a headlight on your saw. Tape a penlight-type flashlight to the front of the saw so the beam is aimed down right in front of the blade's path.

Wasn't it Richard the Handyman who said, "My kingdom for a sawhorse"?

● When working with a sawhorse, you usually have to put small tools and other items down on the ground, and that means a search when you need them. I mounted tin cans on my sawhorses to act as tool and parts holders. I use a regular-size vegetable can for tools, and a flat tuna-fish can for nails and screws. They are mounted with nails at each end of the top crosspiece, and are set so they don't stick up over the top to get in the way.

● To a sawhorse I added a sort of shelf that acts as a tool caddy. I nailed the shelf to the bottom of the crosspiece that braces each pair of legs. The shelf has holes drilled in it so various tools can be dropped in. It also offers enough flat surface so other tools can be laid down on it. This helps me keep better track of my tools and keeps them handier. A handy neighbor liked my idea, but put his shelf down at the bottom and attached it to all four legs.

● Very few home handymen have a saw holder on the sawhorse. When I made my sawhorse, I let the crosspiece extend about six inches beyond the legs on one end, and made a saw cut in the end of this extension. This slit becomes a holder for my handsaw. The blade fits in the slit with the handle resting on the crosspiece.

● Cut a one-by-ten board to the same length as the horse and nail it to the top rail. The sawhorse still works as it did, but now there's a shelf that gives work space, and a place on which to lay tools.

● For a removable pad for a sawhorse, cut six-inch sections from an old tire. One on each end of the cross stringer of the sawhorse forms a padded work area, but still leaves a firm base.

● On a wooden sawhorse, lumber has a tendency to slip around. I remedied this by stapling a piece of rubber from an old inner tube around the top of my sawhorse. Staple underneath so there's nothing to scratch the work.

● Sawhorses are a pain to store in my small garage. However, by adding two screw eyes to the side of the top rail of the sawhorse, I can hang it on a pair of large cup hooks in the garage wall. The hooks are up high enough for the legs of the sawhorse not to be in the way, but not too high for me to reach . . . sort of a high horse.

● Clamping a miter box to a sawhorse is OK, but not really that convenient. I mounted a pair of hinges to the side of the miter box and the side of the sawhorse. By removing the hinge pins, the miter box comes off. The hinge plates left on the sawhorse are on the side and out of the way. The pins stay in place in the hinge halves on the miter box so they don't get lost.

● A full sheet of plywood or paneling will often sag between two sawhorses. Cut a notch in the top rail of the two horses and install a brace that runs across from one sawhorse to the other and acts as a support for the wide workpiece. A one-by-one brace with a notch tailored to its size is plenty sturdy enough.

● When working on those four-by-eight sheets of plywood, regular sawhorses aren't wide enough. Add extension arms that double their width. The arms are two-by-fours hinged at each end. When working on big sheets, fold them out. When not, they fold back together to rest on the top rail and serve as the work surface.

● Rather than drag out sawhorses to hold a sheet of plywood for sawing with a circular saw, I place the sheet on the ground over an area with lush grass and set the blade so it just barely goes through the plywood. Then I get down on my knees on the plywood and saw away. I don't have to reach over when I get toward the end of the cut. The blade doesn't get down to the dirt, and so can whiz right through the grass. This is particularly convenient when work is being done away from the shop.

VISES

● When you install a vise on a workbench, position it so the stationary jaw sticks out over the edge of the bench. This will let you put work in the vise vertically as well as horizontally.

● Right next to my vise I keep a scrap piece from an old inner tube. Anytime I'm going to grip something that could be botched up from the vise jaws, I use the inner tube as a blanket to protect the work. It is flexible, can wrap around anything, and still gives the vise a strong grip.

● Slit garden hose or radiator hose sections can be slipped over vise jaws to protect work.

● When you put a threaded metal object into a vise, there's always the danger that clamping pressure will botch up the threads. Protect the threads by winding a piece of soft solder wire around the object, down in between the threads. Cover enough of the threaded portion so there is plenty of room to grip. The soft solder will allow you to apply as much force as is needed without damaging the threads.

● When drilling a hole in the threaded end of a bolt so it will accept a cotter pin, a careless handyman can botch up the threads. To be sure this doesn't happen, predrill a hole through a nut to fit. When the nut is positioned on the bolt and both put into a vise, the drill bit will go through the bolt without being able to crawl around; and the vise can't chew up threads.

CLAMPS

There are hundreds of different sizes, shapes, and types of clamps used to hold things steady while you work. They hold pieces together until you fasten, and apply pressure for gluing. Not all clamps are store-bought, however.

● For gluing a big piece of veneer or laminate, you need to weight down the area while the glue sets up. A big tub can be placed on top and then filled with water. Or several containers can be spotted around.
● In some cases, I've driven my car on top of big pieces being laminated to provide weight during the gluing. Of course, you must protect the work.
● When gluing something with an irregular surface, fill an old icebag with sand. It can then be placed on the surface being glued and formed around the irregular parts to apply the weight that will make the two surfaces stay together.
● Here's a makeshift clamp for a picture frame. I made two loops of soft rope. Then with the new glue in the joints, I put the two loops diagonally across the frame with one loop on each side (Figure 111). Then, operating the loops like tourniquets, I used a pencil to twist and tighten my clamps. By putting corrugated board in the frame, the pencil has a surface to rest against and can't unwind.

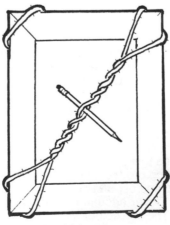

FIGURE 111

● Or, use elastic bands cut from an old inner tube.

● If you ever use a rope or heavy cord to hold odd-shaped pieces together while glue hardens, dampen the rope just before tying it. Then as the rope dries, it will shrink a little and increase the clamping pressure.

● Save plastic-laminate scraps. This very thin material makes excellent pads to go between a clamp and the work. It lets you use good pressure from the clamp without fear of marring the work. It's also rigid enough to spread the pressure a little.

● I added inch marks to the long crosspiece on my bar clamp. It is often a big help to be able to measure against it.

DRILLS AND DRILLING

Here's a "hole" lot of drilling help.

● Now that I'm retired and no longer need my metal lunch box, it's become a case for my power drill. I lined the bottom with foam rubber, and the drill fits nicely in here. I replaced the thermos with a can with a screw-on top, and it holds all my bits. They are rolled in an oily rag to protect them.

● When I need to drill to a specific depth, I use a faucet washer as a stop gauge for most small drill bits. The rubber washer already has a hole in it, so it slips right on the bit. It won't mar the work when it comes in contact with it.

● For a drill bit that slips in the chuck, try putting a small strip of emery cloth around the bit with the grit side against its shank. Then chuck it, and it'll stay put.

● I found that a tiny drill bit wouldn't hold in my old chuck no matter how much I tightened the thing. However, I wrapped a small drip of solder around the bit and then rechucked it, and the soft solder allowed the chuck to hold the bit.

● When drilling holes in plywood, the drill bit usually comes through the bottom and leaves a splintery hole. Drill only partway through, and then drill through from the other side. Center the drill bit by drilling all the way through with a tiny drill, and use this small hole to center the bit when starting a new hole on either side. If you're using an auger bit with a screw point, drill until the screw point breaks through, and use that as a centering point when coming back through.

● If you ever need a miniature buffing attachment for your power drill, use a cotton-tipped swab. Cut off one end and put the swab in the chuck. It can be dipped into polishing compound or used dry. Bring the side of the swab against the work. Check often to see that the cotton doesn't wear down to the plastic or wood.

● Make buffing pads for use with a power drill from carpet scraps. Use the rubber wheel as a template and cut the circle. Rubber-backed carpet won't ravel. Then punch a hole in the center and attach it just like you would a sanding disc.

STAPLER

● Staples have replaced tacks and nails in lots of projects. If you've ever removed a bunch of staples, though, you know you have a job of picking up all the little wires afterward. If you'll use a screwdriver with a magnetized tip to pry with, you'll have all the picking up done as you remove the staples.

● I converted an old kitchen fork into a very useful staple puller. I cut the two outside tines completely off and filed down the two center tines until they were only about a quarter inch long. Filed thin and pointed, these stubs get under staples, and the handle of the fork gives you leverage to pry them right out.

FILES AND RASPS

File these hints away for future use:

● For files without handles, a sponge-rubber ball can be speared by the tang (sharp point).
● A pair of wooden spools can be glued in place.
● The rubber part from a bike pedal is great (Figure 112).

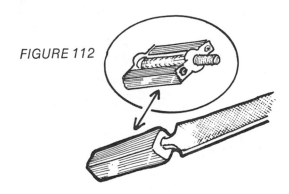

FIGURE 112

● For tiny files, a rubber valve stem from a tubeless tire.
● A doorknob with a set screw can be secured to a file as a handle.
● Self-sticking–foam weather strip can be wrapped around for a file handle.
● A large metal washer or the plastic lid from a coffee can will act as a hand guard when using a file to sharpen an axe (Figure 113).
● A file gets clogged with metal particles. One of the best tools I have found for cleaning a file is a suede brush for shoes.
● Toothbrushes are good file cleaners.
● Before using a file on soft metal, rub the end of a candle stub over the file to fill the teeth with wax. When you start filing, the wax will move out of the way to expose the ends of the teeth. However, there'll still be

FIGURE 113

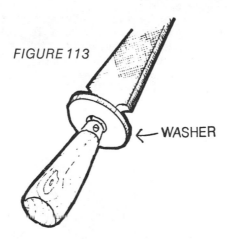

←WASHER

enough wax to keep the soft metal filing from clogging the file. When you're through, hold the file over a flame for a few seconds to melt the wax, leaving the file clean and unclogged.

Or rub chalk or graphite powder over the teeth.

● A good substitute for a round rasp is a long threaded bolt. The threads will do a pretty good job of eating away at most woods.

MEASURING, MARKING, AND LEVELING

● If your shop yardstick has a way of straying off so you can't find it, make a holder that keeps it always handy. To the workbench leg, nail a pair of small frozen-juice cans with both ends cut out. The yardstick will stay upright and ready to use.

● By gluing a section of wooden yardstick to the top of my ladder, I have a handy measure right in front of me.

● In a pinch, you can turn a tape measure into a rigid ruler. Just apply a heavy coat of spray starch and press it out straight.

● A handy place for a yardstick is on the side of your sawhorse. I picked up a pair of the free ones from the paint store and tacked one on each side of the horse.

● The calibrations and markings stamped on metal rules and squares can be made more legible if you brush across them with white paint. Then take a rag barely damp with solvent and lightly rub across the surface, removing the paint on top but not any that's down in the markings.

● An old ball-point pen that has quit writing is ideal for use in carpentry work. Mark a line to be sawed with the ball point. It will make an accurate mark. It works smoothly against a straightedge. The indentation can easily be seen, and your saw blade will tend to follow in the groove better than if there were just a pencil mark there. Then after the sawing is done, there's no graphite to contend with if the wood is for looks.

● A level is a sensitive shop tool, yet most of us stick the smaller ones in the toolbox along with everything else. To protect my torpedo level, I cut two sections of leftover garden hose the same length as the level. They were then slit and fit over each long side. A pair of rubber bands holds the pieces in place. This not only protects the bubble vial, but also keeps the perfect edges from getting nicked up (Figure 114).

FIGURE 114

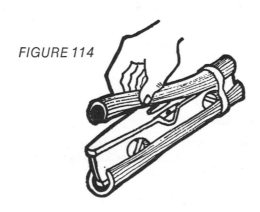

● Needing a level while installing some shelves, I made do with an envelope and a string. I tied a weight to the string and let it hang down like a plumb bob. When the edge of the envelope lines up with the string, the top of the envelope is level.

● When your project calls for transferring an angle from one surface to another, your folding zigzag ruler will usually come to the rescue. Place it down on the angle and adjust two sections of the rule to the angle. It will stay in place for the transfer.

● When a project calls for the use of a large compass, drill a pair of holes in a wooden yardstick. One hole is for the pencil point to go through, the other is for a nail which will act as the center of your circle. Space the holes as far apart as the desired radius of your circle. The holes won't be a hindrance to measuring later on.

LADDERS

Many do-it projects require that you get up to where the problem is, and the best way I know to get high is with a ladder. Don't try to get by with a stack of books on a chair or by standing on a bar stool. That's asking for trouble.

Every time you use a ladder, give it a visual inspection. On a wooden ladder, look for splits or cracks. Be sure rungs and steps are clean.

A seldom-used straight ladder can be tested by placing it flat on the ground and walking on each rung. If a rung breaks at ground level, you won't get hurt.

After the ladder passes muster, use it safely. A straight ladder must be leaned against something solid and must be on firm ground. The surface mustn't be slippery. The angle is also important. The base should be out one foot for every four feet up to the point of support. Since rungs are a foot apart, it's easy to figure the angle.

Don't climb with your dancing shoes on. Clean, dry, nonslip shoes are a must. Some people add an L brace at the bottom as a foot scraper. Just be sure it won't be in the way to trip you as you come back down.

With the straight ladder in place on firm ground, step up on the first rung or so and bounce your weight to be sure it's all set.

As you climb, face the ladder. Try to climb with both hands and hoist tools up when you're in position. As you work, keep your hips between the side rails; when you have to reach to the side, have both feet on the rungs.

If you can't hold with one hand, hook a leg over a rung so you can't fall back.

When using a stepladder, be sure the braces are securely locked in place. Never stand on the top step or even the next one down.

Don't put any ladder in front of a door that could be opened into the ladder.

Be sure extension-ladder locks are securely hooked in place, and always have at least a two-foot overlap between sections. Here are some other ladder hints:

● When using a straight ladder, I insert each ladder leg into an opening in a concrete block. The blocks have a rough surface, plus enough extra weight so the ladder can't move while I'm on it.

● A sandbag against ladder legs prevents their being able to scoot out on a slick surface.

● To prevent slipping, I put a pair of overshoes on the legs of the ladder (Figure 115).

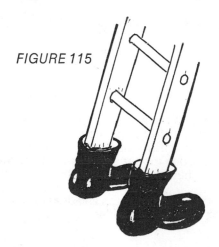

FIGURE 115

● Using a straight ladder in soft ground can be dangerous since the sides can sink in the ground, making the ladder unlevel. Retard sinking by clamping a two-by-four across the bottom from one leg to another. What little sinking occurs will be uniform and still leave the ladder level. It is also a good idea to drive a stake into the ground (Figure 116) to make sure the soft ground doesn't allow the ladder to slide away from the house.

FIGURE 116

● If you worry about the strength of an aluminum ladder, measure the inside diameter of the rungs and select doweling that will fit snugly inside. Cut pieces of the doweling to the proper length and drive them into the rungs. This will let the rungs take an even greater load.

● To prevent a straight ladder from damaging the surface it leans against, slip your work gloves over the ends.

● Or, staple carpet scraps over the ends.

● Rather than carrying an armload of tools up with you while you are climbing a straight ladder, place the tools in a bucket and tie a rope to the handle. Then loop the rope over a rung at the top of the ladder and hoist the tools up after you're safely in place. Tie the rope in place when the bucket is up, and you have a holder for the tools while you work, as well as a dumbwaiter to let them back down.

Better still, get a helper to pull the rope from the ground.

● When working on a straight ladder, put a couple of blobs of putty on the top rung. I can put down small, lightweight hand tools; press them into the putty; and they will stay there.

● Attach a large C clamp to the top step, and your stepladder has a handhold to steady yourself with.

● Since the top step is really a shelf, you can put tools and parts down on it. However, they usually roll off. I built a lip all around the edge with scrap molding and have a tray that corrals everything.

● I ran a bead of silicone rubber sealant all around the edge of the top step. When it set up, I had a retaining wall that won't let anything roll off.

● Drill assorted holes in the top step and drop tools in there instead of on the floor. It doesn't weaken the ladder.

● From an old carpenter's apron, cut off all but the part with the pockets. Then staple this around the back edge of the top step of a ladder (Figure 117), and the pockets hold all those parts and tools that normally drop.

FIGURE 117

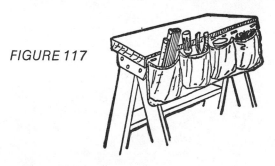

● Probably the best stepladder tool holder is a paint-roller tray. This tray is designed to fit on the top step of a ladder anyway, and stays in place without any special clamping.

● The fold-out shelf on a stepladder is a handy place for a bucket of paint—unless something accidentally hits the shelf arm and tips the shelf. This, of course, spreads the paint a little quicker than you had in mind. With a screen-door hook and eye put in the proper place on the ladder rail and the shelf arm, the shelf can be locked into place. Even if you aren't going to put anything on the shelf, this also gives the ladder greater stability.

● With the fold-out shelf in place, put a wire file basket down and position a pair of cup hooks on the back rails. The cup hooks will hold the basket in place so it and the tools it holds can't fall off. When the ladder is folded up, the basket comes off and the cup hooks are not in the way.

● I mounted an old aluminum cake pan to the shelf, and a paint can fits right into the pan. This makes the paint tip-proof and also catches drips that run down the can.

● I got tired of barking my shins on my stepladder and put a cushion on the front edge of each step. The cushion is some leftover foam-rubber weather stripping of the self-sticking kind.

● A screen-door hook and eye can prevent a stepladder from springing open when it's being carried.

INDEX